M.G.P

Monster Girl Prison

Written by

Chuck B. Smith

Book Format

Acknowledgment

This book exists because certain people showed up when it mattered, and stayed when it would have been easier not to. I want to take a moment to acknowledge their efforts.

To those who challenged my thinking, sharpened my resolve, and reminded me that growth is not always comfortable, thank you. Your presence helped shape this work more than you know.

To the readers, thank you for giving this story your time, your attention, and your imagination. If anything in these pages made you feel seen, unsettled, or intrigued, then it has done what it was meant to do.

Special Note: A heartfelt thank you to California Book Publishers and its team for their exceptional guidance, editing, formatting, publishing, and management throughout the entire process.

I would like to extend a special thanks to Anna Williams for her outstanding efforts in carrying out the editing process smoothly and to Jordan Mascarenhas for his dedication and precision in brilliant project management.

Prologue

Monster Girl Prison: The Intake

The verdict hit him like a hammer, though there had been no time to absorb it. Guards seized him the instant the judge's gavel cracked through the stale courtroom air, dragging him out before he could even lift his head. The world blurred into harsh lights, rough hands, and echoing footsteps that swallowed any trace of dignity he once had. By the time the doors sealed behind him, he was already being delivered into the depths of *The Monster Girl Prison*, a maximum-security labyrinth designed to contain the most dangerous and volatile monster girls in existence.

They stripped him of everything. Clothes, possessions, and identity. All of it was replaced with a stiff orange jumpsuit that clung uncomfortably to his skin. The number was stamped on the back of the jumpsuit. #4721. It felt less like identification and more like a curse.

Milena, the catgirl guard, was assigned to escort him. She happily watched the process with a predator's amusement. Her tail flicked lazily behind her, but her amber eyes were sharp and assessing. She stepped toward him, her boots clicking against the cold concrete floor as she approached with a small metallic bracelet in hand.

"You'd best follow our orders if you value your life. And don't try to remove this bracelet, human." Her voice slithered through the air. She sounded wicked and low, carrying an edge that brushed like claws down his spine. She hissed something about the surprises waiting within these walls, her sadistic tone dripping with a dark promise.

Before he could respond, she snapped the unusual-looking bracelet onto his wrist. The device tightened instantly, adjusting to his pulse with an unsettling precision.

It was sleek… too sleek. As the bracelet took hold of him, he felt a faint warmth seep into his skin, almost intimate. The display flickered to life, revealing his fate in merciless clarity: *Prisoner #4721, three-year term, assault against a monster girl.*

2

Small green lights pulsed around its circumference, blinking in a steady rhythm like a heartbeat monitoring his every move.

He lifted his arm slightly, watching the device glow in the dim corridor light. It felt less like technology and more like a brand.

Milena's lips curled.

"Don't even think about breaking any rules, or we'll make sure you regret it. Now let's find you a new home, boy."

She tapped her baton with a slow, taunting rhythm as she began to escort him deeper into the prison. The sound echoed ominously, each tap marking another step toward whatever waited in the shadows.

As he continued staring at the bracelet, the warmth grew almost uncomfortable; it was alive, somehow. The corridor felt colder by comparison, a sharp contrast to the metallic heat clinging to his wrist.

Milena's voice cut through the air again.

"Like what you see, human? That little beauty is waterproof, shockproof, and tamper-proof." She moved with a fluid, predatory grace beside him.

At 5'8", lean and muscular build beneath her uniform, she radiated a quiet threat. Her canines glinted, sharp and unapologetic, as her feline ears flicked with cruel amusement. Her tail swayed behind her in a slow, deliberate rhythm, as if she were hunting.

"Try to remove it, and it'll send enough voltage through your body to make you piss yourself." She smirked, watching as the fear in his eyes built up.

"Try to escape, and we'll know exactly where to find you. It also monitors your vitals, so we'll know if you're getting too…excited around the inmates."

She punctuated the warning with a cold laugh, tapping a clawed finger against the bracelet. The metal felt even hotter beneath her touch, as though reacting to her presence.

"Welcome to your new life, meat." Every word that came from her mouth was a threat, a warning. "I suggest you get comfortable with that

3

little accessory. It's going to be your closest companion for the next three years…assuming you survive that long."

He swallowed hard, trying to force a breath past the tension in his chest. Anxiety buzzed at the back of his skull, but instinct made him attempt humor anyway. "Will you be keeping me company, or will someone else for the next 3 years? Haha"

The reaction was instant.

Milena's ears flattened, and in a blur of motion, she gripped his jumpsuit collar and slammed him against the wall. The impact stunned him, knocking the air from his lungs. Her face hovered inches away, heat rolling off her coffee-scented breath laced with something metallic and feral.

"You think this is funny, human? You think we're going to be friends?"

Her growl vibrated against his throat. Her pupils constricted to razor-thin slits. She didn't fully extend her claws, but she didn't need to; even the tips pricked through the fabric and scraped lightly against his skin. "I'm not your company. I'm your nightmare if you step out of line. As for who you'll be bunking with…"

She shoved him away with casual force, releasing him as though he weighed nothing. The corridor beyond seemed to shift, growing darker as the prison's sounds pressed in around them.

Voices rose on both sides. Taunting, curious, and hungry. Limbs of every shape and origin reached through the bars. Clawed hands grazed the air beside his head. Something slick dragged across his shoulder before retreating with a hiss of disappointment.

Milena gestured with her baton toward the looming block ahead.

"Cell Block D is where you're headed." She told him, her voice still metal and furious, "You'll be sharing with three others. And they're very excited to meet the new human."

Her smile sharpened into something feral as she spun the baton lazily.

"Let's see if that sense of humor survives your first night. Move it!"

She jabbed the baton against his back, not enough to hurt, but enough to make the message sink in.

He quickened his pace, eyes darting around the prison as he walked. Every shadow felt alive. Every voice seemed to whisper his number. The bracelet's warmth pulsed against his wrist like a reminder: *he was marked, monitored, and owned.*

And his new cellmates were waiting.

The prison corridor stretched before him like the throat of some mechanical beast. It was long, narrow, and humming with predatory anticipation. The harsh fluorescent lights overhead crackled and flickered, throwing jagged shadows onto the filthy floor. Each step he took echoed through the hall, swallowed almost immediately by the low rumble of inmates whispering, calling, and hissing from behind steel bars.

Milena's baton prodded him forward without mercy. Every shove carried her particular brand of sadistic delight, the kind that made her tail swish lazily as though she were herding prey. In the cells lining the hallway, monster girls pressed forward with their hands, claws, tentacles, and stranger things reaching through the bars as he passed.

Some watched with hungry eyes.

Some with curiosity.

Some with something far more dangerous.

Table of Contents

Chapter 1

"First Interactions at Monster Girl Prison"

The eyes never left him, as he moved forward through the prison, it almost felt as if the air vibrated with feral tension.

Milena, the cat girl guard, flicked her tail against his leg as he dared to glance sideways.

"Eyes forward, human! Your admirers will get their turn soon enough."

Her dark chuckle reverberated in the space between them, coated with malicious amusement. She guided him through a heavy security door marked *BLOCK D* in peeling red paint.

The moment it slid open, a new wave of scent hit him. This strange scent was thick, musky, and undeniably monstrous. Pheromones clung to the air like smoke.

The atmosphere here was heavier. Darker. Hungrier.

"Here we are. Your new place." Milena stopped at *Cell D-17* and rapped her baton against the bars with a sharp metallic crack. Inside, something shifted, three silhouettes rising from the shadows like predators disturbed in their den. Her amber eyes gleamed as she keyed in a code on the lock.

"Ladies! Special delivery. Try not to break him on the first day... paperwork's a bitch, you know." She announced as the cell door slid open with a deep, industrial clang. The sound felt final, like a verdict.

The space inside was cramped and suffocating.

Two bunk beds hugged the far wall, the thin mattresses worn and stained. A small toilet sat exposed in the corner, offering no privacy at all. And in the middle of it all were three monster girls turned toward him, their attention sharp and immediate.

He swallowed, forcing a weak smile.

7

"Um… guess I'm your new roomie for the next 3 years." A nervous laugh escaped him; he let out a slow giggle.

The door slammed shut behind him, locking him in with the three figures who now regarded him like a new toy, or maybe a new meal.

The dim cell lights flickered to life, throwing their forms into clear view.

The first was a *blue-skinned oni*, lounging lazily on the bottom bunk. Nearly seven feet tall even while seated, she radiated brute power. Tribal tattoos rippled across her muscular arms. Small horns protruded from her forehead, and a jagged scar cut across her cheek like an old battle trophy.

Zara, the oni's lips curled.

"Well, well… look at the fresh meat," she rose, towering over him, cracking her knuckles with slow, deliberate menace, "a human with jokes. How cute." Her laugh was sarcastic, or maybe demonic.

Above her, perched elegantly on the top bunk, the second inmate descended with a grace that felt too smooth to be human. An *Arachne*, slender but deadly. Her human upper half was poised and almost regal; she was contrasted sharply by the eight spindly legs emerging from her waist, their tips clicking rhythmically against the concrete.

Nyx, the Arachne's dark eyes glittered, "three years? That's assuming you survive the first month."

The third inmate stood by the barred window, a *harpy* with vibrant crimson feathers adorning her arms and shins. Sharp talons tapped against the floor as she shifted her weight. Her bright yellow eyes studied him unblinking, avian and unnervingly perceptive.

Kira, the harpy, tilted her head. "At least he's not crying like the last one. I hate when they cry."

The comment was so casual that it chilled him more than the threat implied.

Zara stepped closer, her shadow engulfing him, "So what'd you do to end up here with us degenerates, roomie?"

Mockery dripped from the word "*roomie.*"

8

He lifted his wrist, showing them the glowing bracelet.

"Says here," he muttered.

The three inmates leaned in immediately, surrounding him. Their bodies crowded against his space... too close, too warm, and way too different. Zara's muscular arm brushed his shoulder, radiating heat that bordered on uncomfortable.

She smirked, "Assault on a monster girl, huh? Didn't think a scrawny human like you had it in you."

Her crimson eyes scanned him with new and dangerous interest.

Nyx circled behind him, her eight legs creating an unsettling rhythm on the floor, "How... disappointing. I was hoping for something more creative."

Her long and pale fingers, tipped in sharp black nails, traced the edge of his collar. The touch was featherlight but undeniably possessive.

Kira clicked her talons, feathers ruffling, "Who'd you attack? Bet it was someone weak. Humans always go for the weak ones."

Her wings fluffed out, showing the razor-like feathers at her joints. Scars slashed across her face like warnings.

Zara jerked her chin toward the bunks, "Top bunk's mine. Bottom one's Nyx's. you can have that one."

She pointed at the last remaining bed, the bunk above Nyx's. The mattress sagged, stained with years of previous occupants.

Nyx's gaze sharpened, "and don't even think about touching our things. The last cellmate who did..." Her lips parted into a cold smile, revealing venomous fangs glistening faintly in the cell's dim light, "Well, let's just say the guards found pieces of him for weeks."

He forced a smirk, though his heart thudded painfully beneath the jumpsuit.

"Aww," he began speaking, looking up at Zara. "Big girl doesn't want a new teddy to snuggle?"

He then glanced at Nyx, "Surprised you don't have a web spun in a corner for me to be wrapped in?"

Then his gaze snapped toward the harpy, deliberately provoking, "Oh, and harpy… She wasn't weak, unlike how you look."

The cell fell silent.

Three monster girls stared at him.

And the night began to shift.

A dangerous silence flooded the cell. A silence that was thick, suffocating, and alive. It was the kind of silence that preceded violence, the kind that made the air itself tighten like a drawn bowstring.

Zara's expression shifted first. The oni's crimson eyes ignited with a furious glow, heat radiating from her towering form as her massive hands curled into fists. The tribal tattoos carved into her blue skin seemed to pulse with each steady throb of her anger, illuminating faintly beneath the dim cell lights.

Behind him, the rhythm of clicking legs grew faster and sharper, in a way that was precise and predatory. Nyx's arachnid limbs scraped against the concrete in a staccato pattern, a warning as clear and visceral as a rattlesnake's tail.

Zara stepped forward, the light bending around her enormous silhouette until he stood fully in her shadow.

"You've got a death wish, human," her voice rumbled low, a promise carved from stone. A thick vein pulsed along her neck, straining beneath the weight of her rage.

Nyx's gaze sharpened like a blade.

"Such bravado. How… misguided," silk spilled effortlessly from her spinnerets, shimmering in the faint light as she gathered and manipulated the strands with delicate, practiced motions. Her expression remained unreadable, but her intent was unmistakable.

But it was Kira who moved first.

With a piercing screech that ricocheted off the metal walls, the harpy lunged. A violent burst of crimson feathers erupted around him as her talons slammed him against the cold concrete. One hooked claw pressed against his throat. Light enough to restrain, sharp enough to kill.

Her face hovered inches from his, wild yellow eyes blazing. "I've gutted monsters three times your size for less disrespect, meat-sack!"

Her breath washed over him... hot, animalistic, carrying the scent of raw meat and blood. The talon at his throat dug in just enough to break skin. A thin line of warmth trickled down his neck.

Zara cracked her knuckles, watching with a grin that held no kindness. "Let him go, Kira. If you kill him now, we don't get to have any fun."

There was a cruel promise in her tone, one that suggested *fun* meant something entirely different to each of them.

But instead of flinching, instead of begging or trembling like the last human who'd landed in this cell...

He straightened up.

Pain lanced through his neck, but he didn't break eye contact with the harpy. His muscles tensed, heat curling through his spine as he rolled his shoulders back and-crack.

A sound was heard across the cell.

He cracked his neck, the sound echoing through the tense air. When he lifted his head again, his pupils glowed with a sudden flare of crimson... something unnatural, sharp, a predatory hue that had not existed minutes ago.

"Now," he said calmly, voice low. "Let's finish with the flirting. I have had a long day. And you beauties will need your beauty rest at some point, right?"

The reaction was immediate.

Kira faltered. The talon at his throat trembled, not out of fear, but out of pure confusion. Her head tilted in a sharp, birdlike motion as she jerked back a few inches, feathers rising along her arms. "What the hell...?" Her voice carried a new edge, not one of aggression, but wariness.

Zara froze. The oni's red gaze widened slightly as she studied the glow in his pupils, the flicker of something inhuman behind them. "Flirting? You've got some nerve, human."

But the anger in her words softened into something else, something intrigued, almost amused. She crossed her muscular arms, the motion causing her tattoos to ripple across her sculpted blue biceps.

Nyx stepped closer, silk retracting back into her hands with a liquid grace. "How... curious. The file didn't mention anything special about you."

Her eight legs shifted, bringing her within arm's reach. She lifted a pale hand, long fingers hovering near his cheek as though studying a specimen under glass. "Perhaps there's more to our new cellmate than meets the eye." She stopped just short of touching him, withdrawing her hand with an unreadable smile.

The tension thickened, but its nature had changed. No longer the crackling threat of immediate violence, but something heavier, more deliberate. A shift in the unspoken hierarchy.

The three monster girls exchanged a wordless series of glances, a silent conversation forged through months of shared confinement. Whatever conclusion they reached was mutual...and unsettling.

Zara smirked, almost indulgently. "Get some sleep, human. Tomorrow's when the real fun begins."

She stepped back, giving him space, but her gaze never left him, nor did the other monster girl's.

The cell, once hostile, now watched him with a new kind of hunger. Not just for blood. Not just for dominance.

For answers. And for whatever he'd just revealed in those crimson eyes.

Zara returned to her bunk with slow, deliberate steps, but her crimson gaze never wavered from him. She watched him like a storm waiting for a crack in the earth, calculating, predatory, yet now tempered with something new.

Curiosity. Wariness. Interest.

The threat hanging in the air had not vanished, merely shifted; it was becoming sharper, more complicated.

He exhaled quietly and reached for the zipper of his jumpsuit. The metal slid down with a soft rasp, and he shrugged the top half off his shoulders before tying the sleeves around his waist. The fabric hung loose, revealing a torso sculpted through hardship rather than vanity. Under the dim cell lights, faded scars traced pale lines across his skin as evidence of conflicts long before this prison ever claimed him.

He stretched, his muscles flexed beneath skin that was still warm from adrenaline. His gaze dropped to the bracelet clinging to his wrist. Its green lights blinked steadily, unfazed by the chaos of the past hour.

His features softened as he spoke. "I may have been rude, and I'm sorry to all three of you. I just don't want to be viewed as weak."

His pecs tightened with the stretch, his abs contracting and relaxing. He glanced up at the bunks, then back toward Zara and the others. "I don't see the ladder to the top bunk. Mind if I have an assist to gauge the distance from the ground and not step on your bunks?"

The atmosphere shifted again... but this time it was subtly charged with an unexpected tension as the three cellmates assessed him anew.

Zara grunted softly, rising from her bunk with surprising grace for someone of her size. Her crimson eyes swept down his torso, tracing the definition there. "Well, well...not as scrawny as I thought."

Her hostility melted just enough to reveal a spark of appreciation, dangerous in its own way.

"I'll give you a boost, fresh meat." She stepped close. Her presence felt overwhelming.

When her hands settled at his waist, her touch was shockingly warm, her calloused fingers pressing firmly into his skin. The heat radiating from her palms seeped into him, an almost intimate sensation.

From her bunk, Nyx tilted her head, legs folding neatly beneath her, "How diplomatic of you to apologize."

Her voice was smooth silk as she studied him, her eyes lingering on the scars across his torso, "though I doubt sincerity factored into it."

13

The words dripped condescension, yet beneath her cold tone lay a glimmer of curiosity.

Kira perched again on the window ledge, feathers settling as she resumed preening. But her bright yellow eyes were locked on him. "Smart move. Weak ones don't last long here."

Zara tightened her grip and lifted him effortlessly. For a moment, her massive form pressed closer, her breath brushing his cheek with a faint hint of spice, something warm and intoxicating. "Sleep light, human. First nights are always...eventful."

Her tone blended warning and promise, a low purr beneath the words. She set him onto the thin, worn mattress of the top bunk.

He held her gaze, eyes steady and intense, "Thanks for the warning."

He tested the mattress beneath him; it was lumpy, uneven, but serviceable. Then he looked toward the window ledge where the harpy sat.

"Ya, always the first night sleep troubles."

He leaned back slightly. "By the way, I don't know your familiarity with human communications, but I actually was being sincere. If we're all gonna be stuck together, we better make do, so insulting was not my intent, just harmless flirting."

His attention shifted to Nyx, curiosity flickering across his face. "Curious, I didn't see a red hourglass on you."

Zara held his stare for several long heartbeats. Something softened around the harsh planes of her face... just slightly, barely-there, but real.

"Harmless flirting, huh? Nothing's harmless in here, human." Her lips twitched in faint amusement as she folded her muscular arms, tattoos rippling along her skin.

A soft chirping sound came from Kira. "He thinks we're going to be friends! That's adorable." Her feathers ruffled playfully, the earlier hostility dissolving into something almost teasing.

But Nyx had the strongest reaction.

For a brief, startling moment, genuine surprise flashed across her features, quickly smothered beneath practiced coldness. She rose slightly on her eight legs, bringing her pale face closer to his bunk.

"I'm not a black widow, human. I'm a Jorogumo. Different species entirely." She extended one slender arm, revealing delicate blue and gold patterns tracing the underside of her wrist, hidden markings that shimmered faintly under the weak lighting.

"Though the confusion is… understandable from someone of your limited knowledge." Her voice was condescending, yes. But there was an unmistakable edge of pride, and perhaps… appreciation.

Zara stretched, bones popping faintly. "Get some sleep while you can. The guards wake us at five for count."

She returned to her bunk, but like before, her eyes lingered on him, watchful, assessing, intrigued. And in the quiet that followed, the cell hummed with an unspoken question:

Who exactly had just been locked in with them?

Zara returned to her bunk with a heavy thud, the metal frame protesting beneath her weight with a long, echoing creak. As the sound faded, a dense stillness settled over the cell, uneasy, taut, but no longer openly hostile. It was the kind of quiet that grew teeth in the dark.

Beyond the bars, Monster Girl Prison muttered and growled to itself. Metal doors slammed shut in distant halls. A prisoner screamed somewhere far down the block, cut short just as quickly. Patrol boots marched their cold rhythm up and down the corridor, each step a reminder that even the night had watchers.

He lay back on the thin mattress, eyes drifting up.

The ceiling above him told stories… scratched tallies marking the passage of time, crude drawings carved with desperate hands, the names of inmates who had slept, cried, or died in this very bunk. And in one corner, delicate strands of webbing clung to the concrete, shimmering faintly in the dim emergency lights. Nyx had claimed this territory long before he arrived. Even above him, Arachne's presence lingered.

Below, her eight legs shifted against the metal frame with a soft *Click.* *Click. Click.* a steady rhythm that vibrated up into his bones. The oni's slow, rumbling breaths filled the cell like distant thunder, steady, deep, but never quite peaceful. From the window ledge, the harpy's bright yellow eyes caught the moonlight, shimmering like predatory lanterns as she watched him with a tilted head and a quiet, birdlike curiosity.

Finally, Kira broke the silence.

"First night's always the longest, human. Wondering what got you here…must've been something special to land you with us." Her voice had lost its earlier bite. It was still sharp, still dangerous, but now tinged with something closer to conversation.

Nyx's voice floated up from the bunk below, cool and silken. "Don't engage him, Kira. Humans are manipulative by nature."

Despite the warning, there was unmistakable curiosity beneath her words. Her pale face tilted upward, dark eyes glinting in the low light. She wanted answers just as much as the harpy did.

Outside the cell, the guard patrol approached, heavy boots, slow and deliberate. A shock baton tapped the bars of each cell they passed, sending faint vibrations through the metal.

He waited, silent, until the footsteps drew even with their cell, then continued past.

Only then did he speak, voice low and honest in the hush.

"Humans are manipulative narcissists. I know because I was one of them. I haven't changed, but I know my flaws, and the charges are based on false pretenses. I was accused and convicted because I broke up with her. That's all. Doesn't matter, because I'm here now, and thinking about it won't fix a thing or"

He lifted his fingers in mocking quotes, "make me innocent."

A heavy quiet followed.

The baton's rhythmic tapping faded away. The moon cast faint bars of silver light through the window, striping the cell floor like a cage within a cage.

Kira clicked her beak softly, "A scorned lover's revenge? That's... disappointingly common." Her feathers rustled as she shifted into a more comfortable position, settling like a crimson shadow against the wall.

Nyx's voice drifted upward again, soft and unsettling, "and yet, I detect there's more to your story."

A single slender leg tapped the bunk's frame directly beneath him. The vibration was delicate but deliberate, "False pretenses rarely lead to maximum security. Especially not to our particular cell block."

Zara stirred, turning toward him. The dim light made her tribal tattoos look alive, writhing patterns across her blue skin. "Everyone here is 'innocent,' human. But they don't put innocents with monsters like us."

She sat up fully, crimson eyes reflecting the faint light with a hungry gleam. "Whatever you did, it earned you respect from someone important, or fear from someone powerful."

The three exchanged a glance. A glance that was silent, sharp, and unmistakably unified.

He shrugged into the moonlit darkness. "What can I say, I've only been with a demon," he said casually, as he chuckled.

The temperature in the cell seemed to drop.

Zara froze.

Nyx went perfectly still.

Kira's feathers flattened tight to her body in a reflexive display of shock.

Zara's voice dropped into something low and dangerous. "A demon?"

Her tribal markings pulsed faintly, as though reacting to the word itself.

Kira narrowed her bright yellow eyes. "That explains it. Demons don't take rejection well."

Her talons dug into the ledge, scraping lightly.

From below, Nyx leaned forward, her eight legs arranging themselves in a poised, predatory stance. "Which clan?" The question cleaved through the dark, direct and sharp.

From deeper within the prison, a scream erupted, violent and abrupt, cut off almost instantly. No guards intervened. Not at night. Not unless someone died. And even then, not always.

Zara tilted her head, studying him with new calculation. "You've got more guts than brains, human. Demons play long games of vengeance."

But beneath the warning lay something else. It was respect and a reluctant hint of concern.

He exhaled slowly. "I'll be honest, I was a narcissistic idiot and didn't pay attention. I was filled with lust, and I loved the way her dark red skin felt against mine. We knew the contract we signed. We were free to do and be as we pleased, just together was all."

He continued the story, "She brought me into the world of 'Monsters,'" he mimed air quotes at the word of *Monsters.*

"As humans say, I was happy. I'm a reject from all. Plus, we trained together, fucked together, everything together."

He shrugged. "Might as well call me a monster too, cuz I don't know any better."

Another silence descended; it was different from before. Heavy. Considering.

The three watched him with eyes no longer mocking or hostile, but studying, reevaluating.

Zara leaned forward slightly. "Trained together? What kind of training?"

Suspicion and intrigue rippled through her voice.

Nyx traced a faint glowing thread through the air, her voice dismissive but curious. "A human who considers himself a monster, how quaint." Yet her eight legs relaxed, no longer poised to strike. "Though it would explain why they placed you here rather than in the human wing."

Kira clicked her tongue softly. "Red skin? Sounds like a Lilim or one of their direct bloodline."

Zara and Nyx turned toward her with equal surprise. Kira ruffled her feathers defensively, "What? I worked in intelligence before…this."

A distant bell chimed. Three hours until morning count. The prison quieted, sinking deeper into its nocturnal hunger.

Zara stretched, leaned back, and said to him, "Get some sleep, demon-lover. Tomorrow you'll meet the rest of the block. Some won't be as… welcoming as us."

As he stared at the dark ceiling, the words slipped from him almost absently. "Ansatsuken training."

The effect was immediate.

Zara's eyes snapped wide.

Nyx stilled, her limbs locking in place.

Kira's feathers flattened in instinctive alarm.

The cell froze.

Zara whispered, "The assassin's fist? That's… not a human discipline."

Nyx's voice was quiet, hungry with curiosity. "Interesting. Very interesting."

Kira tilted her head, yellow eyes gleaming. "Or they know exactly what they're doing."

The dynamic shifted again; it was a shift in power rebalancing and reshaping.

Zara nodded once, slow and deliberate. "We should all get some sleep. Tomorrow will be… eventful."

He let out a slow breath and allowed his eyes to close.

Sleep came in fragments. Shallow and restless.

Nyx's soft clicking.

Kira's whistling breaths.

Zara's deep, rumbling snores.

Shadows curled behind his eyelids.

Red skin.

A contract.

A kiss like a wound.

A promise broken.

And somewhere in the prison's depths, something watched.

A violent buzzer ripped him out of sleep, rattling through the concrete walls like the roar of some awakened beast. The harsh fluorescent lights snapped on overhead, bright enough to sting his eyes, unforgiving enough to make every shadow retreat into corners where danger still lingered.

Morning had arrived in *Monster Girl Prison.*

The cellmates stirred one by one.

The PA system crackled to life, static hissing before the mechanical voice droned from hidden speakers.

"All inmates, prepare for morning count. Cell inspections to follow. Any contraband found will result in immediate disciplinary action."

The announcement echoed down the corridor, bouncing between metal bars and cold stone.

Zara stretched first, her massive blue arms reaching toward the ceiling. Her tribal tattoos rolled across her muscles like living ink, flexing with her slow exhale. Nyx descended from her web-like hammock with haunting elegance, eight legs coordinating in a dance too perfect to be human. Kira hopped from her window perch, talons clicking sharply on the metal frame as she folded her crimson wings neatly.

The harpy's voice was smoother than last night; she sounded almost playful, "Rise and shine, assassin. First full day in paradise."

Outside the cell, voices swelled, other inmates calling out, doors clanging open, the heavy footfalls of guards on patrol. The building felt alive, stirring with restless, predatory energy.

Nyx smoothed her uniform with long, practiced strokes as if the ragged fabric were silk. "Remember to stand at attention for the count. The guards don't appreciate…creativity during morning routines."

He stretched, feeling joints pop and muscles warm beneath the morning chill.

"Great," he muttered as he dropped lightly from the bunk, landing with barely a sound.

His movement drew attention.

Zara let out a low, appreciative grunt. "Light on your feet for a human."

Heavy footsteps approached the cell, shaking the floor with each impact. Two guards appeared, one towering, the other aflame.

The minotaur's horns gleamed beneath the fluorescent lights. The salamander's skin flickered with controlled fire, heat shimmering around her like a warning.

Guard Taurus barked orders, voice deep and professional. "Against the back wall, inmates. Count time."

The salamander eyed him openly, lips curling into a predatory smile. "So, this is our new human. Settling in well?" She asked, her baton tapped rhythmically against her palm.

His cellmates aligned instantly, backs to the wall, chins raised. He joined them with the same automatic discipline drilled into him years ago.

Nyx spoke clearly, voice smooth as spun silk.

"Cell 217, all present and accounted for, ma'am." The minotaur scribbled something on her clipboard. The salamander did not look away from him.

"Breakfast in ten minutes. The new one has orientation with the Warden afterward." A flame danced between her fingers.

He stared back, unflinching, cold.

The flame guttered, shrinking under his glare. The guard's smirk faltered.

Guard Ember clicked her tongue. "Watch the attitude, human. That might have worked on the outside, but in here…"

She left the threat unfinished.

Guard Taurus snorted. "Move along, Ember. We've got twenty more cells to count."

The guards moved on. Kira let out a soft whistle. "Bold move, staring down Ember on your first day. She's not one to forget a slight."

Zara's voice rumbled like distant thunder. "The Warden, though…that's concerning. Special plans usually mean special problems."

A second buzzer blared. Cell doors throughout the block slid open in perfect unison, the metallic clang shaking the air.

Nyx clicked her mandibles thoughtfully. "Come. Breakfast first, then your… appointment."

Her eight legs glided toward the hallway. "Stay close. The dining hall can be…territorial."

He smirked. "Ooh, consent from a spider?"

He winked at Zara.

Her laughter boomed through the hallway. "Hah! Got some spirit after all! I like that."

She slapped his shoulder, hard enough to floor a normal human. He absorbed the hit, muscles damping the impact with practiced ease.

Nyx shot him a sharp look. "I was merely suggesting prudence, not…whatever you're implying."

But her cheeks flushed a faint lavender before she masked it.

Kira strutted into the hall. "Better watch that mouth in the dining hall. Not everyone appreciates humor at their expense."

They entered a river of inmates flowing toward breakfast. Monster girls of every shape and danger. A lamia glided past with hypnotic coils. Two werewolves walked in sync, eyes scanning for threats. A tattooed cyclops towered above them all, her single eye rolling with disinterest.

Zara leaned in, "Welcome to the parade of the damned. Try not to stare too obviously at anyone."

He tightened the jumpsuit around his waist and lowered his head, staying close to the group.

The dining hall opened before them, massive, echoing, humming with energy. Long metal tables bolted to the floor. Enchanted suppression runes glowed overhead. Guards stood at every corner, weapons ready.

Heads turned the moment he entered.

Zara led them to the serving line, where kobold workers shoveled unrecognizable food onto trays.

Nyx accepted her tray with dainty precision. "The food is designed to meet nutritional requirements for all species. Taste is…not a priority."

Zara claimed a table in the corner, her back to the wall, eyes on the room. Strategic. Protective.

Kira leaned close. "Three o'clock. The table with the mantis and the kitsune. They've been watching since we walked in."

He glanced discreetly. Scythe, the mantis girl, sat sharpening her forearms. The kitsune beside her grinned with too many teeth.

Zara muttered, "Ignore them. Eat quickly. The Warden doesn't appreciate tardiness."

Her voice dropped low. "And whatever she offers you…consider carefully before accepting."

He glared at the food.

"Yay," he whispered. "Not a mantis…"

Kira chuckled darkly. "Mantis girls…bad news. That one's Scythe. In for multiple homicides. They say she keeps trophies."

The protein cubes glowed faintly blue. The oatmeal twitched.

Nyx slid a small packet toward him. "Flavor enhancer. Contraband, technically… but the guards look the other way. Makes this slop almost edible."

Before he could reply, a shadow eclipsed their table.

23

A lilim stood before him, beautiful and terrifying. Purple skin, curved horns, wings folded neatly against her back. Her uniform bore the insignia of administration.

Administrator Lilith spoke in a voice like velvet steel.

"Inmate #4721. The Warden is ready for you now."

"Good luck, human," Zara grunted.

Dozens of eyes followed him as he rose.

Scythe dragged a blade across her throat in a silent threat.

He cracked his knuckles and glared back.

The mantis clicked her mandibles sharply.

Lilith said nothing, but her smirk betrayed amusement as she led him out.

The deeper they walked, the more the facility transformed. Rough concrete became polished stone. Harsh lights softened into a warm, magical glow. Guards stood at attention, each a powerful monster chosen for lethal efficiency.

Lilith's wings shifted as she walked, the thin membranes pulsing with life.

"The Warden doesn't often request personal meetings with new inmates. You've caught her interest." Her voice was calm, almost too calm.

"A word of advice: answer truthfully. She knows when you lie."

They stopped before a massive door of dark wood, silver runes glowing faintly across its surface. Power radiated from it, heavy, ancient, and undeniable.

Lilith knocked once.

Then pushed it open.

The Warden's office was nothing like the rest of Monster Girl Prison.

Warm wood-paneled walls rose on all sides, lined with shelves of ancient tomes bound in leather and stranger materials. A massive desk of polished obsidian dominated the center of the room, its glossy surface reflecting the faint light like a pool of black water. Tall windows overlooked the prison grounds, where distant figures moved within the reinforced walls like pieces on a board.

Behind the desk sat the Warden.

Her beauty was the dangerous sort, the kind that could kill a man as easily as any blade. Alabaster skin, smooth and flawless. Crimson eyes that glowed with cold intelligence. Silver hair that spilled down her back like liquid moonlight. Two small horns curved from her forehead, subtle but unmistakably demonic, and bat-like wings were folded neatly behind her chair in a posture of controlled power.

Warden Morrigan's lips curled faintly.

"So this is our human guest. How...refreshing." Her voice poured through the room like velvet over steel, cultured, measured, with an undercurrent that promised consequences. She gestured toward the chair opposite her desk.

"Please, sit. We have much to discuss about your...unique situation."

He moved without hesitation, crossing the room and taking the seat. The chair was unexpectedly comfortable, its cushioning molding to his weight. A choice, he realized. Comfort as a weapon. Comfort as bait.

Morrigan watched him with eyes that had clearly seen centuries come and go. Her fingers, tipped with perfectly manicured claws, tapped a slow rhythm against the obsidian.

"Your file makes for...interesting reading." She lifted a folder embossed with his prison designation, holding it delicately between two fingers.

"A human with your particular skillset is rare within these walls. Most of your kind who commit crimes against monster-kind are opportunists, driven by fear or hatred. But you..." She leaned forward, crimson gaze sharpening until it felt as though she were peeling back his layers one by one. "Your crime was calculated. Professional. Almost...respectful in its execution."

Administrator Lilith stood by the door, silent but impossible to ignore, her presence a reminder that escape was not only foolish but suicidal.

Morrigan set the file down with careful precision.

"This presents me with an unusual opportunity. This facility houses the most dangerous monster criminals in the region, and maintaining order requires…special talents."

She rose from her chair with effortless grace, moving to the tall windows. Below, in the exercise yard, monstrous shapes moved in confined arcs, some sparring, some watching, all dangerous.

"I'm offering you a position of limited authority. You'll work directly under Administrator Lilith, helping to manage certain aspects of prison operations. In exchange, you'll receive privileges and protections not afforded to regular inmates."

She turned back to him, her expression hardening. "The alternative is the general population. With your history, I imagine many of our residents would be quite…eager to make your acquaintance in the most unpleasant ways."

The crimson glow simmered in his pupils again as he met her gaze, unflinching. "Why, Warden, I'm intrigued and flattered. Now, does this offer come as a personal favor or is the professionalism a foundation for a further, shall we say, career change?"

For the first time, a flicker of genuine surprise crossed her perfect features. It vanished quickly, replaced by something far more calculating. The abnormal red light in his eyes clearly did not escape her notice.

She glided back to her chair, every movement fluid, predatory. "How perceptive. Most inmates would simply grasp at any lifeline offered."

She steepled her fingers, studying him with renewed intensity. "Let's call it an investment in potential. Your file indicates abilities that transcend typical human limitations. Abilities that mirror certain…ancestral traits I find familiar."

Her eyes narrowed faintly. "As for career change…this facility has served as a stepping stone for those with ambition and loyalty. Administrator Lilith began as an inmate herself, did you know?"

By the door, Lilith shifted just enough to betray that she'd heard, but her face remained flawlessly neutral.

Morrigan's tone cooled. "I reward competence and punish failure with equal measure. Prove your worth, and doors may open. Disappoint me..."

She let the unfinished threat hang in the air like a noose, lips curling just enough to reveal the fine points of her fangs. "Do we understand each other, 4721?"

A slow, fiendish grin spread over his face.

"I ask you not to flatter me with such beauty in those pearly whites, my Warden. I will say, truthfully, that" his grin shifted into a faint frown.

"I do hope by accepting your offer you don't have high hopes for me, cuz I may actually not meet them. I can say honestly that if accepted, I will do my best and nothing more, as I've said to many who've offered me..." he glanced briefly toward Lilith, then back to Morrigan "opportunities." His wit completed the sentence.

Administrator Lilith's brows ticked up a fraction at his tone.

Morrigan, however, looked genuinely amused now. A rare softness touched the corners of her mouth as she leaned back, the leather of her chair creaking quietly.

"Honesty. How refreshing." She reached for a crystal decanter resting on the desk, its contents a deep, dark red. She poured two glasses, the liquid slid, thick and glossy, and she slid one toward him across the obsidian surface.

"I don't expect miracles, 4721. I expect survival. Those who survive in this place are already exceeding expectations."

The substance in the glass caught the light oddly, too dense to be wine, too translucent to be fresh blood. Morrigan raised her own glass in a mock toast. "To modest ambitions, then. Administrator Lilith will brief you on your duties and arrange your new accommodations."

She took a measured sip, watching him over the rim. "One last thing. Those eyes of yours...they suggest heritage beyond mere humanity. Something you might want to explore during your time with us."

With a small, dismissive gesture, she indicated the door, an unmistakable sign that the audience was at its end.

27

"This way, please." Administrator Lilith's voice slipped into the quiet, smooth, and controlled.

He rose, turning toward the lilim, only to pause when the Warden's voice slipped through the room one more time.

"Oh, and 4721? Do try to avoid antagonizing Scythe further. She's been known to remove limbs before guards can intervene."

He stopped dead.

Slowly, he turned back to face her. The distance between them closed with measured, deliberate steps as he approached the desk again. He reached out, fingers brushing the cool glass she'd slid toward him earlier. Lifting it, he brought it to his lips and downed the contents in one smooth motion.

The liquid burned.

It slid down his throat like heated velvet laced with iron and something ancient that coiled in his chest. His eyes darkened as he swallowed, then he lifted his gaze. Menacing. Unwavering.

"I'm not prejudiced at all, but I will defend myself, and it will cause trouble for everyone around if she tries against me. I only mean to do my time," his gaze flicked down her form in the chair before returning to her face, "and what you've now asked me to do, but if she threatens me again, it'll be either her arms or life removed. I will avoid her kind at all costs, but I'd ask" his eyes lifted briefly, then lowered again, "a favor if u will, to keep distances between us…please."

The silence that followed was sharp enough to cut.

Lilith's eyes widened a fraction. Even she seemed taken off guard by his boldness, returning to the Warden's desk uninvited, issuing a warning about one of the prison's most dangerous inmates.

Morrigan's crimson gaze glimmered. "Fascinating," she said.

She rose from behind the desk, her full height and presence suddenly overwhelming. Her wings unfurled slightly, dark membranes stretching in a subtle but unmistakable display of dominance.

"Most would cower at the mention of Scythe's reputation. Yet here you stand, making demands."

Her smile sharpened. "I'll arrange a buffer zone, but understand this—I do so not out of mercy, but curiosity. I want to see what you're capable of when truly pressed."

She extended one pale hand toward him, her nails lengthening as he watched. Shifting from elegant points into something closer to claws, the gesture was equal parts invitation and test.

The room seemed to hold its breath, waiting to see whether he would take it.

Warden Morrigan's crimson gaze lingered on him a heartbeat longer before her expression cooled back into its usual mask of controlled elegance. The faintest curl of her lips suggested amusement...or warning.

"Your assignment begins now. Administrator Lilith will show you to your new quarters. They're considerably more comfortable than general population cells, though still...secure." With a slow, controlled motion, she retracted her hand. The dismissal was unmistakable.

He rose smoothly to his full height and offered a light bow. Respectful, but with the same faint edge that had defined the entire exchange.

"I thank your generosity," he said, straightening, turning, and as he stepped toward the door, he cast a seductive glance back over his shoulder, a final spark of defiance or charm, depending on who was interpreting it. Then he followed Administrator Lilith out into the corridor.

The Lilim's wings fluttered behind her as the office door sealed shut with a heavy, rune-locked thud. If she was flustered, she hid it well, but the subtle agitation in her wings betrayed something. Her heeled boots clicked against the polished stone floor, echoing the rhythm of her thoughts. She didn't look directly at him at first, but the sideward glances she stole were sharp and calculating.

"That was...unorthodox. Few survive speaking to the Warden that way." Her tone walked a line between disapproval and intrigue.

They passed through three security checkpoints in quick succession. At each one, different species of guards stood watch, a hulking ogre whose

29

brass knuckles glinted under the lights; a tall snake-woman whose forked tongue tasted the air as they passed; a harpy holding a rifle, talons tapping impatiently against the weapon's frame. Every guard bowed subtly to Lilith, a sign of her authority.

"Your quarters will be in the administrative wing. Not quite staff accommodations, but far removed from the general population." She stopped at a reinforced door fitted with a biometric scanner that glowed faintly with demonic sigils.

Lilith placed her palm against the reader. The device hummed as it absorbed her energy signature, runes reacting in a cascade of purple light.

"You'll be expected to assist with inmate management, conflict resolution, and certain…specialized tasks that require a human perspective. The Warden rarely offers such positions."

The door unlocked with a soft hiss.

Inside, warm lighting spilled over a modest but shockingly comfortable room. A real bed, not a cot. A private bathroom. A small oak desk. A bookshelf filled with worn, eclectic volumes ranging from magical theory to monster cultural anthropology.

It may not have been freedom, but it was a world away from metal bunks and hostile cellmates.

"Your duties begin tomorrow at 0600. I suggest you should rest."

Lilith stepped into the doorway but didn't immediately leave. Her violet eyes searched him, curious, analytical, almost predatory. "Those eyes of yours…they're not typical for a human. The Warden noticed too. You might find answers in the prison archives, if you earn the privilege to access them."

He gave a half-smirk, looking around the room with mock appreciation. "Thank you, I'd ask if you'd want to stay and personally help me settle in, but alas," he turned toward her with exaggerated resignation, "you must be busy with other duties with no time to spare."

Surprise flickered across Lilith's face, quickly replaced by something cooler and more controlled. Then her tail flicked once, betraying her amusement. She leaned against the doorframe, framed by the harsh light of the corridor behind her.

"Bold, aren't you? First the Warden, now me." Her violet eyes sparkled with interest as they passed over him, lingering on the faint red glow still haunting his irises.

"I have precisely seventeen minutes before I'm due to oversee evening lockdown. Not enough time to…properly settle anyone in."

Her smile deepened, a dangerous and knowing one.

With a subtle adjustment of her fitted uniform, which emphasized every curve of her demonic form, she stepped back.

"Rest well, 4721. Tomorrow will test your adaptability in ways you can't anticipate." She turned, then paused once more, casting a final glance over her shoulder.

"A word of advice… don't attempt to charm every powerful female you encounter here. Some will take it as a weakness, others as an insult. And a few…" Her lips parted just enough to reveal the tips of delicate fangs. "A few might take you up on it, and you may find yourself…drained of more than just energy."

The door slid closed with a decisive click, followed by the locking sequence engaging behind it.

Silence settled.

He exhaled heavily, tension dripping from his shoulders as he muttered: "Whelp, now that I'm alone, I'm gonna get naked and sleep."

He stripped the jumpsuit off in one smooth motion and practically collapsed onto the bed. The cool fabric of the sheets embraced his bare skin, far softer than anything he'd expected in a maximum-security facility.

The small camera in the corner blinked red, constant surveillance, even here, but for the first time since entering the prison, he felt something close to privacy.

He lifted his wrist.

"This is going to be uncomfortable for a while."

31

The bracelet pulsed softly, its cool metal hugging his skin. A faint blue light shimmered along its edges, and every so often, a subtle vibration traveled up his arm, like the device was reacting to the blood beneath his skin. Or what was in his blood.

Outside the small reinforced window, night had settled across the prison yard. Guard towers stood like dark sentinels under a purple-hued sky, silhouettes unmoving and watchful. A siren wailed faintly in the distance, marking the final stages of lockdown. Below, the clanging of cell doors echoed like a metallic heartbeat.

Despite everything, danger, uncertainty, and new responsibilities, the solitude was a rare gift.

Exhaustion tugged at him, but he allowed it.

His breath slowed. Muscles unclenched. The strange bracelet pulsed in rhythm with his heartbeat.

And in moments, he drifted into sleep, swallowed by darkness and the quiet hum of a prison that never truly rested.

The night in Monster Girl Prison passed in uneven fragments of sleep, broken repeatedly by strange, unsettling noises that echoed through the reinforced walls. Some were screams. Some were moans. Some were the kind of sounds that lived in the uneasy space between pleasure and pain.

The bracelet on his wrist pulsed faintly in the dark, growing warm, then cooling, then warm again, almost as if it were syncing itself to the rhythm of his heartbeat… or monitoring something deeper.

At exactly 0530, the overhead lights brightened slowly, shifting from faint twilight to sterile white. A soft chime sounded from a speaker near the door.

The Automated System announced, "Inmate consultant 4721. Prepare for morning duties. Breakfast will be delivered in ten minutes. Administrator Lilith will arrive at 0600."

Ten minutes later, a small panel slid open in the wall, revealing a tray of food. Real food. Not gruel. Not cubes. Actual scrambled eggs, lightly toasted bread, and a steaming cup of coffee whose aroma momentarily washed the cell's antiseptic smell away.

Behind the reinforced window, the yard stirred to life. Guards cycled into position. Inmates shuffled into their morning routines. Off to the far side, isolated and flanked by minotaur sentries, Scythe's tall silhouette stalked the perimeter; the Warden had kept her distant as promised.

He scarfed down the food with quick efficiency. "That arachnid wasn't kidding, lacks taste still," he muttered to himself.

Then he grabbed the jumpsuit, slipping it on halfway, tying the sleeves around his waist.

His muscles flexed rhythmically as he pushed against the floor, the routine offering a semblance of normalcy in this bizarre situation. The bracelet on his wrist pulsed more rapidly with each exertion, its blue light intensified as if it was feeding off his physical activity.

The sweat began to bead on his back, the half-worn jumpsuit leaving his upper body exposed to the cool air of the room.

At 0600 on the dot, the door slid open.

Administrator Lilith stepped inside, framed by the doorway, violet eyes immediately catching the cadence of his exercise and the state of his half-dressed form. Her wings adjusted with a subtle, reflexive twitch.

"I see you're already…warming up for the day." Administrator Lilith said.

She entered, her tail swaying with deliberate control.

"You have five minutes to make yourself presentable. Today you'll be shadowing me through morning inspections, then assisting with a conflict resolution between rival inmate factions."

She tapped her tablet.

The bracelet buzzed in response.

"I've updated your security clearance. That bracelet now grants you access to administrative corridors and certain common areas. Abuse this privilege, and you'll find yourself in the general population with no protection whatsoever."

Her eyes trailed over him again, as if she was studying his form, intensely, professionally, yet deeply curious.

33

"The Warden has taken a particular interest in your case file. Unusual, considering how many inmates pass through these walls." She told him, her gaze intense.

He rose to stand in front of her, sweat glistening across defined muscles. His breath was controlled but heavy, pupils shifting as the red overtook the grey.

"I'll be honest, I didn't see a closet for clothing, so I just put the jumpsuit back on."

Lilith's gaze flickered at the change in his eyes. Her polished demeanor trembled for only a heartbeat before settling again.

Administrator Lilith replied, "The storage unit beneath your bed contains additional clothing. Standard issue, but clean."

Her wings stretched slightly behind her, stretching before folding again in what might be an unconscious response to his proximity. The air between him and Lilith seemed to charge with an unspoken tension as she took in his sweating form.

"Your…physical condition is better than your file suggested. That will be useful for your duties here."

She stepped back, creating a distance as she glanced back at her tablet.

"Finish dressing. We have a schedule to maintain, and the first stop is the Arachne wing. Their silk production has been…inconsistent lately. The Warden believes a human perspective might reveal what our guards are missing."

Her eyes lingered on the unnatural red in his irises.

"And 4721? I'd advise controlling whatever is happening with your eyes. Some inmates would interpret that as a challenge…or an invitation."

She glanced at him again, this time she could not look away as he untied the sleeves of his orange jumpsuit and let it drop to the floor, fully exposing his muscular, strong body that was long halfway toward an erection.

His voice carried no apology. "My eyes change with my mood..." He continued toward the storage, pulling out the standard-issue black uniform and heading into the bathroom.

"When I'm in a bad mood, they'll go red, when I'm depressed, they'll go blue, indifferent is black." He wiped down his body and put on the uniform.

He stepped out, buttoning the tight uniform, eyes locked on hers.

"Grey eyes ARE a threat, and all who see it are in danger. Words to the wise, no matter the species, *don't piss me off.*" He emphasized, "I'm fun and flirtatious, but I'm also a professional... so watch whom you threaten with a good time, I haven't found my reserves yet."

He leaned close enough for her to feel his breath.

Then straightened.

"So? Shall we commence?"

Lilith's cheeks darkened faintly before her composure returned. The violet eyes traced his movements with predatory focus, her wings flexing once behind her-the demonic equivalent of a controlled breath. "Impressive display of...confidence. Though I should warn you, in this facility, flaunting yourself like that could be interpreted as offering tribute."

She stepped aside as he approached, struggling to maintain her distance, despite the charged and heated atmosphere.

"Your eye condition is noted. As for threats...this isn't one. It's simple prison economics, power, favors, and consequences."

The door opened at her approach.

"The Arachne wing awaits. Stay close, speak only when addressed directly by me, and observe everything. The Warden believes your unique...perspective...might reveal what we've missed."

They walked through the administrative corridor, obsidian walls absorbing light as the facility pulsed with quiet menace. Hellhound guards, minotaurs, and salamanders all snapped their attention toward the human consultant with equal parts curiosity and suspicion.

Lilith guided him down the long passageway.

"The Arachne wing houses seventeen inmates..." she explained, "all convicted of crimes involving their silk, illegal binding contracts, assassination fibers, cocooning travelers."

She gestures toward a massive reinforced door at the end of the corridor.

"They're valuable to the prison economy-their silk is worth a fortune on the outside. But production has dropped thirty percent in the last month. Interrogation has yielded nothing useful."

A reinforced door opened to reveal a deeper truth of the monster girl prison, something that was only to be known by the inmates. The *criminals.*

A towering chamber revealed itself, alive with webs and movement.

Chapter 2

"When it Begins."

The meetings began, and there she was, standing like a mighty force. Fearless, strong, and something more profound... the first glance said a lot.

Arachne scuttled across suspended lattices, their human torsos poised above massive spider bodies. Silk threads shimmered in ambient magical light as they worked, guarded from all sides by elevated walkways.

He studied them carefully.

"Intriguing, now, are they?" he gestured to the Arachne, "getting fed appropriately what is necessary to their glands so as to help in the production of desired silk? Or are they just on food rations like everyone else? In order to maintain or increase productivity, those mining or laboring must have the proper equipment... in their case, sustenance for natural production."

Lilith stopped abruptly, turning to study him with a newfound interest. Her violet eyes narrowed slightly as she considered his observation. The tip of her tail flicked in what might be surprise. "An...astute observation. They receive standard nutritional supplements, but nothing specifically formulated for silk production."

Her claws danced across her tablet.

"The previous administrator believed hunger motivated productivity. I've had...doubts about that approach."

Above him, the Arachne hive seemed to pause and listen.

One of them, larger than the rest, halted mid-spin. Her spider half was a deep midnight blue that gleamed in the ambient light, while long white hair fell around her human shoulders like spun frost. All eight of her eyes turned downward, the dim glow reflecting in each glossy surface as she studied the human standing beside Administrator Lilith.

Around her, other Arachne slowed their work. Threads hung half-spun as attention shifted from silk to the unusual visitor who spoke as if he had any right to comment on their conditions.

Lilith's voice came low and thoughtful. "Their diet could be adjusted. What would you recommend, specifically? And be aware-they're listening to every word."

She gestured subtly upward.

More Arachne had stopped working now. Multiple eyes locked on him from every angle, silent and intent.

He lifted his head, gaze finding the largest of them. "You! Please come here, I have a question, and I do believe only you can properly answer me."

His voice carried cleanly through the chamber, bouncing off stone and woven silk.

For several heartbeats, nothing moved. Then the massive midnight Arachne tilted her head. Her eight eyes blinked in sequence. With practiced ease, she anchored a thick strand of silk and descended toward the floor, her human torso poised and regal as her spider body carried her down.

She landed without a sound.

Her front legs folded beneath her in a posture that felt almost ceremonial. Up close, he could see the tattoos that wrapped her human arms, shifting glyphs and symbols that almost seemed to ripple. Her face was elegant, with high cheekbones and full lips drawn into a thin, assessing line.

"The human addresses me directly? How…unusual." Her voice was melodic, though threaded with suspicion. Even partially folded, she dwarfed him, her spider abdomen the size of a small vehicle.

"I am Weaver Nyx, former Royal Silk Mistress to the Spider Queen. What question could you possibly have that Administrator Lilith cannot answer?"

Beside him, Lilith shifted her weight minutely. One hand hovered near a control device on her belt, a silent reminder that this meeting took place inside a very real threat radius.

He stepped closer, lifting his chin to meet the many eyes fixed on him.

"Such beauty," he breathed, almost to himself, before raising his voice so it carried throughout the chamber. "So! as someone whose expertise is in silk, what would ACTUALLY be needed to help your physical body to produce the appropriate amount of silk as per demand or more, but wouldn't cause harm to you or anyone else?"

For the first time, all of Weaver Nyx's eyes widened at once. Her rigid posture loosened, just slightly. Above, on the webs, other Arachne leaned closer. Silvery strands quivered as they shifted, the entire chamber holding its breath.

"The human asks about our needs rather than our output? How...refreshing."

She straightened her upper body, considering.

"We require proteins-fresh meat, not the processed substitutes we're given. Calcium-rich minerals for web strength. And most critically, nectar from the Demon Realm's night-blooming flowers, particularly Lunar Dew blossoms. Without these, our silk lacks elasticity and luster."

She gestured toward her abdomen, where the shapes of inner glands faintly bulged beneath chitin.

"Our bodies can produce basic silk on minimal resources, but premium silk-the kind worth harvesting-requires proper nourishment. The previous administrator believed deprivation would force quality. He was...incorrect."

From above, legs tapped against webbing in an odd, syncopated rhythm. Their version of agreement, maybe even approval.

Lilith watched, eyes narrowed, tail perfectly still now. "Interesting. Very interesting indeed," she said.

He turned back toward her, though his presence still faced Nyx as if he stood between the two.

"So, what they need should be provided within reason so as to help with production. I would say limit the demon blossoms, I shouldn't have to reason why on that, but still, all things should be provided," he said, then glanced over his shoulder at Weaver Nyx.

"Crimes shouldn't be rewarded, but if you're going to be utilized properly, you should be accommodated properly to be used, am I right, Nyx?"

Weaver Nyx's expression shifted again, something complex and thoughtful moving behind those many eyes. Her front legs tapped a measured rhythm against the stone.

"Utilized properly...accommodated properly. You speak like someone who understands the balance of punishment and productivity."

She leaned in just a fraction.

"The Lunar Dew blossoms contain mild intoxicants-pleasant but not debilitating. I understand your caution."

Around them, the other Arachne slowly resumed their spinning. Threads stretched and connected once more, the soft hiss of silk returning as a steady background song. Still, many of them continued to glance toward the human at the center of the floor.

Lilith's gaze returned to him, sharper and more calculating than before. Her tail moved again, lazy and thoughtful.

"A pragmatic approach. Not sentimental, yet not needlessly cruel." She entered several quick notes into her tablet, claws tapping briskly.

"I'll implement dietary changes immediately. Protein sources will be improved, and calcium supplements added. The Lunar Dew extract will be administered in controlled doses, twice weekly."

Weaver Nyx straightened, head tilting in a subtle sign of respect and approval.

Lilith turned slightly.

"Come. There's more to see...and I believe you've just proven your usefulness."

He nodded once.

"Ah, yes, one more thing," he said, stepping close to Weaver Nyx.

He lifted his hand and, with deliberate care, rested his fingers beneath her chin. The gesture was gentle and steady, a quiet contact rather than a grab or a command.

"You're welcome, and thank you for your cooperation." He closed his eyes for a heartbeat, then opened them as he turned away and began to follow Lilith.

The effect was immediate.

A shiver ran through Weaver Nyx's massive body. All eight eyes widened again, pupils dilating at the unexpected human contact, this time with something like shock. The entire chamber faltered as silk lines trembled and Arachne paused in mid-spin to stare.

"You…dare touch me?"

There was no anger in her tone, only astonished confusion. It sounded like someone who had not been touched gently in a very long time.

As he walked away, one slender hand lifted to brush the exact spot where his fingers had rested, as if confirming it had really happened.

Lilith saw it all.

Her brows arched high, tail giving a single startled flick. "Fascinating. Most humans would be too terrified to make physical contact with an Arachne."

She turned and guided him toward the exit. Just before the heavy door sealed shut, he caught a glimpse of Weaver Nyx moving back to her web. Her motions were faster now, silk flowing with renewed vigor as other Arachne clustered around her, their voices a soft, excited chitter.

In the corridor, the door thudded closed behind them.

"You've certainly made an impression. I wonder if that was wide…or dangerous."

He answered without missing a step.

"It was both, this is a prison, and respect needs to be given AND earned. Also, I am still" he lifted his fingers in mocking air quotes "'human'. I do still have the weakness of lust; luckily, that lust induced her vigor, so it's a win-win, but that won't work all the time. Show no fear, but be respectful."

Lilith's eyes gleamed as she led him deeper into the dim hall. Her tail swished in a slow, thoughtful pattern. The echo of her heels on stone created a steady rhythm beneath the distant clanks and muffled shouts of the prison.

"Lust as a management technique? How...delightfully human."

Her soft chuckle carried a velvet edge. "You understand something fundamental that my predecessors missed. These creatures may be criminals, but they remain monsters with needs and desires. Deprivation breeds resentment, not productivity."

They reached a junction where the corridor split three ways. Overhead lights bathed each path in a different color. Red to the left. Blue straight ahead. Green to the right.

Lilith paused, letting him take it in.

"I'm beginning to think your assignment here wasn't entirely...coincidental. Tell me, what were you before your incarceration? Your approach suggests experience with management or perhaps...manipulation?"

The prison murmured around them. Somewhere far off, a scream cut short. Closer, the hum of machinery and magical wards filled the spaces between her words.

He gave a small, crooked smile.

"Both. Let's go with the green hall of envy, shall we?"

Her lips curved. "The green hall of envy...how appropriate. You have good instincts."

She turned toward the emerald-lit corridor. The strange green glow painted her features in a richer, more infernal shade, picking out the soft curve of her horns and the edge of her cheekbones.

She walked ahead, and as he followed, her tail occasionally brushed his leg. It could have been accidental contact. It could have been testing boundaries. In this place, intent was rarely simple.

The air grew cooler as they continued to advance. A damp, earthy scent rose to meet them, moss and stone and something older that clung beneath the prison's concrete shell.

Whatever awaited in the green hall of envy, it already felt very different from the world he had left behind.

The green-lit corridor widened as they walked, the damp air thickening with the scent of moss, blooming nectar, and something deeper, an undercurrent of ancient forest magic barely contained beneath prison steel. Lilith's steps slowed, the echo of her heels shifting from stone to metal grates as they approached a vast domed chamber.

"This section houses our plant-based inmates. Alraunes, Dryads, Mandragoras...beautiful but deadly. Most were convicted of environmental terrorism or using their pheromones to manipulate high-ranking officials."

The greenhouse chamber opened like a hidden biome inside the prison's metallic skeleton. Thick foliage thrived behind transparent containment walls, each enclosure a small ecosystem under strict control. Roots coiled through nutrient beds. Flowering bodies swayed faintly despite the still air. Some inhabitants watched with serene indifference...others with predatory hunger.

Lilith's voice continued as she guided him forward:

"Management and manipulation...a dangerous combination. I'm beginning to think you might be more valuable outside a cell."

She stopped before one of the largest containment enclosures.

Inside, an Alraune sat enthroned within a spiral of colossal petals, rich violet layered with streaks of venomous green. Thorns the length of daggers spiraled up her vine-like limbs. Her humanoid torso rose gracefully from the center of the bloom, her lavender skin glistening with dew, her hair a curtain of petal-soft purple.

Her beauty was intoxicating. Her danger was unmistakable.

He exhaled softly.

"Ooh, look, my favorite color and favorite female comic character; Poison Ivy hahaha."

He raised his hands in mock surrender, "Calm down, that's a joke, I promise it's a joke, Alrauna."

The reaction was instant.

Petals flared open like a predator baring its fangs. Her black, irisless eyes fixed on him, swallowing his reflection whole. Vines lashed against the containment glass, each impact leaving streaks of corrosive residue that hissed faintly as they slid down the barrier.

The Alraune's lips parted in a smile too sharp to be warm, "Come closer, little human. I haven't tasted man-flesh in so long…"

Her voice glided through the audio ports in the glass. She sounded silky, dangerous, and edged with hunger. Spores puffed softly from her petals, drifting like glowing dust motes before dissipating harmlessly against the barrier.

Lilith stepped beside him, tablet in hand. "This is Hemlock. Former royal gardener who poisoned three nobles and nearly collapsed an entire duchy's governing structure. Her toxins can cause hallucinations, paralysis, or even death. It all depends on her mood."

She tapped her tablet. A vent hissed open above Hemlock's enclosure, releasing a pale mist. The Alraune shuddered, her tendrils slowing, calming, settling back around her base like serpents curling to rest.

"We've been experimenting with various compounds to neutralize their pheromones. Limited success so far."

Lilith glanced sideways, evaluating his reaction to the creature that would happily devour him whole.

He stepped forward instead.

"Hemlock," he said, moving to the glass, "Be a dear and answer me a question truthfully?"

The greenhouse fell quiet. Leaves stilled. Blossoms tilted.

Hemlock's dark gaze sharpened, her tendrils pressing against the barrier like fingers eager to pierce flesh. "A question? How...novel. Most visitors just stare or shudder."

Her petals shifted, revealing more of her humanoid form. The luminous buds at her base glowed softly, pulsing to her breath. "Ask your question, little human. Truth is all I have to trade in this...greenhouse prison."

Lilith raised her tablet slightly, recording. Her tail coiled in a slow, calculating arc behind her. "Careful. Her definition of 'truth' has proven...flexible."

He ignored the warning and began to ask, "When was the last time you had fresh water or been properly seeded?"

Hemlock froze.

Every vine stilled mid-sway. Every bud tightened as though bracing for impact. Her black eyes widened, and something unguarded like fear, longing, and grief flashed through their void-dark depths. "Fresh water? They...they give us recycled nutrient solution. Filtered, sterilized...dead water."

Alraune's vines curled inward, protective. "As for seeding...three years, two months, and sixteen days. The guards fear pollination. They think we'll create spore-children to escape."

Lilith shifted uneasily, her jaw tightening as if the truth scraped against her professionalism.

"The protocols are necessary. The last time an Alraune was properly pollinated, her offspring infiltrated the ventilation system. Three guards were hospitalized."

Hemlock pressed closer to the glass, voice low and sharp. "Why do you ask such things, human? To taunt? To ...understand?"

Around them, other plant creatures pressed nearer to their barriers. Leaves rustled. Petals quivered. Mandragoras peeked through their soil beds with glowing eyes.

They were all listening.

He didn't flinch. "I'd say give her fresh water at least biweekly, and what the hell did y'all seed her with?"

"Fresh water?" Lilith blinked at him... *actually* blinked, startled out of her usual cool detachment. "That's...not in the standard protocols. The nutrient solution is scientifically formulated to-"

Hemlock broke Lilith's sentence with loud laughter. A bitter, cracking sound like a branch snapping under frost. "Science! They know nothing of what we need. Rainwater. Stream water. Living water with minerals and microbes."

Lilith scanned her tablet again, visibly uncomfortable. "The last seeding was...controlled. Pollen from non-sentient plants. It prevents reproduction while maintaining basic biological functions."

Her lips thinned as she looked at him. "Fresh water could be arranged, I suppose. But why would you care about the comfort of a convicted poisoner?"

Every living plant-woman in the chamber leaned toward the conversation. Hope was blooming like a dangerous seed.

He answered flatly: "I don't."

The bluntness struck harder than raised voices ever could, but he continued speaking. "Y'all are using her for a reason, and if you're going to seed her, it needs to be with a non-compatible entity to decrease her killer mood but still satiate to get proper results. She's right, science. I guess knowing science does mean I'm a bit soft and caring, but I also like appropriate results."

The greenhouse air shifted around him, thick with humidity and something else... an awakening, perhaps.

Hemlock's expression transformed as she studied him: first surprise, then something far more dangerous and intimate flickered across her violet-tinged features. The venomous barbs lining her vines retracted in a slow ripple, a reflex she clearly had not intended to reveal. Behind her, bioluminescent buds pulsed brighter, blooming with internal light as though stirred from dormancy. "The human understands...fascinating." She said.

Lilith's crimson eyes narrowed in appraisal. She shifted her weight, heels clicking softly on the metal grate as she made several quick notes on her tablet. "You have botanical knowledge? Interesting. Most humans sent here barely understand monster physiology, let alone specialized care requirements."

With a flick of her wrist, she entered a command. A small panel opened in the wall beside Hemlock's enclosure, presenting a narrow, vial. Some internal nutrient sample. Lilith regarded him with growing intrigue. "Perhaps you'd care to elaborate on your...scientific approach? The prison's research division might find your insights valuable."

Around the greenhouse chamber, every plant monster had gone unnervingly still. Dryads swiveled in their soil beds. Mandragoras peeked partially from their burrows, leafy tendrils twitching. The entire ecosystem held its breath, evaluating the human who dared speak of their needs.

Hemlock leaned closer, petals brushing the containment glass, her voice a sibilant whisper rich with warning. "Don't trust them, human. They'll drain your knowledge like they drain our vitality."

He looked up at her, his gaze was steady and deep. He stared lustfully for a complete moment. "Then I'll finally feel something if they do." He grinned devilishly, turning back to Lilith like nothing had just happened.

Hemlock reacted like a creature touched by lightning. Her petals flushed to a darker, richer purple, and her vines writhed against the glass in agitation...or a different kind of excitement. A dust of shimmering spores lifted around her bloom, swirling like luminous smoke. "Bold words from prey...you might be more interesting than the usual specimens they drag through here."

Lilith watched this exchange with a hunger for data, not flesh, though her curiosity was unmistakable. He noticed a small camera repositioned overhead, responding to a hidden command from Lilith's tablet.

"Fascinating response pattern...most humans cower when Hemlock displays interest." Administrator Lilith stepped closer to him, her tone lowering into the private register of someone evaluating more than his knowledge. "The research division has been attempting to develop more...effective methods for managing our botanical inmates. Your apparent knowledge, combined with this unusual rapport, might be valuable. Would you be interested in a temporary reassignment to this section? With appropriate safeguards, of course."

Inside her enclosure, Hemlock began a slow, hypnotic movement, a type that craves attention. Her vines rippled along the soil as she swayed, petals shifting like unfolding velvet. The other plant monsters retreated deeper into their habitats, granting her space, as though instinctively recognizing dominance in display.

He leaned forward toward Lilith, lowering his voice to a whisper meant only for her.

He leaned in closer to her, breathing into her ear, "It'd be a fun fling, but it wouldn't last, and the heartbreak would cause this prison to flip upside down. Let's keep moving, dear." He snapped back. Gathering his composure, he turned to Hemlock.

"Until next time, dear, if you're good, we may get privileges so I can seed you myself." He winked at her. "Hahaha, joking, joking," he raised his hands and turned to walk away.

As he exited, he gave a deeper, more intense stare, "Or am I?"

Lilith's composure faltered momentarily. Her pointed ears twitched, and a faint flush crept across the high bones of her cheeks. Her tail gave a quick, betraying flick before resuming its disciplined arc.

She cleared her throat softly, forcing her voice back into immaculate professionalism. "I...see. Let's continue the tour then."

Behind him, Hemlock trembled in visceral reaction. Her vines writhed and curled tighter around her bloom, releasing a burst of glowing spores that filled her enclosure with radiant haze. "Such promises from a caged bird! I'll remember your words, human. Perhaps I'll even...behave." Her laughter chased him into the corridor like a living rustle.

The other plant monsters watched his departure in silence; their predatory gazes softened into something contemplative like curiosity where hostility once thrived.

Lilith guided him toward the exit, boots clicking in a quickened rhythm. She dismissed a notification on her tablet, though her eyes lingered on his profile with new calculation. "You've certainly made an impression. That's…unusual. Most inmates don't respond to visitors with anything but hostility."

She led him through the greenhouse's airlock and into a sterile metal corridor, the green glow fading behind him. "Where would you like to continue our tour? The general population area or perhaps the workshop facilities?"

He didn't hesitate. "Workshop. Let's see if there's dwarf mechanizations at play."

Lilith's eyes lit with a genuine spark of interest, her professional mask slipping for a moment to reveal enthusiasm. "The workshop? Excellent choice." She answered, "We have quite the operation there."

She led him through a series of increasingly complex security checkpoints. Each barrier required not just her palm, but a swirl of lilim energy traced in glowing runes. The air shimmered with each authentication. Finally, she reached the last door, a great slab of reinforced enchanted metal.

She placed her palm on the reader and sketched an intricate sigil in the air. The lock disengaged with a deep metallic rumble.

The door slid open, revealing a chamber blazing with forge light and the clangor of enchanted machinery.

And the unmistakable boisterous laughter of dwarven engineers.

The workshop unfolded before him like an industrial cathedral, alive with noise and heat. Sparks leapt from anvils in bright sprays, runes glowed along steel girders, and the rhythmic thunder of hammers echoed beneath the high, vaulted ceiling. The air was thick with the metallic tang of iron mixed with sulfur and faint traces of arcane residue, the atmosphere vibrating with the ceaseless alchemy of creation.

Rows of workbenches extended into the depths of the chamber, each occupied by dwarf-type monster inmates. They were compact in stature but formidable in presence. Their bodies bore the marks of their monstrous bloodlines: skin of metal or stone, runes carved into their arms, gemstone-studded beards, ember-glowing eyes, tools growing directly from

49

fingertips. Power emanated from each of them, the raw, disciplined strength of true artisans.

Lilith walked at his side, her violet eyes gleaming in the forge-light. "Our engineering division. Primarily staffed by Dwarf-type monster girls. Highly skilled, though temperamental."

At the nearest bench, a copper-skinned dwarf lifted her hammer, the muscles in her arms rippling beneath burn scars and tattooed schematics. Her beard - yes, she had a beard, and it was braided and glimmering with luminous gemstones; it shifted as she turned toward him. Her forge-fire eyes assessed him with a heat all their own.

Grimhild, the Forge Dwarf, said, "brought another gawker, Administrator? This one at least doesn't look like he'd faint at the sight of proper metalwork."

She eyed him appraisingly, her muscular arms crossed over her leather apron. Burn scars and intricate tattoos on her body depicted mechanical designs covering what skin is visible.

He stepped toward her without flinching, lowering his tone so the words vibrated like coals settling in a firepit. "I actually like metal work. If done properly, it can make fine weaponry, homes, or even…" He leaned slightly closer, his voice dipping dark and low. "…life."

A hush fell around the immediate workstations. Grimhild's eyes flared brighter, her hammer stilled mid-air. Other dwarves slowed their movements, sensing a shift in the room's temperature.

She reached beneath her bench and produced a small mechanical bird, delicate gears humming softly beneath its metallic plumage. With a twist of a key, the creature sprang to life, its wings fluttering with uncanny grace. Its jeweled eyes gleamed like miniatures of her own. "Life, is it? Bold words." Her smile was bold and sarcastic. "Most humans think we just make pretty trinkets and prison shackles."

She let the bird hover between them for a moment. "This one knows the old ways, Administrator. Might be worth something after all."

Lilith made a notation on her tablet, her lips curving faintly. "Grimhild rarely shows her personal objects to outsiders. Consider yourself…privileged."

A dwarf whose obsidian skin reflected the workshop's fiery glow approached, her fingers splitting seamlessly into precision tools as she wiped grease from her apron. Mechanism Dwarf, the Cogwheel said: "What's this then? The new meat appreciates proper craft? Or just talking pretty to get favors?"

Her tone had the sharp edge of challenge, but curiosity pulsed beneath each syllable.

He studied the mechanical bird, admiration softening his expression.

"Hmm, birds are fine. But I personally think ornithopters show true versatility." This time, he let genuine appreciation color his voice. "It's beautiful. Gotta love the smell of ironworks and sulfur, eh, Lilith?"

Lilith's nose wrinkled delicately, though amusement glimmered in her eyes. "I prefer the scent of ancient tomes and soul energy myself, but…there is something primal about this place."

Grimhild barked a delighted laugh. "Ornithopters! Ha! The human knows his mechanisms. Been years since anyone mentioned those to me."

The mechanical bird shifted, panels sliding, wings expanding with whisper-soft clicks, transforming into a miniature ornithopter boasting flawless articulation.

"Never show all your gears at once. That's what my dad taught me."

Cogwheel circled him, her gear-shaped pupils spinning with the mechanical precision of a lock assessing a key. "You've worked forge before, human? Your hands don't look it." She asked.

She gestured to a complex contraption on her workbench, one that appeared to be a security mechanism with multiple moving parts. "We're not just making pretty toys here. Every lock, every security system in this prison, we have designed them all. Making escape impossible…unless you know the maker's touch."

She winked, a dangerous glint in her gear-shaped pupils.

He dropped to one knee, palms up in offering, his posture honest and unguarded. "Aye. I'm no blacksmith. But I know a hard day's work. And I respect the art."

Grimhild examined his palms with expert scrutiny. The workshop seemed to hold its breath, dwarves pausing mid-hammer strike, molten metal cooling unheard in their crucibles.

Out of curiosity that she couldn't hold, Grimhild asked, "Not forge-hands, but not soft either. What's your craft then, human?"

Lilith answered for him, her voice tinged with something unreadable. "Our new inmate has quite a diverse background. His file indicates experience with…various trades."

Cogwheel's lips quirked. "'various trades' usually means thief or worse. Still…"

She reached into her pocket and withdrew a small cog, intricately etched with runes that pulsed softly in the forge-light. She pressed it firmly into his palm. "Anyone who appreciates proper craft deserves at least one token. Might come in handy someday."

The guards shifted, tense, but made no move to interrupt. The air shimmered faintly as warding runes responded to the exchange.

He rose to his full height, studying the tiny masterpiece in his hand. "I accept graciously. And no, I'm no thief."

A wry, self-deprecating smirk tugged at his lips. "I suck at picking a lock… or properly caressing a clit." He chuckled, slyly.

A beat of silence and then the workshop erupted.

Dwarven laughter rolled through the chamber like an avalanche, loud and full-bodied. Grimhild doubled over, beard shaking. Cogwheel snorted so hard her pupils spun in reverse. Even the stoic steel-scaled dwarf cracked a grin.

Lilith flushed a faint violet and cleared her throat sharply, wings flicking once. "That's…quite enough of that. We should continue the tour."

Before he could move, a dwarf whose arms were covered in overlapping metallic scales approached. Heat radiated from the freshly hammered metal she held in one hand, her molten-orange eyes glowing with appraisal.

Ironheart, the Steel Dwarf, said, "You've got nerve, I'll give you that. Most newcomers don't last a day talking like that."

His voice lowered, sincerity threading through the rough humor. "It is my own personal custom to be upfront and brutally honest. Still, while maintaining some respect and if I falter, I correct appropriately. I'm not perfect. If I were, I wouldn't be here."

Ironheart's metallic scales shifted and clicked as she nodded, the sound reminiscent of chainmail sliding into place. She was taller than most of the other dwarven inmates, almost a towering figure for her species, with a network of glowing orange veins pulsing beneath her skin like molten metal racing through forge channels. When she crossed her arms, the light beneath her scales rippled in subtle waves.

"Honesty. Rare commodity in here." Ironheart said, "Most come in lying, leave lying, if they leave at all." She extended a hand toward him.

Her palm bore a perfectly circular scar, glowing faintly from within, evidence of a forge-born wound healed by her own craftsmanship rather than any healer's touch. "They call me Ironheart. Not because I'm soft inside, because I forged my own replacement after... a workplace incident."

Beside him, Lilith checked her timepiece. The device was etched with shifting arcane symbols, the markings spiraling and rearranging in patterns only she seemed to understand. Her violet tail tapped once against the floor, a subtle cue that their schedule pressed forward. "We really must continue. The workshop crew has actual assignments to complete, and our new inmate has much more to see."

Grimhild returned to her bench, but not without a gesture of respect. She thumped her fist twice against her chest, a salute from the forge. "Come back sometime when the Administrator isn't hovering. We'll show you what real crafting looks like." She winked playfully.

As Lilith turned toward the exit, Cogwheel cupped her hands around her mouth and shouted after him, sparks dancing in her mechanical eyes. "Practice makes perfect, human! On both skills!"

Laughter erupted once more, louder than before, echoing like rolling thunder through the industrial cavern.

He slipped the rune-etched cog into his left pocket, then clasped Ironheart's burning-hot hand with his right. His grip was firm, resolute, unflinching despite the heat that would have blistered most men. Ironheart's molten-orange eyes widened at the unexpected steadiness.

"My pleasure," he told her evenly. "And if plausible, I will return."

Releasing her grip, he straightened, shoulders squared. He turned toward Cogwheel with a wicked grin.

"Hey, Cogwheel! Maybe next time you can show me some help on both skills, hahaha."

The dwarves roared again.

He followed Lilith out as the security door sealed behind them with a deep, resonant *thud*. The noise swallowed the workshop's warmth, leaving only the sterile cold of the administrative corridor.

Ironheart's voice rumbled behind the door, faint but unmistakably approving: "Hmph. Maybe you'll last a week after all."

Cogwheel shouted one last parting taunt through the wall's audio vents: "Bring chocolate next time! Works wonders for both lessons!"

Lilith's wings fluttered with mild exasperation as she led him down the hall. Her heels clicked sharply, the sound punctuating the quiet like metronomic strokes.

She tapped her tablet, adjusting settings that caused the corridor lights to shift subtly in hue. "You've made quite an impression. The forge crew rarely warms to newcomers, especially humans."

She tilted her head slightly, eyes narrowing. "The little token that Cogwheel gave you... I'd keep it well hidden. Not all inmates appreciate fraternization with the maintenance staff. Some see them as extensions of prison authority."

He only nodded. Her gaze lingered on him for a few seconds longer before she resumed walking. "Our next stop is the mess hall. Perfect timing for the midday meal... and your first real introduction to the general population."

He cracked his neck with casual finality. "Let's proceed." His voice held no fear.

The corridor stretched long and sterile ahead of him, shifting subtly between shades of purple and gray, as if reacting to Lilith's presence. Security runes glowed faintly with each checkpoint they passed. Lilith walked with practiced grace, her heels striking a steady rhythm against the polished floor.

Lilith gestured toward the approaching entrance where oversized runes pulsed with a warning glow. "The mess hall can be…overwhelming for newcomers. Each species has distinct dietary requirements and territorial tendencies." She further showed him around. Welcoming, warning, "we've had three riots this month alone over seating arrangements. The lamias refuse to sit near the Arachnes, the dragons demand extra space for their tails, and the slimes… well, they tend to get everywhere."

The massive double doors opened with a metallic hydraulic hiss.

Inside was chaos.

The mess hall was a sprawling cavern of long tables and feeding stations, filled with hundreds of monster inmates. Voices clashed with hisses, guttural laughter, snarls, and the symphony of clattering dishes. Scents intermingled with charred meat, exotic herbs, pheromones, and the raw musk of predatory species.

Lilith leaned closer, her voice low. "Welcome to the beating heart of Monster Girl Prison. Choose your first meal companions wisely because first impressions tend to stick." Her smile was equal parts warning and amusement, eager to see what's coming.

He stepped forward and stopped cold.

Silence rippled outward as dozens, then hundreds, of monster girls turned toward the newcomer. Their eyes glowed in myriad hues. Conversations faltered. Some inmates leaned forward. Others bared fangs. A few simply stared, assessing the human who dared cross their threshold.

"They always notice fresh blood." Administrator Lilith pointed subtly.

An obsidian-furred minotaur stood from her seat, towering above all others with a brutal, imposing presence. Tattoos crawled across her thick arms, and her horns were filed to lethal points; those horns caught the overhead light with a gleam meant for intimidation. A gold ring pierced her nose, and the air around her vibrated with dominance.

"Ravager." The name whispered across nearby tables like a spark catching dry tinder.

She snapped a metal spoon between her fingers without looking away from him.

Another warning came from Lilith, "That's Ravager. Three life sentences for what she did to the last human who crossed her. I'd recommend staring elsewhere."

But he was already moving, leaving her at the threshold.

"Well, I'll leave you to it. Guards are stationed at each corner if there's trouble. Good luck." She said, not with fear but another amused warning.

He didn't stare elsewhere. He locked eyes with Ravager. And strode forward.

Conversations died instantly. Hard gazes tracked his steps. Some inmates leaned forward as though scented blood.

He stopped only a few feet from the minotaur's towering form and exhaled sharply through his nose, a deliberate, animalistic snort.

The room stopped. Silent, frozen.

Ravager rose to her full height; she was nearly eight feet, and her shadow swallowed the light around him. Her nostrils flared as she took in his posture, his scent, his lack of fear. The broken spoon clanged against the table as it fell from her grasp.

Ravager, the minotaur, glanced at him with something more than anger in her eyes, a challenge, "You lost, little man? Or just eager to die?" Her voice was deep, melodic, and chillingly composed.

Behind her, her gang stirred. A scarred minotaur with a jagged, broken horn grinned like a predator catching familiar prey.

The Scarred Minotaur stepped in, "Boss, let me break him in. been too long since we had fresh meat."

The hall held its breath.

Ravager raised one massive hand, and the motion alone was enough to silence the scarred minotaur at her side. The half-spoken threat died on Gorehorn's lips as the boss kept her gaze locked on him. Slowly, deliberately, Ravager leaned forward, bringing her broad, bovine face closer until he could see the faint scars along her muzzle and the tiny imperfections in the gold ring threaded through her nose. Under the harsh mess hall lights, it gleamed like a warning.

Her breath washed over him, a mix of spice, raw meat, and something metallic that spoke of blood spilled and battles won. "You've got bigger balls than brains, human. I respect that. Doesn't mean I won't hang your intestines from the ceiling fans if you're wasting my time."

Her dark eyes narrowed as she studied him, and behind the brutish power, there was sharp awareness, intelligence honed by years of surviving and ruling this place.

He met that gaze with a devious glint of his own, lips curling at the edges.

He did not look away, "I'd rather not waste your time, but I do love your fur. If I have free time, I wouldn't mind trying to work out or train with you. Everyone else may be scared, but I love a challenge, and there are no failures, only lessons."

A ripple of murmurs swept across the surrounding tables. Some inmates twisted in their seats to stare openly, others froze mid-bite. A few simply watched with predatory stillness. Ravager's eyes widened for the briefest instant before narrowing again, the motion of her thick tail behind her a single, slow sweep that could have been irritation... or amusement.

She straightened to her full height, shoulders rolling back. "You've got a death wish or you're truly stupid. Either way, entertaining."

She snorted, a harsh blast of air, then barked out a laugh that cut through the tension and abruptly took the edge off her gang's bloodlust. With a lazy sweep of her arm, she gestured to an empty space at the table. "Sit. Eat. We'll see if your muscles match your mouth."

Gorehorn growled low in protest, the broken-horn minotaur tensing as if ready to challenge the decision.

Ravager split her with a glare so sharp it might as well have been a blade, "Shut it, Gorehorn. I decide who sits at my table."

He stepped forward into the shadow of their territory, aware of the eyes tracking his every move. At a nearby table, a lizardwoman dragged a claw across her throat in a silent prediction. Up by the guard station, he caught sight of a mantis-type warden sliding what looked like a betting chip toward her colleague, both of them glancing in his direction with interest.

Ravager slammed a tray down in front of the empty place at her side, more a challenge than an offer. A massive hunk of rare meat, still bleeding and barely cooked, lay on the metal plate. The smell of iron and fat rose from it in a hot wave.

"Training yard. Tomorrow. 0600 hours. Don't be late, or I'll hunt you down myself." She jerked her chin toward the meal. "Let's see what you're made of, little man inside and out."

Her gang erupted in coarse laughter, but beneath the noise, there was something new in Ravager's gaze, curiosity wrapped in challenge, a predator deciding if the prey in front of her might be something else entirely.

His eyes glistened with something between anticipation and hunger as he took in the meat. "Mmm, I'd prefer a knife, but I don't mind feasting like a…" he lifted his fingers in mock air quotes "monster."

He dropped onto the bench at the spot indicated, grabbed the slab of meat with one hand, and tore into it with a brutal bite, ripping through flesh and sinew.

The table went silent.

Blood slipped down his chin, warm and thick. The meat fought his teeth, dense and resistant. Clearly prepared for jaws stronger than a human's. He chewed and swallowed without breaking eye contact. "Well, well…the human's got teeth."

Gorehorn snorted, but the derision in her expression had softened, uncertainty creeping into her eyes. Another minotaur, one with complex carvings etched along her horns like a maze of scars and glyphs, leaned forward to get a better look at him.

The Carved-Horn Minotaur said, "Where'd they catch you, human? What'd you do to end up here?"

Ravager tore off a chunk of her own meal, chewing slowly and thoughtfully as she listened, her dominance over the table stamped into every motion.

The prison tattoo on her shoulder, a labyrinth cradling a tiny human figure at its center, caught the light when she shifted. "Must've been something special. They don't waste cells on petty criminals."

She leaned in again, her massive bulk folding over the table, shadow swallowing him whole. Her voice dropped low, a private rumble meant only for their immediate circle. "Fair warning, fresh meat. You've bought yourself a day by amusing me. But tomorrow in the yard? That's where I'll decide if you're worth keeping around or if you're just another stain on my record."

Her huge hand came down on his shoulder, the impact strong enough to jolt him on the bench. It bordered on a blow, but there was weight in it that felt more like a test than an attempt to crush him. Respect, in this place, sounded like pain.

He leaned slightly closer, meeting that challenge with steady eyes as he lifted the meat for another savage bite. "I warned you, only lessons never fail. What I do is out of respect for you, not a challenge, but" he tore another gouge from the meat, speaking around the chew, "take that as you will."

Ravager inhaled sharply through her nose, nostrils flaring. The other minotaurs watched him now with focused attention, no longer simply amused, but measuring. Ravager leaned back, crossing her massive arms over her chest, tattoos flexing over powerful muscles. "Respect, huh? Been a long time since I heard that word in here."

She held his gaze a moment longer, then bent to draw a crude shiv from her boot. Across the room, several guards stiffened, hands hovering near their batons.

Ravager ignored them. She used the blade only to spear a chunk from her own tray, a dense piece of meat, thicker, darker, more prized, and dropped it onto his plate with a heavy smack. "Heart. Best part. You'll need the strength."

Gorehorn shifted uneasily, clearly unhappy with the favor being shown. The carved-horn minotaur leaned in close, her voice dropping into a conspiratorial murmur. "Name's Labyrinth. The last human who sat here left in a body bag. You've got the boss curious, that's rare."

Ravager pushed back from the table in one sudden, fluid motion, towering above them all. Conversation around the mess hall dipped again; even those not directly watching could feel the pull of her presence. "Tomorrow, human. Dawn. Don't disappoint me."

She turned away, her heavy hooves thudding against the floor as she strode off.

Her gang rose with her, following in her wake like armored satellites, everyone except Labyrinth, who remained where she was, eyes still fixed on him. She said with a straight face, "Word of advice, whatever game you're playing, be ready to finish it. Ravager doesn't forgive disappointment."

He gouged another bite of meat from the heart she'd gifted him, chewing with quiet satisfaction. "I needed the protein, she understood that. I gave her respect, and she answered accordingly. This is no game. When you step into a ring with a bull, you mustn't back down lest you be skewered. Plus, she's gorgeous, I couldn't help myself."

Labyrinth's eyes widened, then a slow, dangerous smile crept across her broad face. She leaned back, shoulders shaking faintly with a low laugh as one thick finger traced a pattern along the carved grooves of her horn. "Gorgeous, is it? Bold words. Most inmates would sooner call a hurricane 'refreshing'"

Her chuckle rumbled through her chest, warm and dark. Around them, the mess hall gradually returned to its usual din, but more than a few gazes still drifted toward him, toward the empty space where Ravager had stood. Curiosity now colored those looks, alongside confusion that he was still in one piece.

Labyrinth's voice dropped, becoming more intimate, more dangerous. "You know what happened to the last inmate who complimented Ravager? She ripped his tongue out and said she wanted to keep the part that made pretty lies."

She leaned closer, thick forearms braced on the table, her bulk blocking him from the casual surveillance of the guards. "But you...you're different. I can smell it. Just don't mistake her interest for weakness. Ravager didn't become the top bull by being merciful."

She rose slowly from the bench, towering over him one last time, her expression turning thoughtful. "Rest well tonight, human. Tomorrow will test every bone in your body."

With that, she turned and followed in Ravager's wake, leaving him seated alone at a table most inmates wouldn't even look at for too long.

He finished another bite of meat, feeling multiple sets of eyes on him.

From across the hall, a slender Arachne with violet skin and long, graceful limbs lifted what appeared to be a glass of wine in his direction. Multiple eyes glinted with dark amusement, each pair reflecting a shard of his reckless choice.

She toasted him silently.

The Arachne watched him with layered interest as she drifted past his table, her violet skin catching the mess hall's cold lighting like polished amethyst. Dozens of delicate eyes glittered with amusement as she lifted her glass in acknowledgment. Silk folded across her shoulders like a handmade shawl, elegant despite its prison-issue nature. Six tattoos, one on each visible arm, marked her as a long-term inmate, each symbol etched with meticulous precision.

He returned the gesture with a nod, chewing steadily as he closed and reopened his eyes in a gesture meant to appear respectful. She smiled faintly before moving on.

The last of Ravager's offering disappeared between his teeth just as a harsh bell rang through the mess hall. Conversation shattered into motion. The guards were hulking or sleek, feathered or furred. They moved through the rows with trained efficiency, their presence restoring order with practiced ease.

The Mantis Guard exclaimed, "Move it, prisoners! Recreation hour's over! Back to your cells for count!"

The Arachne glided past him on her way to the disposal bins, moving with predatory elegance despite the restraints binding her lower limbs. When she drew level with him, she paused just long enough for her voice to slide into his space like silk drawn across skin.

"Quite the spectacle, darling. Ravager doesn't share food, not even with her lovers. I'm a Widow. Find me in the library if you survive tomorrow." The Arachne said, and with a final flick of her silk shawl, she vanished into the crowd.

A mantis guard stalked toward him from the guard station, mandibles clicking sharply with impatience as her scythe-like arms gestured toward the exit, "on your feet, human! Cell block D awaits its newest resident."

He rose to his full height and lifted his wrist, displaying the bracelet with its newly encoded clearance sequence, allowing the blue glow to catch the guard's unfriendly eye.

His head cocked sideways, a dangerous glare sharpening his expression. "Thought I wasn't part of the common rabble."

The guard froze mid-step, her antennae flicking forward in irritation and something like unease. She leaned closer, examining the bracelet's codes with a sudden shift from contempt to suspicion. Around them, inmates slowed their exodus, collectively sensing potential conflict.

The Mantis Guard said, "Special assignment prisoner? Why wasn't I informed?"

Her scythe-arm shifted position instinctively, half defensive, half contemplative, as she stepped away to activate her thorax-mounted communicator. Her chatter became a series of low, precise clicks. After several tense seconds, her posture stiffened. "Follow me, human. Seems you've got...accommodations elsewhere."

The murmurs behind him thickened instantly. Widow paused in the crowd, her slender body half-turned, multiple eyes narrowing as she assessed the situation with renewed interest.

The mantis guard led him through an auxiliary corridor reserved for personnel with advanced clearance codes. Her chitin clicked rhythmically with each step, echoing off the walls in sharp metallic cadence. "Warden Arachna doesn't usually take special interest in new arrivals. Consider yourself...fortunate? Or perhaps not." This was a warning.

She brought him to a fortified elevator requiring multiple security authorizations. Her tone shifted as she raised a claw to the panel. It was less of hostility and more of warnings. "Whatever game you're playing, human, tread carefully. The Warden doesn't tolerate disappointment."

He stared at her with the same cold intensity he had worn since entering the hall. "Mind yourself around me. I still don't trust a mantis." He stepped into the elevator.

She followed, her mandibles clicking softly, not quite amusement, not quite irritation. "Smart human. My species does have...certain appetites."

The elevator sealed shut with a hiss. The air grew cooler, the lighting sterile and bright. Her exoskeleton gleamed under it like lacquered armor.

She slid a specialized key into the system, and the elevator surged upward, bypassing floors most inmates would never see. "But don't flatter yourself. Prison-issued suppressants keep our more...primal urges in check. Besides, the Warden would have my head. Literally." She emphasized, "If I damaged her new project."

He caught glimpses through the small window: sealed containment units pulsing with sigils, arcane labs veiled in wards, and administrative quarters that looked like part of an entirely different world.

The Mantis Guard said, "Curious bracelet you have. Only seen that code sequence once before. That prisoner didn't last a week."

The elevator slowed to a stop.

When the doors slid open, the corridor beyond seemed to belong to another realm entirely. The floors were polished stone, smooth as obsidian and carved with faint web-like patterns. Ambient lighting hummed in soft violet tones, casting flowing shadows across the walls. The silence here held weight; it was the silence of authority, of power.

At the far end stood an ornate door made of dark wood carved with arachnid motifs, moths, webs, and segmented limbs woven into a design that felt both ancient and new.

"End of the line, human. The Warden awaits. And a word of advice: When she offers you tea, accept it. It's considered…impolite to refuse." She advised him, or perhaps it was yet another warning.

He stepped out of the elevator, boots echoing through the unnatural quiet.

The corridor stretched ahead, longer than physics should allow. The walls shimmered subtly, as if woven from threads of silk infused with dim starlight.

As he reached the door, it swung soundlessly open, not by hinge but by will.

The office beyond defied everything he'd come to expect from a prison. Plush burgundy carpets muted his steps, antique shelves lined with rare books rose along the walls, and the polished obsidian desk at the room's center gleamed like stagnant water beneath a moonless sky.

Behind that desk waited Warden Arachna.

Her exoskeleton gleamed a deep, oil-slick black etched with crimson markings that pulsed faintly in the dim lighting. Eight jewel-toned eyes, each a different color, each reflecting him from a unique angle, tracked his every movement. Her human torso wore a tailored blazer, elegant and aristocratic, while her enormous arachnid lower half remained hidden behind the desk, shifting with subtle, predatory grace.

The air itself changed as she regarded him.

As though the room recognized her authority and demanded he do the same.

Warden Arachna regarded him with cool amusement as he stepped deeper into her office, the glow of her multifaceted eyes shifting through subtle shades of ruby, jade, topaz, and amethyst. Her voice slid through the air with aristocratic ease. "Ah, our newest…acquisition. Please, take a seat."

She gestured toward a high-backed chair upholstered in dark velvet. A secondary hand, one of the four that moved with hypnotic grace, lifted a delicate teapot and poured steaming liquid into bone-fine porcelain.

Her movements were fluid and refined, yet held a predatory undertone that hinted at the creature beneath her administrative veneer. "I've been watching your first day with great interest. Most humans cower in their first week. You've managed to intrigue Ravager and Widow in mere hours. Quite the achievement."

She slid the teacup toward him with an elegant flick of her wrist, all eight of her jewel-toned eyes focused unblinking upon him. "Now, let's discuss your…unique situation, shall we?"

He sighed softly in appreciation, lifting the cup with a murmur of casual charm. "Ooh, I prefer having Earl Grey, jasmine, and citrus with a hefty amount of protein I just consumed." He chuckled lightly, then added with a small bow of his head, "Thank you."

He accepted the tea and sank into the chair.

Arachna's mandibles clicked lightly in amusement as she studied him over the rim of her own porcelain cup. One of her hands drifted beneath the desk and returned holding a crystal vial filled with shimmering liquid. She poured a measured amount into his tea before setting the vial aside. "How fortunate. This particular blend happens to be Earl Grey with jasmine notes. The…protein supplement is my personal touch."

He drank while watching her exoskeleton glisten beneath the lamplight.

Warden Arachna said to him, "Most prisoners don't recognize the opportunity when they're brought to my chambers. They see only the spider, not the web of possibilities I can weave for them."

Rising higher behind the desk, her lower body revealed itself. She looked sleek, powerful, and marked with the insignia of prison authority. There were symbols carved along her abdomen like lacquered armor, each sigil glowing faintly with arcane energy.

"Your file makes for fascinating reading. The crime that brought you here was…unusual. And your psychological evaluation suggests adaptability beyond the typical human range. Tell me, do you know why you've been assigned that particular bracelet code?" Her gaze dropped to his wrist with chilling focus.

He sipped the tea again, eyes dark and unfazed as he murmured under his breath, "You are gorgeous." Then, in answer to her question, he said evenly, "So, I do not know why I've been assigned as I have been."

The Warden's mandibles clicked again, this time in clear satisfaction. "Flattery will get you…everywhere and nowhere in my prison, human. But I appreciate the sentiment." Her eight eyes slightly softened, but her attention never wavered. "That bracelet marks you for my special projects division. You see, this facility serves multiple purposes beyond mere incarceration. Some prisoners become test subjects, others labor resources, and a select few…"

She tapped a finger against the obsidian desk, each tap echoing like a drop of water in a cavern. "…a select few become assets. Your particular crime against monsterkind, combined with your psychological profile, suggests you might be more valuable outside a cell. I need individuals who can navigate both human and monster societies with…flexibility."

Her elegant brow lifted, "You'll remain an inmate officially, but you'll work directly under my authority on certain sensitive matters. In exchange, your accommodations will be considerably improved, and your sentence potentially shortened. The alternative is twenty years in general population, where I suspect Ravager's interest in you might become problematic."

He tilted his head slightly, the corner of his mouth lifting. "Hm. Didn't I already just make a similar deal?"

The shift in the room was instant.

Arachna's eight eyes narrowed into razor-thin slits. The air grew tight, colder. Her movements became precise, deliberate, and dangerous. She set her teacup down with a click that echoed louder than it should have.

"Similar deal? How…interesting." She rose, fully this time, towering above the desk as her formidable arachnid body unfurled. The ceremonial dagger strapped to one of her legs glimmered with a warning gleam.

"There are no other 'deals' in my prison except those I personally authorize. Perhaps you'd care to elaborate on this…arrangement you believe you've made?" Her legs clicked softly against the floor as she circled him. One hand reached toward his bracelet, examining it with chilly precision.

"This is my personal authorization code. Someone has been very presumptuous indeed. Was it Ravager? Or perhaps one of my more ambitious guards?" She leaned closer, an intoxicating blend of exotic perfume and something older, more primal was rolling off her skin.

He kept his posture relaxed as he answered: "Try the other warden?"

Arachna went still. Unnervingly still. Her mandibles snapped once, sharply. Each of her eight eyes dilated and constricted in rapid succession before flattening into slits of pure fury.

"Other…warden?" She moved with sudden predatory grace, circling him faster, her shadow cast in eight directions across the room.

"There is no other warden in MY facility. Only Deputy Wardens who answer to ME." Her hand slammed onto a glowing crystal orb, and streams of security footage flickered within it. Hallways, containment cells, workshops.

"Someone is playing a dangerous game. Impersonating prison administration is punishable by…well, let's just say even monsters fear the consequences." Then, her fury shifted, refined into something colder, sharper, fully controlled.

"Describe this 'other warden' to me. Every detail. This could be more valuable than you realize, human. And if you prove useful in uncovering this deception, your position here will improve…considerably." Her hand drifted near her dagger, though she made no move to draw it.

He took one more sip of the tea, slowly, deliberately, and said: "Warden Morrigan."

The reaction was explosive.

Arachna's exoskeleton tightened, cracking faintly under sudden tension. The teacup in her hand shattered, black liquid spilling across the obsidian desk like venom. Her eyes burned with recognition.

"Morrigan." The name left her mouth as a hiss.

She swept aside the broken porcelain with a contemptuous motion and reached for a concealed compartment within her desk. From it, she withdrew a small, ornate key engraved with runic sigils.

"The Eastern Wing is not under my jurisdiction. It operates…independently. A political arrangement I've been forced to tolerate."

She slid the key across the desk toward him.

"This facility was built on ancient ruins with…unique properties. The prison is effectively two institutions sharing the same physical space but existing in different…let's call them 'frequencies.' Morrigan oversees her domain, I oversee mine." Her eight eyes narrowed in unison, luminous with equal parts fury and intrigue.

The web had just become far more complicated.

Warden Arachna's fury had faded into something colder and sharper, an emotion that glittered like venom on the edge of a blade. Her eight eyes focused on him with predatory precision.

"But she has been recruiting from MY prisoner population. That bracelet marks you as MINE. Yet somehow she's already approached you?" Her voice softened into a silken whisper, dangerous in its beauty. "Whatever she offered you, I can double it. And unlike her, I don't collect souls as payment."

He glanced at the ornate key on the desk, then lifted his gaze, but not to her face. His eyes lingered boldly along the edge of her lower abdomen, tracking the gleaming patterns etched into her glossy exoskeleton. When he finally spoke, his tone carried a low, controlled edge.

He set the teacup down with deliberate care, "What's the key for? And what are you offering first?"

Arachna followed his gaze, noting exactly where his attention wandered. Her lips curved into a slow, knowing smile. She moved closer,

68

her spider legs gliding across the polished floor with a grace that defied the size and weight of her lower body. "The key? Insurance. It opens passages between our two…jurisdictions. Should you need to return to me quickly."

Her upper body dipped, reaching toward his teacup, and her fingers brushed against his with intentional delicacy, silken, cool, and stronger than the touch of any human woman. "As for my offer…protection, for one. Morrigan's prisoners face dangers you cannot imagine." She was confidently speaking in a full flow; her tone radiated power. "Secondly, comfort. Private quarters adjacent to my own chambers rather than a cell. Third, authority. You'll serve as my personal liaison, with privileges over other inmates."

Her voice fell to a sultry whisper as she leaned in, her exotic scent coiling around him like a slow-moving spell. "And finally…my personal attention. I'm quite…thorough in rewarding those who serve me well. Morrigan may promise power, but I offer pleasure beyond mortal comprehension."

Then she straightened, professionalism settling over her features like an elegant mask. "All I require in return is information. What exactly did Morrigan offer you? And what does she want from you specifically?"

He leaned in close, his face inches from hers, voice warm with amusement.

"You play on my lust, but I see not where I can make purchase within as I'd like."

He reclined again with deliberate calm.

"As far as her promise, she offered limited authority, working directly under her with an administrator to help manage with privileges and protections not given to regular inmates. So I don't think she's impeding on your territory, so to speak, but giving me her authority to roam with a watchful eye on me in her jurisdiction, just as you are offering me within yours."

Arachna's mandibles clicked in delighted surprise. Her eight eyes gleamed with something dark and entertained. "Such presumption…I find it refreshing."

She shifted her lower body slightly, allowing him a clearer view of the seamless join between her human torso and arachnid form, a shifting line of bioluminescent veins, pulsing like a heartbeat beneath chitin.

"My anatomy may surprise you, human. But that's a lesson for those who prove their loyalty." She circled behind him, her steps soundless. Her voice followed like a whisper of silk.

She was considering his words about Morrigan's offer, "Interesting. So she's mirroring my approach. Typical."

Then she returned to stand before him, offering her hand. "Very well. I propose something unprecedented... dual authority." She said to him, "Carry both our marks, move between our domains, report to us both. You'll have protection in all sectors of the prison, but remember this, human." She glanced at him, deeply. "I was here first. This prison was mine before the veil thinned and her realm bled into mine. When the inevitable conflict comes, remember who offered you honesty from the start. do we have an arrangement?"

He slowly and deliberately took her hand. Her skin felt impossibly smooth, like woven silk over steel. His tone hardened as his grip tightened. "I'd say we have an accord."

Arachna smiled, sharp and pleased, her fangs catching the lamplight. "An accord it is," She replied.

Her thumb traced across his wrist, and the bracelet pulsed brightly in response. The runes shifted, permissions rewriting themselves in real time. "I've upgraded your access privileges. You'll find certain doors now open for you that were previously locked." She said softly, her eyes still unwavering.

She glided to a tall cabinet carved from petrified wood and withdrew a vial of iridescent liquid. The colors swirled inside like trapped auroras. "Drink this before entering Morrigan's domain. It will protect you from certain...influences she might attempt to exert. And it will allow you to remember everything you see there clearly."

He accepted it with a steady hand and without hesitation, swallowed the contents.

Warmth rushed through him instantly; it was honey, spice, electricity, and beneath it all, an unmistakable undertone of *her* scent.

Arachne watched him with predatory satisfaction. "Good. The effects will last several days."

She stepped closer. One slender finger lifted his chin, guiding his eyes upward into hers. "Consider me heavily indeed. I've existed for centuries, human. I've perfected the art of pleasure that would make lesser beings lose their minds." Her stare was something else, a deep trance, "return with valuable information, and I'll show you exactly where you can…make a purchase."

Her voice wrapped around him like silk as she withdrew her hand. "Now go. The eastern corridor will lead you to the boundary between our domains. Use the key when you see a door with dual sigils."

He grinned slowly, confidently, and turned to leave.

As the door closed behind him, the corridor stretched out with eerie transformation. The sterile white walls of Arachne's administrative wing softened into stone laced with veins of glowing crystal. The air thickened with incense and faint ozone, vibrating with an energy ancient and half-forgotten.

Guards watched him pass, not with suspicion, but with wary respect.

A harpy officer murmured to a minotaur guard, feathers rattling softly. "That one's got Arachne's personal mark now. Dual jurisdiction, too, by the looks of it."

The minotaur grunted, folding her massive arms, but her gaze lingered.

Further down, fluorescent lights gave way to floating orbs that drifted like captive spirits. Shadows grew deeper. The temperature dropped, prickling his skin.

He reached the eastern boundary at last.

The door before him was colossal. It was half forged from reinforced prison alloy, half formed from living shadow and pale bone. Sigils spiraled across its surface, some in Arachne's clean geometric lines, others in the whispering spirals of Morrigan's domain.

Where the two halves met, a keyhole shimmered like a pupil contracting in anticipation.

The key in his hand pulsed faintly.

As he turned it, the mechanism produced a click that sounded like distant thunder. The door shuddered, and both halves seemed to breathe before slowly parting inward.

As soon as the doors opened, the rush of cold air washed over, carrying scents of night-blooming flowers and a metallic breath beneath, somewhere. The corridor beyond that door defied conventional architecture. The walls appear to be made of living shadow, occasionally revealing glimpses of stars and distant landscapes that couldn't possibly exist within the prison.

The floor transitioned from concrete to a path of what appears to be polished obsidian, veined with pulsing purple light. There were floating lanterns of blue flame illuminating the way, casting more shadows than they dispel.

As he was still trying to understand the place, a figure materialized from the darkness ahead. It was a slender woman with skin that shone like moonlight and hair that flowed like liquid darkness around her shoulders. Her uniform bore the prison insignia; maybe she was a shadow guard, but that uniform was reimagined in silver and shadow. Her eyes were entirely black, except for her pupils that were violet, assessed with ancient intelligence.

She looked at him and said, "You bear both marks. Unusual." She circled him once; her movements were fluid like water.

"Warden Morrigan awaits in the Umbral Office. Follow the path. Stray, and the shadows will return you... not always intact, though."

She gestured down the corridor with a hand that momentarily appeared to end in talons before shifting back to slender fingers.

He silently walked down the path as it was shown to him.

The path unraveled further into Morrigan's domain. Reality was becoming increasingly fluid around. The walls occasionally rippled like dark water, revealing glimpses of other places... prison cells where inmates slept fitfully, guard stations manned by creatures more shadow than substance, and once, briefly, what appeared to be Warden Arachna's office seen from an impossible angle.

The potion he consumed created a strange clarity amidst the surreal environment, allowing him to perceive details that might otherwise slip past consciousness. He noticed how the shadows themselves seemed to whisper as he passed, how the air tasted of secrets and forgotten memories.

Finally, the corridor opened into a circular chamber. However, unlike Arachna's practical office, this space resembled a gothic throne room that was reimagined for administrative purposes.

There was a massive desk of black wood sitting before a wall of stained-glass depicting scenes of judgment and punishment.

And behind it stood Warden Morrigan herself.

Where Warden Arachna is all predatory grace and spider-like precision, Warden Morrigan embodies elegant darkness. Her form shifted subtly as he watched her; sometimes she appeared as a regal woman in a warden's uniform, in a second glance, she would look like someone with bat-like wings and horns that crowned her head. Her eyes held the same ancient intelligence as her subordinate's, but with an intensity that felt like it was peeling back layers of his soul.

"So Arachne has marked you as well. How…progressive of her." Morrigan spoke. Her voice resonated with multiple harmonics, as if several voices spoke in perfect unison.

"Are you surprised?" He asked at the counter, flexing his confidence in himself.

Warden Morrigan's lips curved into a smile that didn't change the expression in her eyes. She moved from behind her desk with a fluid grace that left trails of shadow in her wake. Her uniform, black with silver accents, clung to her form like a second skin; the material shifted between solid fabric and something more ethereal.

"Surprised? No. intrigued, perhaps. Arachna rarely shares her toys." She circled him slowly, her presence causing the temperature in the room to fluctuate. When she spoke again, her voice came from directly behind him, though he didn't see her move there.

"I wonder what you offered her. Or perhaps...what she sees in you that I have yet to discover."

She completed her circle around him, coming to stand right in front of him, again. Her eyes, now entirely black with pinpoint violet light, were studying his face with unsettling intensity.

"Tell me, human. What do you seek in the shadows of my domain that the light of hers cannot provide?" Her eyes were sharp, hissed almost as he spoke.

"She offered me the same as you, but also provided flesh and truth. I'm merely doing my time here. Within the full scope of this place, I will now be assisting you both." Every word he replied was bold, unwavering, unafraid.

Warden Morrigan's expression shifted, like darkness rippling across her features like ink in water. A soft laugh escaped her lips; it sounded like distant wind chimes, only made of bone.

"Flesh and truth?" she chuckled sarcastically. "How...quaint. Arachna deals in webs of flesh and half-truths. I offer something far more valuable."

She extended a hand, palm up. A small sphere of darkness coalesced above it, swirling with pinpricks of light like a miniature galaxy. "Power. Knowledge beyond the veil. The ability to walk between worlds."

The sphere dissolved, particles of shadow sinking into her pale skin.

"But service to two mistresses is a precarious path, human. The spider and the shadow seldom align their interests." She moved closer to him, her scent enveloped him like the night-blooming flowers and ozone.

"Still, your...adaptability...may prove useful." It was an offer, perhaps. "There's been unrest in the deeper cells. Whispers of rebellion among the more…primordial inmates. I need eyes and ears where my shadows cannot reach."

Her fingertips that felt like winter midnight, brushed against his wrist where Arachna's bracelet sits.

"Then I guess I have one more task before retiring for the day. Where's Lilith as my guide so I may see what's going on. Only then can I make assessments, retire, start the activities for the morrow, and report back as needed afterwards?"

Morrigan's eyes narrowed slightly, and a ripple of shadow passed across her features.

The temperature seemed to drop several degrees as she considered his request. "Lilith? You presume much, human. She is not a guide to be summoned at your convenience." She seemed surprised and intrigued at what he just said.

She turned away, her form momentarily blending with the shadows before solidifying again by a tall obsidian cabinet. Opening it revealed rows of crystal vials containing swirling darkness.

"However…your timing is fortuitous. Lilith has been monitoring the situation in the Abyssal Block. Perhaps having a…different perspective would be beneficial."

She selected a vial and approached you again. "Drink this before you meet her. It will allow you to perceive what lurks beneath appearances. Without it, you'd be blind to half of what transpires in the deeper levels."

The door behind him opened silently, revealing a tall, statuesque demoness with curved horns and wings folded elegantly against her back. Unlike the other inmates, she wore a modified guard uniform with arcane sigils embroidered along the seams. Her eyes, a mix of amber with vertical pupils, regarded him with amused curiosity.

"You called for me, Warden? Ah, the new…assistant. How delightful." Lilith stepped in. Her voice carried notes of honey and venom, each word precisely measured.

"Ah, you take me as presumptuous. My apologies." He accepted the flask and drank from it. "It was she who guided me earlier before lunch, and I thought it was her I'd return to for completing this task, as you wish?" he glared into her eyes intently.

"Already receding from an earlier agreement due to a mention of another threatening power, I see."

The potion slid down his throat like liquid shadow, cold yet burning, tasting of midnight and forgotten stars. His vision blurred momentarily before sharpening with supernatural clarity. The room's dimensions seem to shift, revealing hidden alcoves and passages previously invisible.

Morrigan's expression darkened, and the shadows around her deepened until they swallowed light. When she spoke, her voice carried an edge, "Careful, human. Perception is not understanding."

The air thickened, vibrating with power as Lilith stepped forward. Her silhouette that gleamed elegantly with well-defined horns, wings, and amber eyes was framed in the threshold like a painting of temptation and cruelty. Her presence shifted the room's balance, forcing the shadows to recoil and reshape themselves around her.

"Such spirit. I see why both wardens find you...intriguing." Lilith's voice carried the smoothness of honey poured over a blade. She bowed to Morrigan in a gesture threaded with both obedience and deliberate insolence. "With your permission, Warden Morrigan. I'll escort our mutual asset to the disturbance. The Abyssal inmates have been...restless since the arrival of the new prisoner."

Morrigan offered no more than a dismissive flick of the hand, shadows streaming from her fingertips like smoke underwater. "Go." She gestured, "Report directly to me what you find. Remember, human. In the Abyssal Block, reality is...negotiable. Trust nothing, especially what seems most true."

Lilith extended her arm, amber eyes flickering with amusement and a darker, more evaluative interest. "Shall we descend, then? The abyssal awaits."

He exhaled a quiet, resigned sigh through his nose and dipped into a shallow bow toward Morrigan. His posture returned to full height with a shift of the shoulders, voice dropping into a composed baritone.

"Always so nice at first. Oh well." He straightened fully, offering the Warden a final cool nod. "G'day, Warden…"

Then he turned sharply, cape of shadow still brushing at his ankles from Morrigan's influence, and strode toward Lilith.

Lilith fell into step beside him the moment he left the sanctum's glow.

Behind them, Morrigan's eyes burned with violet fire, watchful, calculating, withholding judgment the way a wolf with a full belly waits before deciding whether to hunt again.

Chapter 3

"The Meeting with the Abyss"

The door closed behind them with a deep, resonant hum, sealing off Morrigan's office as if it had never existed. The corridor ahead twisted downward in a spiral of obsidian and shifting mist. The walls breathed softly, contracting and expanding like giant lungs beneath the stone.

Lilith's steps were unhurried, her gait a predator's glide. Shadows bent subtly toward her, recognizing authority, even here, where the laws of physics bowed to older, stranger principles.

She regarded him sidelong.

"Let's go, Lilith." He said firmly. But her lips curved in a judging, confused smile, comprehending the informal tone he just used to regard her with.

They walked deeper, the light thinning into strands of violet luminescence that clung to the walls like veins. The potion Morrigan had given him sharpened everything, edges clearer, darkness denser, sounds layered with meanings he had never before perceived.

The corridor opened suddenly into a vast shaft that wasn't there before, descending endlessly. A suspended bridge of runed metal spiraled downward along the wall.

The Abyssal Block breathed beneath them, waiting.

The runes lining the spiraling descent pulsed like a colossal heartbeat, each throb echoing through the stone and through him. Lilith guided him down the impossible staircase, its dimensions stretching, contracting, and subtly violating Euclidean reality. Her voice slipped into the shadows around them.

"You play a dangerous game, little human, speaking to her that way. Morrigan collects slights like precious gems, to be savored and repaid with interest." Her wings unfurled slightly in the narrow stairwell. The brush of one leathery edge slid across his shoulder, not forceful, but electric, sending an involuntary tingle across his skin.

Lilith excitedly, nervously added, "The Abyssal Block houses those whose very existence threatens the fabric of reality. Not merely murderers or thieves, but beings who've tampered with cosmic laws. The new arrival, they say, she devoured her own dimension before being captured."

Lilith only offered a faint, knowing smile as the staircase widened into an obsidian corridor, one far deeper than the prison's physical structure should permit. No cells lined this floor. Only smooth, seamless stone broken by circular doors bound in metal and sigils that writhed when not directly observed.

"The disturbance began three cycles ago. Whispering first, then screaming. The guards reported seeing…impossible things. Even for this place." She stopped at a door larger than the rest. Its carvings shifted like living calligraphy across its metal and shadowed surface. "Ready yourself. What lies beyond responds to fear…hungrily."

He shuddered, tone edged with resignation. "This is no game. Her level of respect and motive has changed, and she's upset. Anyways… I'm ready. Let's go."

Lilith pressed her palm to the door. Something ancient clicked, hissed, and inhaled. The portal split open, not into a room but into a cavern of impossible scale, a realm deep within the prison's bowels where gravity was merely a suggestion.

Floating stone islands drifted through a void streaked with auroral light. Shapes moved upon them, humanoid silhouettes and indescribable geometries occupying the same space at once. Morrigan's potion allowed him to see their true forms, superimposed upon the illusions his mind tried to enforce.

Lilith stepped beside him, her wings fully extended now, a protective arc of obsidian leather. "Perception and reality blur here. The potion will help, but trust your instincts above your eyes." The air vibrated with a low, melodic hum, threading into the chambers of his mind.

Lilith pointed toward the largest island, the one suspended at the center of the void. "There. The new arrival."

She sat cross-legged at the island's core. From afar, she appeared delicate with pale blue skin with cascading white hair. But the potion stripped away the illusion: her "hair" was a mass of tentacles, each ending in a small blinking eye, and her skin was a swirling tapestry of galaxies, nebulae, and unfathomable cosmic patterns. "Void Siren Nyarlathotep. They say she sang her world into oblivion, then consumed the remains. The others fear her...or worship her. We need to discover which."

He took several steps forward, and the void beneath him condensed into a crystalline path of starlight. The song intensified, resonating in the marrow of his bones.

Creatures from drifting islands turned their twisted forms toward him, observing, analyzing, hunting.

Lilith's voice lowered with warning. "Careful. The Void Siren's song affects different beings in different ways. Some find enlightenment...others, madness."

A chimera, a woman fused to a writhing shadow, noticed his approach first. Her trio of eyes widened. "A human? Here? Has the Warden grown so desperate?"

Nyarlathotep's humming ceased. Silence rushed in like the breath before an avalanche.

Slowly, her head turned. She began to speak, "The pattern...disrupted. A singular thread among the tapestry. Approach, little singularity. Let me taste your story."

He lifted a hand to his head, plucked a strand of hair, and extended it forward, his voice booming across the void. "If the world-consuming entity wishes, then stand and accept my offer so ye may know my truth."

Gasps rippled outward. Even the dimensional fractures around them flickered.

Nyarlathotep rose, gliding rather than floating, her body elongating in ways that defied physical law. She drifted until she hovered just before him. Her beauty and horror oscillated in mesmerizing intervals. "Bold...or foolish. Perhaps both."

Her fingers... too many joints, too much reach, all of them closed around the offered hair. Every tentacle eye turned toward him simultaneously. Reality itself seemed to lean closer to listen.

80

Lilith stiffened beside him, wings arched. "This is unexpected. She's never shown interest in physical offerings before."

Nyarlathotep shuddered. The ripple sent waves of cosmic distortion through the entire cavern. "Fascinating...a nexus of possibilities. You carry echoes of worlds I've never tasted."

Her lips peeled back into a smile, too wide, too many teeth spiraled inward like concentric rings. "What would you know of me, little singularity? What truth do you seek in the void between stars?"

He met her fractal gaze without flinching, voice sharpening with authority. "I know nothing of you, but I only seek why there's a disturbance, and then I shall leave you be."

Nyarlathotep's amusement deepened. Light fractured around her as if she were the nexus of a collapsing star. "The disturbance...is me. It's this. It's now."

Cracks of prismatic energy splintered through the air when she gestured. The void around them hummed in sympathetic resonance. "I sing, and the walls between dimensions grow thin. I breathe, and possibility bleeds through the cracks. Your wardens call this...disturbance."

She drifted closer until her face hovered inches from his. Her breath smelled of ozone and forgotten galaxies. "But the true disturbance is you, little singularity. Your presence here creates...ripples. Patterns shifting. Futures rewriting."

The void pulsed in response to her words, as if acknowledging a truth spoken aloud for the first time.

The disturbance rolled through the Abyssal Block like the shifting of a colossal beast beneath the void. The inmates, shifting silhouettes shaped from shadow, bone, ether, and nightmares, formed a widening circle around him and Nyarlathotep. Their bodies undulated with a tension that could have been anticipation, terror, or both. The air itself trembled.

Lilith's wings unfurled fully now, casting a sharp and protective silhouette behind him. Her voice cut through the rising hum of the void. "The wards are weakening. She's been testing the boundaries."

Nyarlathotep's laugh followed. It was delicate at first, then spiraled outward into a sound like crystal shattering in reverse, reforming, then breaking again in infinite recursion. "Not testing. Teaching. The void remembers me, and I am teaching it to remember freedom."

She released the strand of his hair. It drifted upward, glowing with a cold cerulean light before dissolving into stardust that disappeared into the cracks of reality. "Tell your wardens: the cage grows restless. The bars remember they were once something else. And I...I remember worlds beyond counting."

Her form folded inward, collapsing through geometries that defied comprehension, angles that shouldn't exist, curves that overlapped themselves. She drifted back toward her floating island, turning her back as though the conversation were already over. "You may leave now, little singularity. Our threads will cross again when the pattern demands it."

But he stepped forward, refusing the dismissal. His voice deepened, commanding, provocative. "Not so fast." He advanced another step, shadows trembling beneath his feet. "Tell me exactly why you're here. I can easily tell that you willed yourself to be taken and brought here. I know you can leave at any time you wish. If this is a private question to be answered, then I shall retire until we can be remote and in isolation enthralled within flesh. Answer me, and I shall leave thee be for now."

The void went still.

Utterly, terrifyingly still.

Even the drifting stone islands froze in place as if suspended mid-breath. Figures that had been shifting in impossible forms became statues of horror. Lilith inhaled sharply, her wings snapping outward in instinctive alarm.

Nyarlathotep's collapse halted, reversed. Her form unfolded toward him again with unsettling slowness, as though savoring each atom of attention he dared to give her. Cosmic patterns brightened across her body, flaring like distant nebulae coming alive.

Her smile stretched far too wide, revealing serrated rings of teeth descending down a throat that spiraled like a black hole. "Perception...sharpened by desperation. How delicious."

She circled him with predatory grace. Her movement left faint afterimages drifting behind her, as if time lagged at her heels. Dozens of tiny eyes blinked across the living tentacles of her hair, studying him with clinical hunger.

"Prisons exist in many forms, little singularity. Some built of stone and steel, others of flesh and bone, still others of law and consequence. I am here because this nexus point... this prison, sits at the convergence of realities." She leaned close, her whisper spilling directly into his mind, bypassing sound entirely.

"The Warden believes she contains me. I allow this belief. For now, I feed on the concentrated suffering, the compressed possibilities, the denied futures of those imprisoned here. Such exquisite sustenance." A single elongated finger traced an arc before his face, a sigil of glowing blue light, lingering like an echo before dissipating.

"When the pattern completes, when the last thread is woven...Then I shall consume this place entirely. And you, little singularity, you are an unexpected variable. A wild thread in my tapestry." She began to fold back into her impossible self, retreating toward her island.

"Return to your Warden. Tell her what you will. The countdown has already begun."

Not willing to let her vanish back into the void, he moved.

In a single decisive motion, he reached out and *grabbed* her.

His hands closed around a body that was simultaneously flesh, energy, memory, and cosmic dream. Her form solidified under his touch; it was warm like starlight, soft as velvet stretched over electric current. Her hair-tentacles reacted with a serpentine shiver before curling around his wrists and forearms, binding him to her in a living, curious embrace.

He pulled her closer.

His voice dropped to a whisper made of gravity. "Embrace me, and no more shall you be disturbed. Show me what I was meant to and then I shall report back." His grip tightened, gentle, but firm… eyes locked on the shifting light behind hers.

The void roared.

A cosmic wind exploded outward, spiraling around them both. Inmates fled, scrambling to the extremes of the realm in pure terror. Lilith shouted his name, but the sound was devoured by the void's sudden hunger.

Nyarlathotep's expression shifted… shocked, then deeply pleased. A purr vibrated through dimensions. "Audacity…such beautiful audacity."

Her voice bypassed sense; it vibrated through bone and blood, directly into his mind. Her face stabilized into a form almost unbearably beautiful, blue skin shimmering like a polished gemstone, eyes deep as singularities, lips curling in fascinated delight.

"Very well, little singularity. Embrace the void." Nyarla's body softened against his.

The tentacle-eyes brushed his skin, each touch leaving a cold kiss that detonated visions inside his mind…

worlds birthing in fire, realms dissolving into dust, civilizations screaming as they collapsed into hungry stars, and behind it all, a hunger as old as existence, as patient as gravity, as inevitable as ruin.

"See what I am. See what awaits." Reality fractured before both of them.

He saw the prison undone, atoms unspooling, sigils detonating, the very stone devoured by a cosmic maw stretching across dimensions.

And he stood beside her as it happened, no longer human, not monster, but something between.

She pulled back slightly, face inches from his, the void of her breath brushing his skin like winter starlight, "Report that, if you dare."

He exhaled slowly, grounding himself against the warping reality. "So, you'll stay in content and keep things in check till then? All I ask, and I've asked much of you as is. I shall go, but I would pragmatically lower the disturbances of this place, lest you give away what I saw too soon."

Nyarlathotep's form rippled like liquid cosmos.

"Pragmatism...from a human? Rarer than you know."

She drew back slightly, her ever-shifting features settled into a semblance of contemplation. The void around both of them seemed to breathe, expanding and contracting in time with her thoughts.

"I shall...moderate my resonance. The disturbances will quieten, for now. Time is meaningless to one who exists between moments, but I understand its value to lesser beings."

Her elongated finger traced a sigil on his forehead, a touch cold as starlight that leaves no visible mark but sends a shiver down his spine.

"You carry my mark now, little singularity. When the final convergence approaches, you will know. Until then..."

She began to fold back into herself, her form condensing and distorting as she returned to her island at the center of the void.

"Tell your Warden whatever truth serves your purpose. The game continues regardless." As she receded, Lilith cautiously approached. Her wings still flared defensively, amber eyes wide with disbelief.

"By all the ancient laws...what did you just do? No one touches the Void Siren and remains...unchanged." She studied his face intently, searching for signs of corruption or madness.

His stare was still stuck on Nyarlathotep disappearing; he looked away, disappointedly, catching Lilith's gaze. He straightened up, "honestly, she left me half-cocked and only tickled my... fancy without fully trying to give me blue balls." He laughed.

Lilith's amber eyes widened momentarily before narrowing with suspicion. Her wings folded slightly, the leathery membranes shifted as she processed his crude deflection.

The void chamber around him gradually returned to its normal state, the cosmic disturbances settling like disturbed water.

"You expect me to believe she just...teased and released you? Men have gone mad from merely glimpsing her true form." Lilith circled him slowly, her tail flickering with agitation. Her nostrils flared as she seemed to scent something unusual about him, perhaps the lingering trace of Nyarlathotep's cosmic essence.

"Whatever game you're playing, human, remember that some pieces get sacrificed first."

In the background, Nyarlathotep had fully returned to her island. Though distant now, her tentacle-eyes remain fixed on him, blinking in patterns that seem almost like code. The other inmates cautiously returned to their activities, though they maintained a respectful distance from both him and the Void Siren's domain.

"The Warden will want a full report. And she'll know if you're lying-she always does." She gestured toward the exit portal, which had reappeared now that the disturbance subsided.

"After you, brave one. Let's see how that silver tongue of yours fares with the Warden." She threw a taunt.

"Well, if you insist, but I assure you that my tongue isn't silver. It's like a pinkish red," he chuckled and walked toward the portal.

Lilith snorted at his comment, a small puff of brimstone escaping her nostrils. Her amber eyes rolled dramatically as she followed close behind him toward the portal. "Your humor won't save you from the Warden's scrutiny. She's been monitoring the Void Siren for centuries."

The portal pulsed with deep purple energy, its surface rippling like disturbed mercury. As he approached, it seemed to react to his presence, or perhaps to the invisible mark Nyarlathotep left upon him, flashing briefly with cosmic patterns before stabilizing.

Behind him, the other inmates resumed their activities, though many cast furtive glances in his direction. Some appeared fearful, others curious, and a few with expressions that might be interpreted as newfound respect.

"Whatever happened between you two, you're changed. I can sense it." She gestured impatiently toward the portal, her wings flexing with tension.

"After you, human. The Warden doesn't like to be kept waiting. And I'd rather not be in her bad graces when she discovers you've been…fraternizing with the most dangerous inmate in the entire prison." The portal hummed with increasing intensity, awaiting his passage to the administrative section where the mysterious Warden awaits.

The portal's surface parts like liquid obsidian as he stepped through, enveloping him momentarily in a cold embrace before depositing him in a stark, pristine chamber. Unlike the chaotic prison sections he had seen before, this room held order and authority. The walls gleamed with polished black stone shot through with veins of luminescent blue, and the floor bore complex runic patterns that pulsed subtly beneath his feet.

At the far end was an imposing desk carved from what appeared to be a single massive piece of dark crystal. And finally, behind the dark crystal, silhouetted against a wall of surveillance monitors, stands the Warden.

She turned slowly to face him, revealing a tall, statuesque figure clad in a form-fitting uniform of midnight blue with silver accents. Her skin was pale alabaster, contrasting sharply with her long raven hair that moved as if suspended in water. Her eyes were the most striking, entirely black except for pinpricks of white light where pupils should be, like distant stars in the void.

"So. You've met Nyarlathotep." She said, finally. Her voice was melodic, too melodic. Each syllable is placed with the precision of a scalpel. "Few return from such encounters with their sanity intact."

Behind him, Lilith emerged from the portal, her wings refolding in a fluid sweep. The moment her gaze fell upon the Warden, she dropped to one knee, amber eyes lowered in reverence that bordered on fear.

The Warden raised one slender hand, "Rise, Lilith. Tell me what you observed."

Lilith obeyed, though the tension in her wings betrayed her unease. Her voice remained steady. "The human approached the Void Siren despite warnings. They… embraced. Spoke. The disturbances ceased afterwards."

For a long moment, the Warden said nothing. She merely watched him, her star-pupiled eyes pinning him in place. He felt her attention like gravity pulling at the edges of his thoughts, something ancient, vast, and distinctly dangerous.

Then she stepped forward.

Each movement was smooth, controlled, predatory, without haste. Standing before him, she loomed an entire head taller, casting a precise shadow over his feet as though even light was obligated to obey her. "Interesting. Very interesting indeed." She expressed how intrigued she was.

His stance tightened instinctively, shoulders squaring, breath steadying. A faint grey shimmer tugged at the corners of his vision; it was the residue of Nyarlathotep's cosmic mark whispering beneath his consciousness. Still, he met the Warden's stare without flinching.

"It's as she says," he answered, tone flat yet firm. "No need for dishonesty."

The slightest curve touched the Warden's lips, less a smile than a mark of professional curiosity, "Bold. But boldness without wisdom is merely recklessness."

She lifted her hand toward his face. Her fingers halted a hair's breadth from his skin, and the space between him crackled with cold, invisible static. He felt the faint brush of her influence as if testing the edges of his soul for fractures.

"Her mark is upon you. Faint, but unmistakable." She said as she circled him with the unhurried scrutiny of someone accustomed to dissecting truths from flesh and aura alike. The soft whisper of her uniform contrasted sharply with the weight of her presence.

Lilith did not move, nor breathe, it seemed. Only her tail flicked once in restrained anxiety.

The Warden's voice unfurled again, calm yet sharpened by a blade of inquiry. "Nyarlathotep doesn't spare humans out of mercy or whim. She is calculation incarnate, chaos with purpose. Tell me, prisoner, what did she whisper to you? What visions did she plant in that fragile mind of yours?"

Her eyes narrowed the slightest fraction, two collapsing stars now focused entirely on him.

Waiting. Weighing. Judging.

The room felt smaller, the air felt colder, and his heartbeat louder.

And the truth, or whatever part of it he chose now, stood balanced on the edge of his tongue.

Morrigan completed her slow, predatory circle around him, coming to stand directly in front of him once more.

Her presence radiated power... vast, cosmic, and cold, and yet beneath the authority in her posture lingered something almost curious, as if he had become a problem she had not anticipated, a puzzle she had suddenly developed the desire to solve. "Speak plainly. Your fate in this facility may depend on it."

He lifted his gaze deliberately, letting it trace up and down her towering form. Heat flickered behind his eyes, tempered by exhaustion and irritation.

"*Speaking plainly*," he emphasized on her words, "I don't think that your presence needs to be imposing or threatening anymore. You've made your point. Stand with me mutually, or sit with me mutually, and I shall convey. I'm tired of these games, as you are the third Warden I've had to report to today, and I've done my best to meet all of your wishes. If it's information you wish to get, I give freely, but enough with the intimidation games. I'm imprisoned here, so let's be practical." He stared at her deeply, fearlessly, "I'm not leaving for the next 3 years."

The shift in Morrigan's expression was subtle, but unmistakable. The star-filled irises in her eyes glittered with a new shade of interest, respect, perhaps, or the faintest ember of surprise. Silence fell across the chamber, thick and taut.

Then her lips curved, the smallest ghost of a smile. "Three years? Your sentence was revised the moment you interacted with the Void Siren."

She gestured with elegant precision, and a sleek obsidian chair rose from the polished floor as if summoned. Lilith stiffened in shock at

Morrigan's offer of something resembling courtesy. "Sit. You've earned that much."

He lowered himself into the chair. Morrigan followed suit, settling into her own with fluid, regal movement. Her long raven hair drifted as though suspended underwater, shimmering in the ambient light.

"I am Morrigan, the only Warden. Those others you met were merely aspects, projections I use to maintain order in different sectors. Few inmates ever meet me in my true form." Her long fingers steepled together, the tips glowing faintly with residual cosmic energy.

"Now, tell me what transpired with Nyarlathotep. Not for my amusement, but because whatever she's planning may affect everyone within these walls." Lilith remained standing at stiff attention, amber eyes locked on him, anticipation and unease mingling in her expression.

He exhaled, leaning back. "Lilith, I'd find a comfortable place. This may take a while."

Lilith blinked. She was caught off guard, then retreated to perch on a crystalline ledge emerging naturally from the wall.

He returned his gaze to Morrigan, "Well, now, you've piqued my interest. If every warden were you, then you've been prodding at my mind lustfully in different forms. Smart and calculated. And I thought I was good at manipulation." He chuckled.

"Ok, basically..." He relayed everything, his first approach, Nyarlathotep's escalating resonance, the whispered patterns, the impossible embrace. Morrigan did not interrupt once, though her eyes brightened at certain revelations. When he finished, she considered him with unnerving stillness.

"So, she's shown you potential futures...interesting. The Void Siren rarely shares visions without purpose." A sweep of her hand summoned a holographic projection above her desk: Nyarlathotep's island, now calm, no longer surrounded by cosmic turbulence.

"You've done more than what was asked. You've accomplished what centuries of containment protocols could not." Her eyes sharpened, pinpricks of light swirling within them.

"Your sentence is indeed changing, but not in the way you might expect. Nyarlathotep has marked you, she has *claimed* you, in her way. And this changes your status here." Lilith's wings twitched at the word *claimed*. "You're no longer simply a prisoner. You're now a conduit, a liaison between the administration and one of our most dangerous inmates."

She leaned forward slightly, lowering her voice.

"The question is: are you prepared for what this entails? The Void Siren doesn't form connections lightly. Whatever she showed you, whatever she whispered…it binds you to her purposes, whether you realize it or not."

He shrugged with irreverent boldness. "Well, again, as I told you, Lilith, at least she didn't get me fully risen and leave me with blue balls."

Lilith made a strangled sound, nearly choking. Embers flew from her wings as she sputtered. "By the nine hells, human! Do you have any sense of self-preservation?"

Morrigan did not flinch. Instead, the faint smile returned with a razor-thin curve of dark amusement. "Crude, but honest. A quality I find…refreshing, after centuries of diplomatic falsehoods."

She rose from her seat, approaching a wall that became transparent at her gesture. Beneath them sprawled the entire prison… layers, wings, domes, and wards, a sprawling labyrinth of stone and magic.

"Your new position grants you certain privileges, but also responsibilities. You will have access to sectors previously forbidden to you. You will serve as our intermediary with Nyarlathotep when necessary." She turned back toward him, cosmic eyes glowing brighter.

"But make no mistake, you remain under our jurisdiction. Should you abuse these privileges or should we suspect the Void Siren is using you against the prison's interests…" The unspoken threat chilled the air around them.

"Do we understand each other?" This time, she glared at him in a way that could tear souls apart.

He stood, rising to his full height, and the sclera at the corners of his eyes darkened crimson, not fully human anymore, and Morrigan recognized it instantly. "You can cut the act." His tone hardened, deep and resonant. "I know full well the consequences and the dangers that threaten not only his posterior of position but also the fabric of THIS reality. This is a prison; she's dangerous. I have lust, but I don't have stupidity. Respect me a little to know I'm more intelligent than that Warden."

The temperature plummeted.

Morrigan's eyes exploded with brilliant white starlight, and her humanoid form shimmered, momentarily revealing something ancient and titanic beneath the façade. The screen monitors flickered violently. Shadows twisted along the walls like serpents.

Lilith flattened herself against the crystalline surface, wings flared in instinctive defense, pupils dilated with terror.

Something vast stirred behind Morrigan's gaze, something that recognized his defiance…and did not dismiss it.

The stars in Morrigan's eyes dimmed to slitted focus as she regarded him, her voice resonating through the chamber in layered harmonics that vibrated against the marrow of his bones.

"Act?" she echoed, the word wrapped in so many tones it sounded like a chorus. "You mistake caution for condescension, human."

The distortion that rippled across her form, those hints of something vast and inhuman beneath the shape she wore, faded as quickly as it had flared. She exhaled once, smoothing the midnight fabric of her uniform with graceful fingers, restoring the illusion of calm authority.

"But perhaps you're right. We needn't dance around the matter."

She crossed the room with unhurried confidence, moving not as a figure of intimidation now, but as an equal, an extraordinarily rare posture for the true Warden of the prison. The shadows obeyed her movements, recoiling or shifting like living things as she approached him.

"Very well. Nyarlathotep is indeed here by choice, as are several of our most powerful inmates. This facility exists not merely to punish, but to contain forces that would otherwise destabilize multiple realities." As she lifted her hand, a small obsidian token shimmered into existence on her palm, runes carved in shifting constellations. It glowed faintly, pulsing in time with her gaze.

"This grants you access to all but the most restricted areas. Use it wisely. Report to me directly if Nyarlathotep communicates anything further." She extended the token, not as an order, but as an offering. "Do we have an understanding...colleague?"

He raised his arm, eyes locked with hers, and spoke with a sharp edge undercutting the fatigue in his voice. "First things first... is the bracelet and its obtuse presence still necessary?"

Morrigan's gaze dipped to the standard-issue bracelet that encircled his wrist. The tiny lights along its surface jittered nervously under her stare. Her fingers hovered just above the device, never touching, yet commanding its full submission. The bracelet flickered from hostile red to soft blue.

"An astute question." She gestured lightly.

The clasp clicked open on its own, and the device dropped into her waiting palm. Where metal had touched his skin remained a faint pale ring, quickly warming back to its natural tone.

"This particular...limitation...no longer serves our purposes." She lifted the bracelet in one hand, the obsidian token in the other, old shackles and new authority, side by side.

"However, this does not mean you go unwatched. The token I offer contains more sophisticated tracking capabilities, but it also grants you authority that the common prisoner lacks." Lilith shifted in the corner, the succubus's golden eyes widening in open disbelief at the display of trust. "Consider it an upgrade rather than a removal. You still remain bound to this facility, only with a longer leash now. Does this satisfy your concern?"

He raised his hand slowly, deliberately, and touched beneath Morrigan's hovering fingertips where the token glowed between them. "I accept." He said.

The moment his skin brushed the relic, light flared, brief as a heartbeat, bright as a newborn star. The runes rearranged themselves instinctively, aligning to the shape of his touch, syncing to his pulse. He felt it settle into him: not just an item, but a bond.

Morrigan inclined her head, "It is done."

She stepped back, watching the token as if she could see unseen threads weaving between it and his aura. "The token will adapt to your preferences; some wear it as a pendant; others keep it in a pocket. It cannot be lost or stolen; it is now attuned to your specific energy signature."

Her attention moved toward Lilith, "Lilith will show you to your new quarters. You're being relocated from the general population to the liaison sector. Consider it a...neutral territory between administration and the special containment wing."

Lilith nodded, extending a wing as a subtle gesture toward the door. "Ready when you are. And...congratulations, I suppose? This is unprecedented."

Morrigan paused long enough for her star-filled eyes to lock with his again, "We will speak again soon. The Void Siren rarely acts without purpose. Whatever she has set in motion by connecting with you...We shall see."

He took a breath, then spoke with pointed clarity. "Lilith, be a dear and give me a moment alone with the Warden. I have a... private question I want to ask her without you. It'll just be a moment."

Lilith froze. Her wings tensed, folded, tensed again. Her tail twitched as her amber gaze darted between the two of them. "I... that's not standard protocol..."

Morrigan lifted one elegant hand. "It's alright, Lilith. Our new liaison has earned a moment of privacy."

The succubus looked anything but thrilled, but she bowed, wings scraping the air. "As you wish, Warden. I'll wait outside."

The door sealed behind her, leaving the chamber way too quiet. Without Lilith's presence, Morrigan's full cosmic weight pressed subtly into the air, filling the space with something vast and ancient.

She turned to him fully. "Well then. What is it you wish to discuss without my lieutenant present?"

She remained standing, posture relaxed yet undeniably sovereign. With Lilith gone, the room felt more intimate and more dangerous. Shadows deepened along the furniture, responding instinctively to her shifting mood.

He drew in a slow breath. His voice lowered, hardened with a mix of vulnerability and defiance. "Be honest and true, if all the other 'wardens'" he lifted two fingers in air quotes "were you, I felt your lust align mine. Am I deceived, or am I only for your lesser forms and not thy true self? If I report to you, then what of everything else I was told?"

The air thickened, charged with the hum of a storm waiting to break. Morrigan's expression did not shift immediately; she only watched him, eyes glowing brighter, constellations shifting in spirals behind her pupils.

Then she spoke. Quiet, resonant, and lethal in its honesty. "Perceptive. More so than I anticipated."

She stepped closer. And closer. Her movement blurred at the edges, as if her body occupied more dimensions than the room allowed.

"Yes, I sensed your...response to me. Just as you sensed mine. The forms you've encountered throughout this facility... the other 'wardens' as you call them are aspects of myself. Fragments I project to maintain order in different sectors."

She lifted a hand. The space around her fingers warped: light bending, reality flexing like softened metal. "As for my 'true self'...few mortal minds can comprehend it without fracturing. This form you see now is the closest approximation that won't...damage you."

Her voice deepened, resonating inside his mind rather than his ears. "What Nyarlathotep told you was not false, merely incomplete. You report to me, yes, but I am far more than just the warden of this prison. I am its architect, its guardian, and in many ways, its purpose."

Her gaze softened. Not with tenderness, but with recognition of someone who had stepped willingly into the orbit of powers beyond mortal comprehension... and had not shattered.

Morrigan's question lingered in the charged air, her voice a velvet thread of cosmic resonance. "Does this...disappoint you? Or perhaps...intrigue you further?"

He stepped closer, closing the distance with muted confidence, his gaze traveling the length of her tall, void-touched form. "I'm only disappointed that I won't be able to take purchase in lust with you."

A smile unfurled across Morrigan's lips, a slow, deliberate, and undeniably predatory smile. Not the measured, diplomatic smile of a warden, but something older... something that understood desire in its primordial form. Heat stirred in the room, an intimate warmth radiating from her body as the stars inside her eyes pulsed in a rhythm that matched the steady thrum of a heartbeat.

Morrigan moved with the ease of someone who had long ago abandoned the need to feign hesitance, "Who said such a thing was impossible?"

Her hand rose, elegant and weightless, fingertips brushing his chest. The contact sent a current through him, not merely electric, but deeper, touching the threads of his being with a shiver that felt like a second heartbeat pressed against his own. "This form is quite capable of...experiencing mortal pleasures. I simply choose my partners with extreme selectivity."

She leaned in closer, her presence overwhelming without ever feeling oppressive. Her scent surrounded him, something unnamable, like the cold of distant stars softened by the warmth of midnight air. "The token I've given you marks you as mine in more ways than one. Should you desire to explore what that truly means...well, my private quarters exist beyond normal space-time. We would have all the privacy the cosmos can offer."

Her lips drifted close to his ear, her whisper cool as starlight, "But first, you have work to do. Nyarlathotep chose you for a reason. Discover it. Then seek me out...if your courage holds."

He slid his arms around her in a slow, deliberate motion, drawing her into his embrace until their bodies pressed together. He lowered his voice, whispering against the curve of her neck. *"I will need to be refreshed by you after tomorrow, my dear."*

His arms tightened, pulling her closer, letting her feel his body rise in answer to her nearness.

Morrigan responded with an unexpected fusion of contradictions, her form soft and inviting, yet beneath it lay the immensity of something cosmic and untamed. The stars in her eyes flared, brightening at the unmistakable contact. "Bold... I appreciate that quality."

Her hands traced along his back with delicate precision. At each point where her fingers touched, ripples of something unfamiliar washed through him, sensations from beyond mortal perception, fleeting glimpses of realities that shimmered with impossible pleasure. "Tomorrow will test you in ways you cannot yet imagine. The Void Siren's call...it changes those who enter."

Instead of withdrawing, she leaned in, her cool breath brushing the shell of his ear. "Come to me afterward. Three knocks on any wall while holding the token. I will know, and I will answer."

She shifted subtly, pressing against him one final time, an intentional tease, a promise wrapped in starlit provocation, before slipping gracefully out of his arms. "Now go. Lilith grows impatient, and we've given her enough to gossip about already."

He cleared his throat and adjusted himself with a practiced composure, deepening his tone. "Yes... You are correct. I do have work to do and a busy schedule tomorrow. Thank you, Ms. Morrigan. I will report promptly as necessary."

He leaned closer, voice dropping to a conspiratorial whisper. "Don't punish my lustful antics."

Amusement shimmered across her features as she returned to her desk, her movements smooth as liquid gravity. The uniform she wore shifted like a night sky disturbed by invisible winds. "Punish? Quite the contrary."

She activated a control on her desk, the office door sliding open with a quiet, seamless motion. Lilith stood waiting outside, posture taut with curiosity she barely disguised. "I find your...directness refreshing. Most beings, human or monster, cower in my presence. They sense what I am beneath this form and recoil."

Her gaze sharpened. "I believe our business is concluded for now. Lilith will show you to your new quarters. Rest well, Liaison. Tomorrow begins your true work here."

He stepped toward the door, but her whisper caught him, reaching him alone, though her lips had not appeared to move. "And I shall look forward to our...debriefing."

He passed through the doorway with a steady stride. *"Ok, Lilith, let us proceed."*

Lilith straightened, wings giving a subtle rustle as she appraised him with sharp curiosity. "Well, that was...unusually private. The Warden doesn't often dismiss me from meetings."

Her amber eyes swept him up and down, searching for any visible sign of what had transpired. She flicked her tail once before turning abruptly. "Your quarters are in the administrative wing, a privilege few enjoy here. Follow me."

She set off down the corridor with brisk steps. The architecture around them shifted subtly as they walked, angles bending in ways that defied mathematics, distances stretching or condensing like the hallway itself breathed in slow, silent rhythms.

Lilith's heels clicked softly against the polished floor as she led him deeper into the administrative wing. Her wings brushed occasionally against the air, stirring faint embers that never fell but hung suspended like fading fireflies.

"I hope whatever arrangement you've made with the Warden serves you well. Just remember, even her favorites aren't immune to the rules of this place." Her tone held the cadence of a professional reminder, yet beneath it a thin ribbon of warning thrummed like a plucked string.

He slowed his pace just enough for a smirk to curve across his lips. "Are you immune to the rules? Or does a succubus get free rein like yourself?"

Lilith stopped so abruptly that one wing snapped outward in a reflexive flare. She turned, amber eyes catching the corridor's light with a sharp glint that bordered on predatory delight. Her tail curled at the tip, flicking once like a serpent poised to strike. "Immune? No one is immune here, human. Not even me."

She stepped closer, her presence unmistakably intoxicating. The warm, spiced scent of her heritage, cinnamon, heat, and something darker, unfurled in the narrow space between them. "But privileges? Yes, I have a few. Earned through loyal service, not through whatever…arrangement you seem to have struck with the Warden during your first day."

Her gaze dipped, unabashed, tracing down his body before rising again with deliberate slowness. "As for 'free rein,' a succubus is never truly free. Our nature binds us to certain…hungers. The difference is whether we control them or they control us."

She resumed walking, hips swaying with controlled grace, tail swishing in a smooth arc behind her. "Careful with that sly grin, Liaison. It might work on the Warden, but I've seen countless men reduced to mindless husks for offering less to a succubus."

He chuckled, not quite softly, but with a dry, raspy edge that echoed faintly down the corridor. "Ha! It's only less right now cuz he's receding. Grower, not shower. But that's a topic we can save for a dreary night, not walking down the halls in earshot of everyone."

Lilith's eyes widened for a brief heartbeat before narrowing with renewed interest. Her wings fluttered once, betraying a flicker of surprise she quickly masked.

A low, melodic laugh that was sultry and dangerous slipped past her lips. "My, my… the human has fangs after all. Interesting."

Her sidelong glance appraised him again, sharper this time, weighing threat and charm in equal measure. "You might survive here longer than I expected. Though whether that's wisdom or foolishness remains to be seen."

The corridor began to shift around them, the harsh steel and concrete transitioning into smoother stone, etched with geometric designs that pulsed faintly when not directly looked at. Softer lighting replaced the sterile glare, bathing the hall in warm, atmospheric hues.

"Your quarters are just ahead. And don't worry about being overheard here, these walls have absorbed far more…interesting conversations than your anatomical boasting." Her tail flicked with playful precision, almost brushing his thigh as she gestured toward a heavy reinforced door with veined black metal.

He moved.

Faster than should have been possible.

In a blur, he cornered her, one arm braced beside her head, pinning her lightly against the door. The sudden shift stole her breath; her wings flattened, her lips parting in genuine surprise. The corridor trembled faintly with his sudden manifestation of power.

Her eyes widened, fear, fascination, and calculation all colliding.

He growled low, a sound not entirely human. "Careful what you say to someone so dangerous. This mere *HUMAN* still has a full deck up his sleeve. You are prey, not a predator. I am here for a reason."

For a heartbeat, the shadows seemed to bend toward him, drawn to the surge of red that flared at the edges of his irises.

When he finally stepped back, his posture cooled, and the red bled from his gaze, returning to its usual dark depth.

He adjusted his stance with controlled precision, "Now, madam, if you'll excuse me, I will proceed to retire."

"Well... The Warden certainly didn't mention this particular quality in your file." She said, looking directly at him.

When he backed away, she remained against the door momentarily, her amber eyes never leaving his as they faded back to black. Her clawed hand rises to straighten her uniform with deliberate slowness.

"Your quarters, sir." Said Lilith. The word *sir* came with an edge of part respect, part challenge, part something she likely hadn't expected to feel.

She laid her palm upon the scanner. With a soft hiss, the door slid open, revealing the chamber prepared for him. "Sleep well...if you sleep at all. I'll be sure to update your assessment in our personnel records."

Something in her voice had changed. She sounded cautious now, yes, but also unmistakably intrigued, as if the human she had escorted through the halls had abruptly transformed into a far more complex creature than she'd expected.

He offered a sly smile, tone shifting into playful velvet. "Thank you, lieutenant. I do hope you get rest as well, we'll both need it for the early light, I'll be looking for a before-dawn... night creature."

Her expression flickered, surprise melting into wariness, then settling into a slow, sharpened amusement. Her wings flexed once, like a creature stretching after being roused too early, and her tail curled into a languid S-shape behind her. "Before dawn? My, aren't we ambitious."

She tilted her head, horns catching the corridor's dim glow like polished stone. A predatory smile lifted her lips, revealing the faintest glimmer of needle-fine fangs. "I'm curious to see if your...performance matches your confidence, Liaison."

With a flick of her clawed hand, she gestured toward the open doorway. "Your quarters are equipped with everything a human might need. If you require anything else, there's a communication panel by the bed. Though I recommend reserving its use for actual emergencies."

She turned as if to go, then paused, glancing back over her shoulder. The look she gave him held equal parts mockery and genuine curiosity. "Sleep well...day-walker."

He stepped inside his new quarters, shutting the door behind him with a quiet click. The room embraced him with unexpected warmth, muted lighting, soft shadows, and the faint aroma of calming herbs that seemed to soak into the air itself. "Oof, ok, I've had enough for one day, I'm getting naked to recharge," he muttered to the empty room.

His uniform hit the floor with a soft thud. The mattress invited him like a dark cloud, absorbing the weight of his body as he collapsed atop it. Muscles unwound as exhaustion claimed him, and his eyelids sank. "I'd better charge up while I can before she comes in here before dawn," he murmured, the last words slurring as sleep overtook him like a slow tide.

His quarters, unlike the stark cells that house the inmates, offered surprising comfort. As he collapsed onto the bed, he noted the room's thoughtful design; it was spacious by prison standards, with subdued lighting that adjusted automatically to his movement. The bed itself held itself pleasantly beneath his weight, conforming to his body with unexpected luxury. The air carried a faint herbal scent, neither masculine nor feminine, but clean and vaguely soothing.

The walls, painted in muted blues, absorbed sound rather than reflect it. A private bathroom adjoined the main space, visible through a partially open door. A small desk with an integrated computer terminal sat in one corner, and a narrow window, reinforced with some kind of enchanted glass, offered a sliver view of the prison grounds bathed in moonlight.

As his consciousness began to fade, he became aware of a subtle vibration, almost imperceptible, running through the floor and walls. It was rhythmic, like the breathing of some massive creature. The prison itself seemed alive around him, monitoring, waiting, perhaps even judging as he drifted into an exhausted sleep after his extraordinary first day as the human liaison in this monster girl facility.

Chapter 4

"The Next Morning"

An electronic chime sliced through his dreams, not shrill, but insistent, designed to wake rather than alarm. Soft light bloomed across the room, mimicking dawn.

5:00 A.M. glowed on the wall display.

Right on schedule.

Then came the knock... three firm, precise taps, unmistakably Lilith's cadence. Her voice followed, lower than last night and edged with the roughness of early hours. "Rise and shine, Liaison. Your presence is required. You have precisely fifteen minutes to make yourself presentable."

He groaned, sitting up slowly and running a hand over his face. "Enter, Lieutenant."

The door slid open without a sound.

Lilith stepped inside, wings folded neatly behind her back, though the early hour lent her an air of sharpened rawness, like a blade not yet polished after forging. Her fitted black shirt hugged her form, the silver insignia gleaming at her throat. Her horns seemed darker in this lighting, absorbing rather than reflecting the glow of the room.

"I'm impressed. Most humans struggle with early rising." Her gaze flicked once over the state of his bed, then to him. He was barely clothed, with hair tousled and expression still adorably half-asleep. A smile tugged the corner of her lips, betraying amusement.

"The Warden requires your presence for an early briefing. There's been an...incident overnight in the eastern wing. Since it involves a human guard and several inmates, your perspective is deemed valuable." She remained near the door, posture crisp despite the hour. "I've taken the liberty of having fresh uniforms delivered. You'll find them in the wardrobe. Five minutes, Liaison. The prison waits for no one, not even its newest curiosity."

He grumbled and rose, stretching, *"Ugh... be out in 3."*

He moved into the bathroom, quick, efficient motions. A flush. Running water. Then he rifled through the wardrobe, tugged on the new uniform, smoothing it out as he stepped back into the main room.

Lilith had not moved from her post by the door.

He closed the distance between them in three strides, one arm hooking around her sharply. He backed her against the door, the impact soft but undeniable, their bodies pressed flush. His scent mingled with hers like a collision of heat, ozone, and cinnamon.

He walked over to Lilith and pulled her in with one arm and slammed the door behind her, pressing her against his body. As the morning wood rose fully again and he started to retreat, smelling her and baring his fangs, hovering over her neck, then receding.

Then he exhaled, a whisper brushing against her skin. "Thank you... I needed that refresher."

For a moment, Lilith froze.

Her body reacted instinctively, wings half-flaring, breath catching, pupils dilating to thin slits. Her claws flexed against the metal door, scoring faint scratches into the reinforced surface. "Playing dangerous games this early, Liaison?"

Her voice came out lower, huskier; the succubus within her clearly stirred. The air tingled between them, alive, electric, fraught with potential and consequences. The temperature between their bodies spiked noticeably.

Lilith held his gaze for a long, simmering beat.

"Whatever you are, I've handled far worse."

She didn't push him away, but she didn't yield either. Her posture remained taut, her pupils slightly dilated, the faint quickening at her throat betraying just how close his fangs had hovered only moments earlier. Controlled. Calculating. And yet undeniably shaken.

"The Warden is waiting. And she's considerably less... tolerant of these little demonstrations than I am."

The warning was unmistakable.

The intrigue was impossible to miss.

He straightened his uniform with measured precision, every movement deliberately calm.

"It is not an antic or demonstration. I told you I'd see you before dawn, and I needed the charge of testosterone for the day." His tone sharpened. "You did your duty and assisted me with that, and I cannot thank you enough."

He stepped past her, confidence radiating from every line of his body.

"Now, we must be on our way. The Warden knows my being and intents, and you are correct, keeping her waiting isn't my plan." His eyes flicked to hers. "Besides, you should've understood by now that I wish not to harm you, only play lustfully with you to fill my physical agenda and to keep your mental barriers in check, since they've yet to be fully tested, I see."

Without waiting for permission, he caught Lilith lightly by the arm, guiding her away from the doorway with effortless strength. His other hand swung the door open wide, metal groaning under the decisive motion.

"Chop chop, let's go."

He set a brisk pace down the corridor.

Lilith followed with precise, controlled strides. Her heels clicked a rhythmic cadence against the polished floor tiles, each step betraying the agitation she refused to show on her face. Her leathery wings adjusted subtly behind her, folding close to her spine. Even her shadow seemed to sharpen as she moved.

The corridor ahead stretched into the prison's pre-dawn blue glow, a light designed specifically for the night-oriented species that dominated the staff.

"The Warden knowing your 'being and intents' is precisely what concerns me, Liaison." Her tone carried only far enough for him to hear, as a passing minotaur guard gave them a curious glance before quickly lowering her gaze beneath Lilith's sharp, warning look.

"Your… methods of 'charging' notwithstanding," she continued, voice laced with icy professionalism, "we have protocols here. Hierarchies. The eastern wing houses our more volatile inmates, those with particular appetites for human flesh or essence."

She lengthened her stride to draw level with him, her amber eyes sliding across his profile with academic scrutiny.

"The incident involves a human guard found drained of vital energies… alive, but barely. The question becomes: predation or consent? Your insight on human-monster dynamics might prove valuable… assuming you can focus on something beyond your morning 'testosterone charge.'"

He didn't break pace.

He did, however, turn his head enough for her to see the anger sharpening his features.

He glared.

"Mind your tongue, imp. That boost gave me the edge I needed, knowing last night that it would be necessary."

Lilith's wings snapped taut for a fraction of a heartbeat, just enough to betray where his rebuke landed.

"Your singlemindedness sounds more incubi than a calculated succubus to me with such a remark," he said coldly. "I thought better of you."

The corridor began to transition into the more ornate administrative wing, with polished obsidian floors, rune-etched archways, and amber lanterns casting long shadows.

"I haven't hidden a single thing from anyone up to this point, and it seems that it still is not intellectually following me," he added, voice low and razor-sharp, "A shame. Guess I will make sure that this is reflected accordingly during the briefing."

Lilith didn't respond.

Not verbally.

But the faint darkening of her cheeks, the tension in her jaw, the flare of something wounded and furious behind her eyes...

He had struck deeper than even he realized.

Her wings folded tight. Her claws retracted. And her expression assumed a mask of immaculate professionalism, but the heat buzzing beneath it was unmistakable.

Exactly as he intended.

Lilith adjusted her pace until she walked even with him again, her amber eyes studying the hard line of his jaw with something like respect. "I meant no disrespect, Liaison. Merely an observation."

Her voice had cooled, tempered back to professionalism, but some softer ember of intrigue lingered beneath it. Her tail swayed once behind her, betraying a thought she didn't voice. "The Warden's office is just ahead. She's... particular about first impressions, though I suspect you two may understand each other better than most."

She gestured toward an imposing door of what appears to be black oak, inlaid with silver runes that pulse gently with magical energy. Two guards flank it-both dragonkin women with scales of gleaming like metallic armor beneath their uniforms, eyes tracking your approach with predatory focus.

"For what it's worth, I do understand your methods, even if I question their timing. You'll find that many here respect power displayed appropriately."

She stopped before the door, awaiting the final approach to the Warden's domain.

He stopped in the tracks, softening his angry tone, "You're forgiven, now open the door to our headmistress, we're early, but she's still expecting us."

Lilith inclined her head slightly, acknowledging both his forgiveness and command. She approached the massive door, placing her palm against a rune that flares crimson at the touch. The dragonkin guards straightened imperceptibly, their scaled tails shifting against the floor in a subtle display of alertness.

"Lieutenant Lilith Ashborne, escorting the Human Liaison for the scheduled briefing." The door parted without a sound.

A wave of cold air slid out, brushing over his skin like the first breath of winter.

The office beyond was vast and severe, yet refined. Dark wood paneling rose to high ceilings, polished to a sheen that reflected faint glimmers of azure magic drifting in slow spirals through the air. Shelves of ancient tomes, relics, and artifacts lined the walls, each one humming with dormant or restrained power. The great desk in the center was a monolith of obsidian carved from a single slab, its surface smooth and pitch-black as a starless void.

Behind it stood Warden Morana.

"Warden Morana, the Liaison as requested." Lilith presented him.

The sight of Morana was arresting.

She was tall, easily seven feet, and her presence filled the room like a tide of winter wind. Her skin was pale as moonlit frost, her hair cascading to her waist in a soft spill of white that shimmered with an ethereal glow. Two crystalline horns twisted upward from her temples, refracting the room's dim light into fragments of icy brilliance.

The air around her was cold enough to sting.

Her uniform was midnight blue, trimmed in silver, which was tailored with a precision that suggested both military discipline and ancient regality. When she stepped forward, the very temperature seemed to obey her.

"So this is our new Liaison. Punctual. I appreciate that." Morana's voice held the crispness of deep winter, like a melodic resonance layered with the threat of a blizzard beneath the surface.

She extended an elegant hand toward the chairs before her desk. "We have matters to discuss before the others arrive. Lieutenant, you may wait outside."

Lilith bowed her head in compliance, backing out with measured deference. The door closed behind her with a hiss, sealing him inside with the Warden.

He stepped silently and deliberately into the room, shoulders squared, posture stoic in the presence of an authority that radiated ancient power. The air seemed to crystallize around him as Warden Morana circled the desk, her glacier-blue eyes studying him with clinical thoroughness, cataloging him, dissecting him, reading him like an open page.

She moved with a fluid yet cold grace that was almost predatory, a creature accustomed to command.

He remained motionless, absorbing her scrutiny without flinching.

For the briefest moment, her lips curved. Not into warmth, but into a faint expression of recognition. *Interest.*

The kind reserved for anomalies.

Creatures who didn't fit neatly into the expected patterns.

He exhaled slowly, the chilled air steaming faintly between them.

Whatever this briefing would entail, it was clear one truth had settled like frost upon the room:

He was no longer being evaluated as a prisoner.

He was being evaluated as an asset, dangerous, unusual, and very much worth the Warden's personal attention.

Warden Morana regarded him with an expression carved from winter itself, her icy stare cutting through the soft glow of her office. Frost crept delicately across the armrests of the ornate chair she indicated, shimmering faintly despite the warmth of the room. "I've been observing your integration, Liaison. Quite...unorthodox methods you employ."

She gestured for him to sit. As he approached, the cold radiating from the chair prickled against his skin, leaving a thin fog of breath in the air. She continued, her voice smooth and sharpened like frozen steel. "The incident in the eastern wing presents a unique opportunity. A human guard drained of life force, not killed, but reduced to a near-catatonic state. The inmates responsible claim consensual exchange. The guard, when briefly conscious, claimed assault."

From her desk drawer, she withdrew a crystalline orb, the sphere glowing faintly as she placed it between them. Within its depths, a haze of shifting images took form: a prison cell, three monster women, and a human guard whose stance already suggested arrogance. "Before my other administrators arrive, I want your unfiltered assessment. You straddle both worlds here. Tell me, do you think monsters and humans can truly engage in consensual exchanges within these walls? Or is predation inevitable?" Her fingers tapped once against the obsidian desktop, and the impact left tiny frost blooms that melted seconds later.

He moved to the chair and sat, the heat of his body softening the ice along its surface. His gaze stayed locked on the orb as he answered, his tone edged with simmering temper. "Actually, it is plausible, and humans are known for their dishonesty when the time suits them. Does this magic crystal show the full event as it's taking place? Cameras maybe? To rewind so as to get an accurate assessment?

He was boldly sharing his opinion, "Honestly, at this point, it's hearsay and her word versus his. Honest opinion, he was guided by lust, thinking he's..." he lifted his fingers, making mocking air quotes, "an 'alpha' and thought he could handle her, upon finding out he couldn't, screams foul. That's classic but in reverse."

A faint smile ghosted across Warden Morana's lips that was hidden almost as soon as it appeared. Frost glittered, then dissolved as she exhaled softly. With a small motion, she expanded the orb's view, sharpening the misted visions, "Perceptive. The crystal captures magical residue, not full events. A limitation of our surveillance system is when dealing with certain species."

The image shifted. The guard entered the cell swaggering, confidence dripping from every movement. The lamia, the hellhound, the lesser succubus, all had positioned themselves in unmistakable invitation.

Warden Morana traced the orb's surface with her fingertip, "The guard bypassed three security protocols to reach this cell block during shift change. We have partial recordings of his...negotiations with these three. He offered contraband in exchange for what he called 'sampling the merchandise.'"

The scene advanced, distorting during the intimate exchange, then clearing again to show the guard collapsed on the ground while the inmates recoiled at the approaching responders. "My concern isn't merely disciplinary. If word spreads that humans can falsely claim assault after willingly engaging, it threatens the delicate balance we maintain. Conversely, if monsters can drain humans with impunity by claiming consent was given..." she added, "I require someone who understands both sides. Your file suggests you have the necessary...experience with our kind. The question remains... how do we proceed with this case?"

He leaned back slightly, though tension coiled beneath his skin. "Honestly, they're both at fault. All three inmates had contraband, willingly and consensually assaulted the guard. The guard is DEF at fault for throwing away his integrity as a guard to initiate, and again, as stated, cry foul when they lose. I say that justifies the means. Honestly, I'd suggest that the guard be put on unpaid leave until fully recovered and a slap on the wrist for the three, but a strong enough slap on the wrist so it's visible that this isn't ok and would go unpunished if repeated."

Warden Morana's crystalline eyes narrowed, ice fracturing at the corners before melting into the surrounding warmth. With a smooth gesture, she dimmed the orb, returning it to its dormant opacity. "Balanced. Pragmatic. The board will appreciate this approach."

She took a silver stylus and inscribed notes onto an enchanted parchment, the glowing ink sinking slowly into the fibers like frost seeping into stone. "The guard is already in medical isolation. As for the inmates...a visible punishment, as you suggest. Perhaps reassignment to the mining detail for a fortnight. Enough to discourage similar incidents without provoking unrest."

She rose in one elegant, gliding motion, her height commanding and her presence chilling the air around her. She crossed to a crystalline decanter, steam curling faintly from its neck as she poured the liquid into two small glasses. "Your assessment aligns with mine, though I suspect for different reasons. I value order above justice; you seem to understand the...nuances of interaction between our kinds."

She lifted one glass, its contents shimmering like distilled winter, "Ice wine. A rarity from my homeland. The others will arrive shortly, but first, a toast to our new working relationship. I believe you'll serve this institution well, Liaison."

She extended the glass to him, hand steady and pale as moonlit frost.

He shook his head, voice steady and respectful, "Sadly, Warden, I must decline drinking this morning. I hope you don't take it as disrespect. I'm still peaking at the moment, and I have an appointment at 0600 that I must keep this body and form in condition for. But I ate with our alignment of thoughts."

Warden Morana paused, fingers still curled around the offered glass. A flicker that looked almost admiration crossed her glacial features before she withdrew her hand, "Discipline. Another quality I value. Your 0600 appointment would be with Combat Instructor Keres, I presume?"

She returned the untouched glass to the side table, frost blooming across its surface where her fingers had held it before fading into nothing.

The Warden's cool voice cut through the charged air between them, each syllable precise as cracking ice. "For a liaison, maintaining physical condition is indeed essential. Many of our inmates respect only strength, or at least the appearance of it."

The temperature in the office dipped a fraction as a soft chime resonated through the chamber. Silver runes embedded along the towering doorframe pulsed once, an elegant warning that visitors approached. Frost crept delicately along the edges of Morana's desk, responding instinctively to her shifting focus. "That would be the board arriving. Before they enter, know that not all share my pragmatic view. Some favor stricter separation between humans and monsters. Others advocate for…greater integration."

Her gaze flicked to the door, sharp, calculating, then returned to him with a piercing intensity that could freeze marrow. "Navigate carefully, Liaison. In this prison, politics can be as dangerous as the inmates."

He leaned in close enough that the cold radiating from her body pricked at his skin like crystalline needles. His whisper slid into the space between them, low and unfiltered. "I'm no typical human, and my lust for monsters is embedded within me, so I don't see the politics of separation as only pragmatic issues of me not being able to satiate my appetite and lust."

He rose to his full height, the shadows of the room hugging the shape of his frame. "Thank you for your hospitality. I will proceed before the arrival of the others. Thank you."

He began moving toward the door with measured purpose.

The air crackled; the Warden's shock was brief but unmistakable. Frost burst in delicate fractals along her cheeks, the closest her kind came to flushing. "Interesting. Your file mentioned... proclivities, but not their extent."

She regained her composure in a heartbeat, the frost melting in a soft exhale as a thin, knowing smile formed. With a flick of her wrist, a crystalline token rose from a drawer and drifted toward him, hovering in the air like a captured star. "Liaison, one moment."

"Your security clearance has been upgraded. This will grant access to the rehabilitation wing and certain...specialized containment areas. For assessment purposes only, of course." The magic shimmering behind her eyes deepened into something sly and glacial.

"Report your findings directly to me. The board need not be troubled with every detail of your...integration efforts." The token pulsed with cold blue light, waiting.

He snatched it with deliberate intent, feeling the surge of chilling magic race up his arm. *"Thank you, Warden."* He fixed her with an intense look, winked sharply, and resumed walking toward the door.

Morana's gaze followed, one elegant brow arching, a rare outward sign of amusement. "Do be careful, Liaison. Some of our more...specialized inmates possess abilities that even your unusual constitution might find challenging."

"The rehabilitation wing has its own rules. Guard Captain Lilith can brief you on the particulars. I expect your first assessment report by week's end." The runes on the door rippled from silver to deep blue, reading his upgraded clearance and releasing the locks with a soft hiss.

As he stepped into the corridor, several imposing silhouettes approached the board.

He straightened instantly, nodding with solemn respect. "Board members."

The procession swept toward him, a stately sphinx draped in ceremonial runes, an enormous oni in tailored attire, a delicate alraune

113

whose petals glimmered subtly, and a hooded figure wrapped in shadows that clung too tightly to be natural. "The new liaison, I presume? Interesting timing for your departure."

The Oni board member "Human. Let's see how long this one lasts."

The Alraune board member also stepped in, "Do give our regards to Captain Lilith, won't you? She's been so…persistent about expanding the rehabilitation program."

The hooded figure offered no words, only pressure, a mental weight pressing against his skull, rifling through surface thoughts like fingers sifting sand.

They swept past him into the Warden's office. The door sealed behind them with a cold pulse of light.

He was alone again in the dim corridor, the token in his hand beating like a second heart, an eerie compass pointing ever forward.

He followed its pull.

He started heading in the direction the crystal led.

Chapter 5

"Restricted Access"

The prison's architecture morphed around him.

The harsh linear angles gave way to smoother walls etched with softly glowing runes.

The air warmed, fragrant with herbal undertones and a sweetness that teased the senses.

Ahead stood a far more ornate checkpoint, arched stone wrapped with arcane sigils. Two guards flanked it: a towering gargoyle carved of living stone, and a lithe kunoichi whose serpentine tail uncoiled behind her like a rhythm.

Both watched him with predator stillness. "Halt. Rehabilitation wing is restricted access," said the Gargoyle Guard.

Her statement halted abruptly when the token in his palm exploded in radiant blue light. The kunoichi stepped forward, eyes narrowing into sharp slits.

The Kunoichi Guard expressed her confusion, "Warden's clearance? For a human?" She moved with liquid grace, studying the crystal without touching it, her tail curling in a slow, deliberate coil. "The new liaison, then. Captain Lilith mentioned you'd be coming...eventually."

Her tone held amusement, warning, and thinly veiled curiosity.

The massive reinforced door behind the guards began to thrum with power, its many arcane locks disengaging one by one. Each seal broke with a resonant pulse of magic, silver sigils dimming as they deactivated in sequence. A deep internal mechanism groaned, letting the heavy structure shift open.

The Gargoyle Guard said, "First time in rehab? Rules are different here. No weapons, no magical dampeners, and..." A grin broke across her stony features, cracking her severe expression like fractured granite. "...no promises about your personal space. These inmates are here by choice. Remember that."

His voice cut through the charged air like a blade. "Thank you both, now move, or I'll make you both into minced rubble of stone."

The response was immediate and starkly different between the two guards.

The kunoichi's scales rose sharply, her instincts flaring. A clawed hand shot toward the hilt of her blade, her fangs lengthening as droplets of venom gathered at their tips. Her body coiled to strike, eyes narrowing to reptilian slits of pure hostility. "Try it, human. I've gutted three of your kind this month alone." She said.

The gargoyle, by contrast, laughed. A deep grinding rumble like boulders collapsing. Her immense stone wings partially unfurled, their span blotting out the lamplight above. Etched tattoos glowed faintly between the cracks of her rocky skin as she looked him over with revised interest. "Aggressive. Captain Lilith will either love you or break you." She stepped aside with a mocking bow, though her massive silhouette still dominated the doorway. "Welcome to rehabilitation, tough guy. First lesson's free."

With a final, thunderous click, the last seal disengaged. The door parted to reveal a corridor unlike any other in the prison. Warm amber light replaced the harsh institutional white. Metal bars were gone, replaced by private chamber doors marked with runic sigils. Soft laughter drifted through the hallways, along with music, murmurs, and sounds far more intimate than anything found elsewhere in the facility.

He took one step forward, then shifted, vanishing from his original position in a blur of motion.

Before either guard could blink, he appeared behind the kunoichi, seizing her wrist and the hilt of her blade in a single fluid motion. She froze, her shock instantaneous and raw.

He cast a dark grin toward the gargoyle. *"The first lesson IS free."*

With a controlled release, he let the kunoichi's arm go, straightened his uniform, and stepped calmly around her rigid form as he walked through the doorway.

Her forked tongue flicked out involuntarily, tasting the air where he had stood.

116

"Impossible..." the Kunoichi said, as her voice tremored with disbelief. The gargoyle's amusement deepened into something akin to respect, her eyes following him with a newly sharpened interest.

"Well, well... Captain Lilith will definitely want to know about this one." Gargoyle Guard stepped in.

As he crossed into the rehabilitation wing, the atmosphere wrapped around him immediately, lush, warm, intoxicating. The air carried exotic scents of enchanted flora and something sweetly dangerous. Magical currents tingled against his skin.

The wing appeared less like a prison and more like a decadent sanctuary. Inmates (if they could even be called that) moved freely. Plush furniture, glowing runes, and living plants filled the space. Conversations paused as he entered; eyes followed him openly, they seemed curious, hungry, and appraising.

A melodic chime drifted through the air, followed by a voice dripping with sultry amusement. The announcement voice said: "Attention residents. Our new human liaison has arrived for assessment duties. Standard protocols apply. Captain Lilith will conduct introductions in the central atrium in fifteen minutes."

The crystal token in his hand pulsed, guiding him deeper into this alluring labyrinth of controlled indulgence.

He maintained a brisk, formal pace, gliding through the halls as he followed the crystal's pull.

The central atrium opened before him, a magnificent octagonal chamber capped by an enchanted dome that shifted scenes of forests, night skies, and distant realms. Tiered seating ringed a central fountain where crystalline water flowed upwards in defiance of gravity.

Every eye followed him.

A tattooed elf whispered to a battle-scarred werewolf whose amber stare tracked him like prey. Twin succubi sipped elegantly from jeweled goblets, their wings, one crimson, one midnight, that were fluttering with subtle interest.

And beside the floating fountain stood Captain Lilith.

A lilim born of sin and royalty, she was striking: obsidian horns framing her face, wings folded in sleek restraint, uniform tailored to accentuate her seductive silhouette rather than hide it. Her gaze locked onto him like a predator recognizing another predator. "Our new liaison arrives precisely on time. How…unexpected for a human."

She approached with liquid grace, scenting the air subtly, her tail flicking rhythmically behind her. "I've been informed of your unusual credentials. The Warden believes you possess unique…qualifications for working with our special cases. Care to demonstrate what makes you so suitable for this position?"

He stepped closer into her personal space; his presence was deliberate and brazen. "What kind of demonstration?"

Lilith's smile widened, revealing the faint glint of fangs. "Bold. I appreciate that in a liaison."

She circled him slowly, wings unfurling just enough to stir the air. Every inmate watched in near-silence, their attention fixed on the tension gathering between the two of them. "The demonstration is simple. Each inmate in rehabilitation has a… specialty. A particular talent or trait that makes them valuable to our research. Your role is to assess these traits, document them, and help determine when they're ready for reintegration."

She came to a halt behind him, warm breath grazing his ear. "But first, we need to know if you can handle them. The guards mentioned you have… unexpected reflexes. Perhaps we should see what else about you is unexpected?"

She stepped away with poised confidence and gestured forward.

Three inmates approached on her command:

The tattooed elf whose arcane markings pulsed like living runes.

A honey-skinned Apophis whose sinuous, serpentine body wove hypnotically across the marble floor.

A petite kitsune with multiple swaying tails and nervous, luminous eyes.

"Choose one for your first assessment. Each has a unique case file. Each requires a different approach." Lilith listed the options.

With a blink that bordered on supernatural, he moved, swiftly and silently as a shadow cutting through candlelight. One moment, he stood before Captain Lilith, the next his body pressed firmly against hers, breath brushing the sensitive curve of her ear.

"I'm still peaking, my reflexes are not as sharp, do not entice my lust at this moment, demon." His whisper threaded heat and warning into the space between them. Just as quickly, he stepped back, shedding the intimacy like a cloak. "Now, ladies, who goes first?"

Captain Lilith's eyes flashed with delighted danger. The flicker of surprise that overtook her was brief, but it was gone in the beat of a wing, not before the hunger beneath her polished demeanor revealed itself. When she recovered, it was with the elegance of a seasoned predator reining in her instincts. "Fascinating. The Warden was right about you." Her voice caressed the air, low and approving.

The three inmates reacted in stark contrast. The tattooed elf maintained flawless composure, though the runes spiraling across her exposed skin momentarily brightened in response to the electric tension.

The Apophis's serpentine body undulated with languid allure, her golden scales catching the light like molten coins. The kitsune, by contrast, flinched, her ears twitching nervously as her many tails curled inward, seeking comfort.

"I volunteer." Each syllable carried a melodic lilt by the tattooed elf. "My assessment is overdue, and I'm curious about the human's...methods."

The Apophis replied, "Always so eager, Sylindra."

Her forked tongue flicked briefly, tasting the air near him. "Perhaps our new liaison would prefer someone who can truly test his...reflexes."

The kitsune remained silent but watchful. Her amber eyes clung to him, uncertain, wide, calculating beneath the tremble of her shoulders. "Ladies, remember protocol. The liaison chooses."

She turned back to him, her lips curving into a smile that was both professional and exquisitely predatory.

"Though I must say, your first assessment will set the tone for your tenure here," said Lilith.

He bowed dramatically, almost flirtatiously, and allowed a teasing grin to touch his mouth.

"Ladies, ladies, you all make me blush, probably in ways a male shouldn't admit around all of you hahaha." He chuckled. "Ahem. kitsune front and center, and stand proud, don't slouch, and stand with grace as the ancient Japanese admire you to be."

The kitsune, Mizuki, blinked in shock. But his words had weight, and she straightened instantly, rising into the dignity of a creature bred from shrine and spirit. Her seven tails spread behind her like an unfolding fan of autumn hues. "My name is Mizuki. Seventh-tail of the Eastern Shrine. I am…I was…a guardian before my incarceration."

Her voice held softness, but not weakness.

The elf sighed with disappointment; Apophis's smile sharpened with interest.

Captain Lilith seemed intrigued, "Interesting choice. Mizuki's case is…complex."

The captain gestured to a private assessment room off the atrium, a space with traditional Japanese elements: tatami flooring, shoji screens, and a small garden visible through an enchanted window.

"Her file indicates unique abilities with illusions and perception manipulation. Her crime involved…well, perhaps she should tell you herself."

Mizuki approached him with measured steps, her traditional kimono in shades of crimson and gold shifting with each movement. Up close, he noticed scars partially hidden by her fur; these looked like deliberate marks forming patterns along her forearms and neck.

"I look forward to your assessment, Liaison-san." She bowed formally, her tails momentarily sweeping the floor before rising again in a graceful arc. "Few understand what I truly am."

He clasped his hands behind his back, flexing all muscles, then relaxing, "As is custom. I will not return your bow, as you are disgraced. I inform you of this so we both have an understanding. State why you're here and what makes you think you've been rehabilitated."

Mizuki straightened up from the bow; her expression was carefully controlled, though her amber eyes flashed with momentary hurt. The other inmates watched with renewed interest as she visibly composed herself. The fur along her neckline bristled slightly before settling.

"I understand, Liaison-san." Her voice remained steady despite the public rebuke. "I am imprisoned for deceiving an entire village with illusions that drove seventeen humans to madness and three to death. I...manipulated their perception of reality until they could no longer distinguish truth from fantasy."

She clasped her hands before her, clawed fingertips pressing into her palms hard enough that he noticed tiny droplets of blood forming.

"As for rehabilitation..." A bitter smile crosses her features. "I don't believe I am rehabilitated. I merely practice control. The urge to create illusions remains, especially when threatened or...dismissed."

Captain Lilith observed the exchange with clinical interest, making notes on a crystalline tablet that materializes in her hand. "Honesty is progress, Mizuki. The first assessment room is prepared for you both."

The kitsune's seven tails twitched with nervous energy, though she maintained her dignified posture as she waited for his next instruction. The tattooed elf and Apophis have begun whispering between themselves, clearly reassessing his methods and their own strategies for when their turn comes.

His voice cut clean through the air. "No. We'll do it here."

A hush rippled across the atrium, smooth as silk, sharp as a blade. Lilith's wings lifted in faint surprise. Inmates shifted in their seats, drawn like moths to the flame of confrontation. "Here? That's...unorthodox, but within your authority." She said.

Mizuki's ears twitched downward before she forced them upright again, her tails going rigid with tension. "As you wish, Liaison-san."

She moved to the center of the atrium and knelt with grace steeped in tradition. Her kimono pooled around her like a spilled sunset, crimson and gold swirling in precise folds. The scars along her neck, like kanji burned into her very fur, shimmered faintly with suppressed magic.

"My rehabilitation involves daily meditation to control my illusion-casting. I've learned to channel my abilities into constructive expressions through the prison's art therapy program." Mizuki said as she extended her hand. Her claws glinted. Her breath steadied.

Above her palm, reality bent.

A miniature cherry blossom tree emerged, illusory yet perfect, cycling through all four seasons in mere seconds. Petals bloomed, fell, withered, and were reborn in an endless fractal of soft pink and ghostly white.

The atrium held its breath.

The tree glowed in her palm like a piece of living memory…or a fragment of madness waiting to bloom.

Mizuki's voice softened, the illusion-tree dimming slightly above her palm as she looked up at him fully for the first time. "I create only what is permitted now. My parole hearing is scheduled for next month, but…"

Her amber eyes locked onto his, direct, vulnerable, devastatingly honest. "I don't deserve freedom. Not yet. The faces of those I drove to madness still visit me each night."

He answered her confession with a stare sharp enough to cut through the illusions she hadn't even cast yet. "I see. So first, why did you do it?"

The question struck her like an arrow. Her seven tails trembled before settling, and the fur along her shoulders lifted as the memory clawed its way through her composure. All around the atrium, the onlooking monster girls hushed as though sensing the shift in air pressure, like the stillness before a storm.

"I was a shrine guardian for centuries. The humans of my village once honored me with offerings and respect. Then…" she started her statement. Her claws curled inward, digging crescents into her palms until drops of bright blood beaded on her fur. "They built factories. Polluted the sacred waters. Cut down the ancient trees. When I confronted them, they laughed. Called me a relic. A superstition."

Her golden eyes darkened, first to amber, then to a violent shade of smoldering orange. "So I showed them what a 'superstition' could do. I crafted illusions tailored to each villager's deepest fears. Made them see horrors beyond comprehension. I wanted them to understand true terror before I allowed their minds to break."

A single tear slid down her fur. It shimmered, catching the glow of the illusion-tree still hovering above her palm.

But her voice... her voice never wavered. "I did it because pride became vengeance. Because I forgot my purpose was protection, not punishment. Because after centuries of being worshipped, I couldn't bear being forgotten."

Captain Lilith quietly recorded, her face unreadable while every inmate in the atrium leaned closer.

His next question landed like a judge's hammer. "Interesting. Now, if put in that same position, would you do it again?"

Silence swelled around the atrium. Even the fountain seemed to still its upward-flowing waters.

Mizuki's breaths grew deeper, slower, each one a battle. Her tails began to sway in a serpentine, dangerous rhythm. The edge of an illusion shimmered faintly around her form, distorting the air. "I…"

She closed her eyes. When she opened them, they glowed softly, beautiful and terrifying. "Part of me would. The ancient part. The part that remembers being divine."

Her voice dropped, becoming a whisper woven with centuries of pain. "But I've learned something here, surrounded by monsters who've all made their own terrible choices. I've learned that revenge is…hollow. Those I drove to madness didn't understand what they'd destroyed. Their ignorance wasn't worthy of my power."

She leaned forward, her whisper carrying unnaturally well. "If placed in that position again, I would find another way. Not because I've become merciful, Liaison-san, but because I've become wiser. Terror is a crude tool. There are more...elegant methods of teaching humans to respect what they don't understand."

Captain Lilith's wings twitched slightly at the answer, though her expression remained disciplined.

But he wasn't satisfied. "I don't believe you. I believe you would do it again cuz you were in a fit of rage, as you stated. You've learned more to handle things and to think things through thoroughly, which I commend, but it didn't prepare you to face it again. What you SHOULD be focusing on is triggers and rage control. I am moved by your honesty and beauty, and you should justly be rewarded, but you are not rehabilitated."

He dropped to one knee before her, grasping her paws in his palms. "You have the ability, but you were being pointed in the wrong direction. Focus now on rage and discipline of how to PROPERLY utilize that aggression instead of lashing out without thought."

The entire atrium inhaled.

His touch broke her composure. Her fur bristled. Her illusions flickered out entirely. Her breath hitched in a small, helpless sound that no creature with divine blood should be capable of making. "You... You're right."

Her voice trembled. "I've been focusing on controlling the expression of my rage, not the rage itself."

Her paws shook in his hands, claws retracting fully, a sign of trust more intimate than any bow. "No one has spoken to me with such clarity since my imprisonment. The therapists focus on my illusions, not the emotion behind them."

Her seven tails went still. Perfectly still.

Not out of fear.

Out of absolute attention.

"I will redirect my efforts as you suggest, Liaison-san. The rage... It's ancient. Older than the buildings here. But perhaps not unmanageable." Mizuki said.

Captain Lilith stepped closer, her wings tight against her back, her interest no longer clinical. "This is…unexpected progress. I'll have her rehabilitation program adjusted accordingly."

He leaned forward, closing the remaining space between him and the kneeling kitsune. The air trembled around both.

He met her forehead with his.

A sound rippled through the atrium: gasps, whispers, the thrum of magic reacting to the intimacy. Mizuki's eyes widened, pupils dilating to full black.

Her tails shuddered, all seven of them. "I believe in your ability and your willingness. You are now on the path to regain thy honor."

He released her paws, cupped her head gently, and pressed his lips to her forehead.

The kitsune froze, trembling, not in fear, but in something closer to reverence.

Then he rose to his full height. "Now rise and take your place on your path to rehabilitation."

The illusion-tree above her palm bloomed once more, this time more vivid, more stable, more alive.

And Mizuki lifted her head…

…reborn in purpose.

The atrium still hummed with the fading resonance of Mizuki's transformation when her voice softened again, a tremor running through her words. "I…"

For once, the eloquent shrine guardian struggled to speak. A lone tear slipped through the fur along her cheek, catching the amber light before falling away like a dying star. "Thank you, Liaison-san."

She rose with the graceful precision of a creature born from myth. The timid posture she'd held only minutes before was gone, replaced by a regal, renewed dignity. The kanji burned into her neck pulsed faintly with golden light, as though awakening to a long-forgotten purpose. "I will not waste this chance."

Captain Lilith stepped forward, her heels clicking sharply against the polished floor. Her expression carried a complicated blend of authority, suspicion, and grudging respect. "That was…unorthodox, Liaison. But effective." She said.

She motioned to the remaining inmates, who watched Mizuki with mixed awe and apprehension, predators recognizing a shift in hierarchy. "Shall we continue with the next assessment?"

The tattooed elf and Apophis whispered to one another, their voices low and sharp. The entire atmosphere of the atrium had shifted, no longer tense but charged with new possibilities.

He swept his gaze across the room before answering, his tone cold but measured. "I will not do everyone in this room at this moment. I do believe one every day is enough to give careful consideration to EACH and every one of you, so that way everyone has a chance to get the care assessment NEEDED that has been disregarded."

He turned to Captain Lilith and stepped into her space. so close their noses nearly brushed. The captain inhaled sharply, her wings twitching in reflexive surprise. "And you, my dear, let this be a reflection of YOUR failure of duties, not caring for each of these inmates appropriately, so that they can be released accordingly. I WILL be reporting this to the Warden as part of my report. Any questions?"

He glared at her, eyes burning with a ruby intensity that bordered on dangerous.

Captain Lilith's wings flared outward, her composure fracturing at his audacity. "You overstep. Liaison." He said.

Her voice dropped to a volcanic whisper, warm enough to sear against his skin.

"I've managed this wing for fifteen years according to protocol. These inmates are dangerous criminals, not misunderstood victims."

But despite her scorching tone, uncertainty flickered in her lavender-and-violet eyes. The other inmates watched silently, the impossible unfolding before them. "Report what you wish to the Warden. But know that coddling these monsters won't rehabilitate them. It will get you killed." Lilith spoke to him.

She forced herself to step back, wings folding with visible restraint, though not fully, her instincts refusing to surrender ground.

"We will continue tomorrow. One assessment per day, as you wish." Lilith's professionalism returned like a snapped mask, but the tension still twisted the air around her. "Guards, escort the inmates back to their cells. Assessment period is concluded for today."

Mizuki cast a final look back toward him, amber eyes glowing with a mixture of gratitude and apprehension, before being guided away.

Once the atrium emptied, the silence grew heavy. He waited, breath low, until only he and the captain remained. "Good."

The doors sealed behind the last guard.

Captain Lilith straightened, her wings unfurling again, not in warning this time, but in primal reaction to the charge between him.

He spoke first, voice rough-edged and simmering. "No shit, they're criminal monsters, they're NOT to be coddled, they're to be appropriately rehabilitated. My approach IS unorthodox, but it gets results."

His blood heated beneath his skin, a dangerous burn radiating up his spine. "And mind you... Remember that I'm no different than every monster in here, including you. I'm no mere human, and if I'm to do my duties, you WILL address me respectfully and not dismissively anymore. I start from the top down with the harshest judgment so that everyone beneath understands the standard."

His neck cracked as he rolled it, muscles trembling with suppressed aggression. "Call me bold, but we're alone now, and I love the heat. Speak your mind, Captain."

His eyes burned ruby, alive with fire, and his anger was no longer hidden.

Captain Lilith reacted instantly. Her wings unfurled to their full span, the membranes glowing from internal flame. Her scales blazed with molten color, heat radiating off her in palpable waves. The tiles beneath her feet cracked as her draconic blood surged. "No different than us? Bold claim, Liaison."

She stalked in a slow circle around him, tail lashing, the air thick with smoke and magic.

"I've watched a dozen 'rehabilitation experts' come and go. Each one thinks they understand monsters. Each one failing."

Lilith halted in front of him, towering and incandescent with fury. "You managed one kitsune. Congratulations. But when you face the Wendigo in Cell Block D, who's eaten seventeen humans, or the Mindflayer who collects memories like trophies…your little forehead touches won't save you."

Her eyes narrowed, studying his burning gaze as though seeing him for the first time. "Though perhaps you're right about one thing. You're not entirely human, are you? The Warden neglected to mention that detail."

A slow, dangerous smile spread across her lips. "How fascinating."

He didn't flinch. "Are you deaf, dumb, or just a rapid promoted imp? I said that EACH ONE IS TO BE CATERED TO ACCORDINGLY. You fool!"

His voice rose, raw and shaking with the force of what surged through him. "I don't intrude as I know better. You wanted a demonstration? I gave you one. You claimed that was the hardest case? I handled it with ease, as you unexpected."

The heat in his blood surged again, vision tinged with red. "Don't threaten me like I'm some mere mortal. I'm flesh, but so are you. I know the color of your blood and how you taste, therefore you're NOT DIFFERENT than me. Stand down NOW."

Captain Lilith froze mid-step.

Her breath hitched, not in fear, but in something sharper, more instinctual. His words rattled her in a way nothing else had.

The flames rippling over her scales dimmed.

Her wings lowered a fraction.

Her claws retracted.

"You…"

Captain Lilith inhaled sharply, steadying herself. "No one speaks to me that way. Not in my prison."

The fire drained from her muscles little by little as his words sank deeper, his presence, heat, and intensity. "The Warden said you were different. I assumed it was bureaucratic nonsense." She studied his trembling, burning form, finally seeing beyond the human shape. "What exactly are you, Liaison? What creature knows the taste of dragon blood yet walks freely among humans?"

Her hand hovered over the alert glyph, but didn't touch it.

Her eyes narrowed in thought, not hostility.

"Perhaps we've both misjudged the situation. I've spent fifteen years watching these walls... watching monsters exploit every kindness shown them. Forgive me if I'm...skeptical of new approaches." Something beyond hatred was brewing inside Lilith.

He was barely listening now.

His breathing had changed, ragged, strained, each inhale trembling with volatile energy barely held in place, "My dear Captain, I've spoken rashly."

His body shook, fighting itself, "I apologize to you as I am peaking more and more, and it's still not even 0600 yet, is it? My levels are getting dangerous."

His voice cracked on the last word.

And Captain Lilith's eyes widened, not in dominance...

...but in recognition.

Something in him was slipping.

And she finally understood.

Captain Lilith's defensive posture shifted the instant his composure cracked. The draconic predator in her, honed by years of dealing with volatile inmates, recognized that this was no longer a dominance game. This was a different kind of threat altogether.

Her wings slowly folded back, the sharp, flared edges softening as she took a cautious step toward him. The anger that had burned in her eyes cooled into something far more clinical and focused: assessment, calculation, concern.

"Your levels? By the Demon Lord..." Lilith's gaze sharpened, shock flickering across her face as she finally named what she was seeing. "You're in transition, aren't you? The Warden didn't just send us a liaison, she sent us a metamorphic."

She darted a quick look toward the surveillance crystals embedded high along the walls. In one fluid motion, she tapped her security badge three times. The faint glow of the warded lenses dimmed, registering the override as a 'security assessment' in the system logs. The room felt suddenly more enclosed, more intimate, with the invisible eyes briefly blinded.

"It's 0547. How long since your last stabilizer dose?" Lilith asked, her tone was anything but calm.

She reached for the pouch at her belt, claws precise despite their taloned tips, and drew out a small silver vial etched with draconic sigils. A faint, acrid heat radiated from it. "This is my emergency suppressant. Dragon-grade, but it should help temporarily."

Gone was the territorial captain ready to tear his throat out; in her place stood someone who understood the mechanics of an overloaded body and a dangerous threshold. "Take it. We can discuss rehabilitation philosophies after you're stabilized."

He shook his head, breath ragged and uneven, but resolve still carved into every line of his body. "No, I need this aggression, I must get to the yard to release this energy accordingly, let me catch my breath, and I must go to the courtyard, I'm anticipated there. Take me into your flesh and help calm me, but I cannot lose this energy and testosterone."

Captain Lilith's eyes widened at that, the words striking across her professionalism like sparks across dry kindling. For a heartbeat, confusion warred with instinct. Then training took over.

She swept her hand toward the main doors, triggering another lock sequence to seal them fully. The rune-studded frame flared briefly as if acknowledging a higher security state. "The courtyard is too exposed. You're in no condition…" Her gaze swept his trembling form, recalculating. "Combat training room. It's empty this hour." It hit her.

She moved to his side with brisk, controlled purpose, letting him lean against the solid, heated strength of her scaled frame. Heat radiated off her, not the wild furnace of rage, but a tempered, grounding warmth that seeped into his shaking muscles, giving them something to anchor to.

"I've seen this before in transitionals. The energy build-up becomes toxic if suppressed too long." Her voice dropped into the cool cadence of experience as she guided him into a narrower, dimmer corridor reserved for staff and high-clearance movement.

"We have three minutes to reach the training room before the next guard rotation." Her wing spread just enough to curve around his shoulders, shielding him from any stray gaze that might pierce the corridor unexpectedly. The scent of stone, sweat, and faint brimstone followed them.

"The Warden should have warned me. Sending a metamorphic into a prison of monsters without proper protocols…" Her jaw clenched, a spark of genuine anger flaring there. "Reckless, even for her."

He forced a laugh around the strain curling through his body, his voice edged with both humor and something more dangerous. "I can control, I just need to hold out," he chuckled, "You think this is bad? You should see when I'm in heat and desire another in heat, haha," he now coughed.

The corner of Captain Lilith's mouth twitched despite herself, though her eyes only grew more serious. "Heat cycles in a prison environment…"

She muttered it like a curse under her breath, shaking her head. "The Warden truly has lost her mind this time."

They reached a reinforced door marked:

COMBAT TRAINING – AUTHORIZED PERSONNEL ONLY.

Chapter 6

"The Warning"

COMBAT TRAINING – AUTHORIZED PERSONNEL ONLY.

Whatever was about to happen, he was ready for it.

Lilith keyed in a sequence of runes with practiced ease. The door slid open to reveal a broad chamber of padded walls, marked rings on the floor, racks of blunted weapons, and an empty observation booth looming above like a dark, glass eye.

"Here. This room is shielded, magical, and a physical containment. You can…release your energy without risk." There was a brief pause. Her next words came more quietly.

"I'll stand guard. The security feed shows maintenance for the next thirty minutes."

She stepped back, positioning herself near the door, wings tight to her spine but eyes fixed on him, weighing threat and vulnerability in equal measure. "What exactly are you transitioning to? If I'm to help manage your…condition…during your assignment here, I should know."

He straightened with effort, breathing rough, a faint sheen of sweat along his neck. His reply came with a cough and a bitter twist of humor. "I'm not transitioning, I'm preparing for combat with…" He coughed mid-sentence, "…the bull."

The effect on her was instantaneous.

Shock rippled through her scales, visible as a brief flare of internal fire racing along the ridges of her neck and shoulders.

Her eyes widened, then hardened into sharp focus. "The bull? You mean Minotaura?"

Her voice dropped low, almost a growl. "The three-time champion of the underground fighting rings? The same inmate who put two guards in the infirmary last month?"

She began pacing in a tight circle, tail striking the padded floor with enough force to send dull thuds reverberating through the room. Fury now had a target, and it was not him; it was the decision that had placed him on this path. "Is this what the Warden meant by 'alternative rehabilitation methods? Pitting you against our most violent inmate?"

She halted, turning that blazing gaze fully on him. "No human could survive that. Which confirms my suspicion that you're something else entirely."

Her hand moved toward her comm glyph, claws hovering over it. Protocol screamed at her to press it. She didn't. "I should report this. It violates at least seven safety protocols."

Conflict shadowed her features. "But I've watched traditional methods fail with Minotaura for years. Nothing reaches her."

She stepped nearer again, the air crackling faintly where their energies overlapped. "If you're determined to do this, I need to know what I'm dealing with. What are you, really? And how do you intend to survive Minotaura's rage?"

He shook his head, more in bafflement than denial, eyes still burning faintly red. "I don't know, I know I'm flesh, but I know I can withstand her. I just have to last until we begin. I'm still not peaked yet, and no, I don't know my true name or the reasons demons feared me on the outside. Or maybe I'm just REALLY dumb and lustful toward the wrong entities hahaha." He coughed.

She studied him with a look usually reserved for weapons of unknown origin. There was no fear in her eyes anymore, only assessment and a reluctant, growing respect. "Demons feared you…"

She tasted the idea, turning it over. "…and now you're deliberately facing Minotaura in combat. Either you have a death wish or…"

Her eyes narrowed, something clicking into place.

"The Warden isn't testing you. She's testing Minotaura."

Lilith stalked to the nearest control panel and activated a series of runes. Blue lines of subdued light sprang up around the perimeter of the room, forming a containment grid that hummed faintly. "These are suppression fields. They won't stop your…whatever this is…but they'll contain any magical discharge."

Her tail flicked again, this time with restless energy rather than rage. "We have twelve minutes before yard privileges begin. Use this time to prepare however you need."

She stepped away, giving him space, though she never took her eyes off him. "I've served in this prison for fifteen years. Seen every kind of monster and aberration. But you…"

Her head tilted slightly, as if trying to see angles that hadn't existed before. "The Warden must be desperate to try something this unorthodox with Minotaura. Her last rampage nearly breached the eastern wall."

He exhaled slowly, forcing the storm inside him into something vaguely disciplined. "Exactly, I faced the void in the basement of the premises, and I ate with the Minotaura's for lunch. I've been preparing mentally, and my body is following. I ran on lust, and I'm still running on lustful anticipation, but I have to hold it within me. Stay or go if u choose. But if you choose to stay, only quelling my lust will help keep this in check."

Her expression hardened instantly.

The warmth she had offered became heated steel. "I see the Warden neglected to brief you on protocol as well."

Her voice dropped to something cold and molten, dangerous for entirely different reasons. "I am Captain of the Guard, not some common succubus to be propositioned. My duty is to maintain order in this facility, not to service inmates or…whatever classification you fall under."

She stepped back, wings flaring in warning, tail snapping once against the floor. The air around her shimmered from the heat spike. "You have ten minutes to compose yourself by appropriate means. I'll escort you to the yard when it's time."

She moved to stand directly before the door, a living barrier, equal parts protection and control. "And for future reference, propositions to staff are punishable by solitary confinement. Consider this your *only* warning."

134

Her tail lashed the padded floor again, the impact echoing like a muted thunderclap, but she did not abandon her post.

He snarled softly under his breath, the heat inside him spiking again, not just with lust but with affront and rising power. "That wasn't..." he growled, "...a proposition."

The training room itself seemed to respond. The air thickened, growing hotter, pressing against both of them like a stormfront. "I know better than to disrespect a dragon in her element."

His eyes brightened into vivid rubies, and for an instant, something not entirely human stared out through them. Ruby flamed like a dart in her direction from his glare.

The fire wasn't literal, not yet, but in the crackling magical tension that snapped between them, it might as well have been.

The captain's command hit him like a blast of cold wind cutting through a furnace.

"Control yourself," her voice had dropped into a dangerous rumble, the ancient growl of a predator older than the prison itself. Even as the heat rippled outward from his body in blistering waves, she refused to retreat.

Captain Lilith stood her ground, planted firmly in the center of the containment chamber, wings drawn back in a stance that was both confrontational and disciplined, "I misunderstood your intent, but that doesn't excuse this display."

The suppression runes embedded in the walls pulsed wildly, their blue light flickering as if straining to hold the atmosphere together. The temperature continued to climb, bending the air in shimmering distortions around him. His breath came in hot bursts; steam curled from his skin, licking upward like living tendrils made of fire and mist.

"Seven minutes remain. Whatever you're becoming, whatever the Warden has planned, remember where you are." Lilith's posture shifted, no longer fully defensive. She studied him with sharp, clinical interest, measuring him the way a seasoned warrior measured the first twitch of an opponent's transformation. Her tail moved in slow arcs across the floor, steady, rhythmically anchoring her composure.

"Minotaura responds to strength, yes, but she respects control more. This wild energy you're exuding? She'll see it as weakness, not power." A thin wisp of smoke escaped her nostrils as she inhaled deeply, modeling the same restraint she demanded from him. The heat radiating off his form washed over her scales in waves, but she stood as if forged for this environment.

What she was preparing him for was beyond any comprehension, "focus. Channel. Contain. Or Minotaura will break you before you land your first blow."

He obeyed instinctively. His eyes closed, lashes trembling as he drew a breath so deep it visibly expanded his entire torso. Every muscle along his arms, shoulders, and abdomen flexed beneath skin that glowed faintly like iron beginning to heat. Steam rose from him in thicker clouds. At first chaotic, then slowly settling into undulating waves as he fought to pull the power inward instead of letting it boil over.

Captain Lilith watched intently, professionalism returning to her like a mantle she'd momentarily shed. Her draconic blood responded to his rising aura; the faint shimmer along her scaled neck brightened, the violet in her eyes deepening to molten amethyst.

Yet she remained calm and assessing. "Better," she said.

Her tone carried grudging approval. Like one warrior acknowledging another's discipline rather than emotion, "Channel it inward. Let it strengthen rather than consume you."

She moved with controlled precision toward a nearby control panel. The runes responded to her touch, deepening from pale blue to a richer cobalt that spread across the walls in concentric ripples. The new containment field hummed against the rising heat, stabilizing the air pressure that his energy strained to unravel.

Lilith remained alert, wings subtly shifting as steam rolled across the floor toward her boots. She didn't step away. Instead, she studied the phenomenon with focused intent.

"Four minutes remaining. Whatever you're becoming, whatever power you're harnessing… Minotaura will test its limits." Her wings gave a slight twitch, signaling both tension and preparedness.

The memory of Minotaura's past victories flickered through her expression. Three years undefeated, and a reputation for snapping bones like dry twigs. "She's been undefeated for three years," she told him, "Broke the arm of the last guard who challenged her authority. The Warden must see something exceptional in you to arrange this… confrontation."

She glanced at her timepiece, the gesture sharp and precise. Her tail swayed once more, a physical metronome marking the final moments before the inevitable battle.

Captain Lilith's wings shifted subtly at his answer, the crimson glow of his pupil-less eyes reflecting in her own. The raw heat rolling off his body made the containment chamber feel smaller than it was, as though the walls themselves were bending closer around him.

"The yard awaits. Are you prepared to face her, or shall I inform the Warden that her experiment requires more…incubation time?"

His breath left him in a low growl, thick steam curling from his lips as he pushed to his feet. Every muscle in his body tightened beneath skin that shimmered with molten tension.

"No, this will not be my way of disrespect. I will arrive promptly. Please assist in my adjustment; my hands are shaking," He rose fully, though the movement lacked his usual precision, his body vibrated with uncontrolled power, his fingers twitching as if sparks danced beneath the skin.

Captain Lilith approached him with deliberation, her steps silent and predatory. Her posture remained rigidly controlled, but her eyes betrayed the truth. She was no longer angry; she was concerned.

"Understood," she said. Her voice came quiet and firm, the tone she reserved for volatile situations. She stopped within arm's reach, the heat radiating from him brushing against her scales like an open flame.

"Stand still," She reached slowly toward her belt, drawing out a pair of ornate restraints forged from dark metal etched with pulsing sigils.

He stood, and the trembling in his hands worsened as she neared. The air between them vibrated, their energies brushing like opposing storm fronts.

Lilith lifted one of his wrists with care, steadying his uncooperative fingers within her firmer grip. The bracers clicked into place with a muted chime, and the runes activated instantly.

Golden light seeped along his veins in delicate lines, threading through the heat surging beneath his skin. His muscles tensed in response, then loosened, the violent trembling easing, though not fully subsiding.

"These are dampening bracers. They won't suppress your... abilities..." she murmured, checking the alignment of the runes, "...but they'll help you maintain control."

She moved to his other wrist, her touch firm yet strangely gentler than before. It was professional, but edged with a muted respect. "Standard procedure for all combatants in sanctioned matches. Even Minotaura wears them."

When both bracers were secured, she stepped back to observe him, wings folding neatly along her spine. The heat still poured off him, but the chaotic bursts had settled into a fierce, focused burn.

"Two minutes. The yard is being cleared of regular inmates. This will be a controlled encounter." Her eyes narrowed slightly, assessing both him and the runes glowing along his arms, "Whatever happens out there, remember that I have authorization to terminate the match if necessary. Don't make me use it."

He swallowed the fire in his throat and managed a ragged, humorless breath, "Terminate if you see me lose control, and an inmate's life is on the brink of death. I trust your judgement, not my own right now."

His trembling hands reached for the bracers as if to adjust them, but he fumbled, and Lilith wordlessly guided his fingers into place, steadying the straps until they latched securely. She glanced up at him once more, expression unreadable.

"Your awareness of the risk is...noted," she turned, her tail slicing through the heated air as she crossed to the sealed door. Several layers of magical locks disengaged at her command, glowing circles collapsing inward like vanishing stars.

Beyond the threshold stretched a sterile corridor lit by harsh magical lamps... the cold, clinical light that clashed with the inferno he carried inside his chest.

"Follow me. Walk three paces behind. Do not make eye contact with other guards or inmates we might pass," her wings shifted, adopting the wide, authoritative stance of a senior officer escorting something dangerous yet vital.

"The yard has been specially prepared. Minotaura is already there, waiting," Captain Lilith led him through the corridor with her usual measured precision, the sway of her scaled tail controlled and rhythmic despite the tension coiling beneath her uniform. The corridor's enchanted lights washed across her obsidian scales as she spoke without turning her head.

"For what it's worth, most who face Minotaura don't request safeguards for her protection. That...distinguishes you from others the Warden has tested," this was Lilith's attempt at encouragement, the most she had in this moment.

He closed his burning eyes, feeling the world tilt in a haze of heat and suppressed aggression. His trembling hand reached forward, fingers brushing the tip of her tail. The touch made the dragon-woman stiffen instantly, a ripple of instinctual fury tightening every muscle beneath her armor.

But he curled his fingers lightly around the warm, flexing muscle and spoke with deliberate calm. "Let the appearance be that I'm weak, I cannot see, so guide me with your tail, please."

The request struck her like a thrown spear. Unexpected, intimate, and uncomfortably vulnerable. For a heartbeat, the corridor's ambient temperature spiked as her instincts flared. But then, slowly, her rigid posture softened.

"An...unorthodox request," her voice held a strange blend of suspicion and reluctant understanding. Still, she did not pull away. She allowed her tail to remain in his grasp, adjusting her stride so its movement guided rather than resisted.

"Very well. The appearance of weakness may indeed serve as a tactical advantage." She spoke as her tail guided him. It was hot beneath his touch, the muscles rippling with controlled power. Her scales felt smooth and hardened, shifting subtly as she walked. Each step she took transmitted faint vibrations through the appendage, letting him sense the path ahead through her body alone.

They passed several guards, each pausing to stare, some with confusion, others with shock. But none dared to speak. Lilith's predatory glare was a sharper weapon than any blade.

"We approach the yard. I can hear Minotaura pacing," her voice grew lower as the corridor opened into a larger staging area. The faint echo of distant hooves striking dirt reverberated through the air, "she's agitated today, more than usual. The Warden's announcement of a 'special challenger' has her…eager to prove herself."

The massive reinforced door to the yard loomed before them, covered in runes of warding that pulsed gently with restrained power. Lilith paused just before it, her tail taut beneath his fingers. "Once we cross this threshold, I cannot intervene unless lives are at risk. Are you certain you wish to proceed with this charade of vulnerability? Minotaura respects strength, not deception."

He released a tense breath, still gripping her tail lightly. "It's not a charade, I legit can't see."

Lilith inhaled sharply, finally turning enough to study his face. The fully crimson eyes, devoid of pupils, reflected nothing, no movement, no light, no life. Only power.

"I see", her voice shifted, no longer irritated or wary… now measured and analytical. She adjusted her stance so her tail braced more firmly in his hand, a physical anchor as she entered a command sequence into the massive door, "This transformation has affected your vision. That complicates matters."

As the door began its slow ascent, a harsh blast of outdoor air rushed inward… dry, dust-laden, and tinged with the iron scent of old blood. Sunlight flared bright across the threshold, though he could not see it.

Lilith narrated quietly, guiding him with her tail. "Listen carefully. The yard has been cleared to a thirty-meter circle. Minotaura stands at the center-approximately 2.4 meters tall, heavily muscled, with curved horns that span nearly a meter across."

The earth beneath his boots shifted to packed dirt, still cool from the night. The heavy breathing ahead grew louder... a deep, animal rumble accompanied by the scrape of hooves and the slow grind of thick muscle.

"She's pawing the ground with her right hoof, a sign of impatience," the door thundered fully open, "I'll guide you fifteen paces in, then protocol requires I release you. The Warden is observing from the north tower."

Her tail trembled barely, but enough for him to feel the tension. "If you truly cannot see, I am obligated to inform her and potentially cancel this match."

Then, softer... almost beneath her breath: "Or I can guide you to a position and trust whatever the Warden has planned. Your choice, prisoner. Decide quickly."

He tightened his grip for a heartbeat, then released. Choosing trust through absence, "Just guide me in, I trust you, now trust me."

Captain Lilith's tail flexed in a rare gesture of acceptance. She stepped forward, guiding him into the blistering open yard as if leading a blindfolded predator into an arena filled with knives.

The moment he crossed the threshold, the world changed.

Heat, dust, and the deep, thunderous sound of massive lungs drawing breath.

"Fifteen paces forward," Lilith murmured, her tail moving like a living compass. An immense presence loomed ahead, hot as a forge, furious as an earthquake.

"Minotaura has spotted us," Lilith whispered. "She's snorting, pawing the ground harder now. Seven more paces."

The earth trembled with each strike of her hoof, "final position."

Her tail slid from his grip like a serpent leaving warm stone. "She stands eight meters directly ahead. The sun is at your back, in her eyes. Whatever happens next...make it count," Then her voice shifted, booming, official, echoing across the yard.

"Challenger positioned! Match commences at the signal!" the announcement was made.

Lilith stepped back, her tail slipping completely from his grasp as she moved away.

The world fell into a hush.

He opened his eyes. And it all erupted into color.

Two incandescent spheres of red flame replaced his pupils, casting a hellish glow across the combat yard. For the briefest instant, everything sharpened: the grit beneath his bare feet, the metallic taste of anticipation on his tongue, the humming vibration of the magical barriers straining against the weight of a hundred monstrous spectators pressing in.

Before him, the arena stretched wide and raw, a circle of compacted earth scored by countless hoofprints, clawmarks, and the darker stains of past battles. Heat shimmered above the ground, carrying the thick scent of sweat, dust, and primal adrenaline.

But all of that fell away when his gaze locked onto her.

Minotaura towered over the space like a living monument to brutality. Her upper half was a woman forged of hardened muscle and tribal scarring. She rose powerfully above a monstrous bovine lower body, the flank muscles rippling beneath short dark fur. Her gleaming black hooves struck the ground with such force that the earth reverberated. The massive horns curved outward like deadly scimitars, polished to a threatening shine. A prison issue tank top barely contains her impressive chest, stretched tight across her torso.

She inhaled deeply, nostrils widening as steam curled into the air. Disdain twisted her lips as she took in the sight of him.

"They send me *THIS*? some glowing-eyed runt?" Her voice boomed through the arena, vibrating the ground beneath him like a war drum. She took a threatening step forward, the packed dirt cracking beneath her hooves. "Captain! Is this a joke?"

From the sidelines, Captain Lilith stood expressionless, with her arms folded, wings tight in controlled tension. Only the rapid flick of her tail betrayed the storm beneath her discipline. High above, in the north tower's shadowed balcony, Warden Morrigan leaned forward, the faintest glimmer of anticipation in her star-filled eyes.

Minotaura snorted again, the sound echoing like a bull's challenge, "No matter. I'll make this quick." She lowered her massive horns; every muscle in her colossal frame coiled like braided steel ready to snap, "Try not to die too fast, human. The others have placed bets."

He did not flinch. Instead, he slid one foot back, grounding himself. His stance widened, thighs locking into a perfect sumo posture. His toes dug into the dirt. His center dropped low. The heat radiating off his body wavered the air around him.

Then he raised both hands, curling his fingers toward her in a universal "come at me" gesture, a deliberate beckon, something that electrified the crowd.

He *welcomed* her.

The arena erupted in howls, cheers, and feral whistling.

Minotaura froze for a fraction of a second, her eyes narrowing with something almost like surprise. Then her lips peeled back into a savage grin, "Playing warrior, are we? cute."

She exhaled, and the air trembled.

Without another warning, Minotaura exploded forward.

The ground quaked beneath her charging weight as two tons of raw destruction barreled across the yard. Dust spiraled in her wake. Her horns gleamed like twin crescents of doom aimed directly at his ribs. She moved impossibly fast, each hoofbeat a thunderous strike, each breath a furious snort of steam.

The inmates roared, slamming against the transparent-walled barriers, some shouting his death, others chanting for blood.

Even Captain Lilith involuntarily stepped forward, her wings twitching open with shock as she realized Minotaura was accelerating past safe-combat velocity.

Her jaw clenched as she whispered under her breath: *This might actually kill him.*

Above, Warden Morrigan leaned farther out over the balcony, the faintest smile ghosting across her lips, her expression locked in clinical fascination.

Minotaura roared "RAAAAAAAAAHHH!" an earth-shaking bellow of primal fury, as she lowered her head fully and committed every ounce of her monstrous power into the charge.

Dust swirled violently.

The ground trembled.

His red eyes burned brighter.

And he held his stance.

The unstoppable force was seconds from collision.

He waited until the very last second... until Minotaura's shadow swallowed his own... before his body moved with a speed no ordinary human should possess.

His muscles coiled, then uncoiled like a sprung trap. He pivoted sharply, letting her colossal weight and momentum become a weapon against her rather than for her.

His hands shot forward, palms slamming onto the very base of her horns.

The impact tore through his arms like the collision of tectonic plates. Raw force meeting immovable will, but he held fast. Using Minotaura's own inertia, he twisted his hips and shoulders, redirecting her unstoppable charge into a devastating fall.

Minotaura's eyes widened in primal shock as her massive body lurched sideways, her legs scrambled uselessly in the dirt. Two tons of furious, bellowing monster crashed into the ground with a bone-shaking *thud* that sent a plume of dust erupting skyward. The earth groaned beneath her weight.

He vaulted over her thick, corded neck and landed astride her shoulders, still gripping her horns. The heat of her breath scorched the ground. Her raw strength trembled beneath him like a storm held barely in check.

He planted his feet and pulled.

"IMPOSSIBLE!" Minotaura screamed, her cry torn from her throat. Not fear, not even rage, but disbelief. A sound that made even the most battle-hardened inmates flinch. As he heaved, spreading her horns apart, he felt the sickening give of bone straining toward fracture.

Minotaura's bellow pitched upward, transforming into a scream laced with humiliation and pain. Her powerful legs kicked and scraped against the earth, but with her head pinned and her horns controlled, she could not find purchase.

Minotaura was trapped beneath him. Completely and undeniably.

"by the Demon Lord…" Captain Lilith's whisper cut through the uproar. Her usually perfect composure fractured as she stared, wide-eyed, at the impossible sight before her. In the north tower, the silhouetted form of the Warden leaned forward, still as death, watching with predatory fascination as her strongest inmate lay helpless beneath a man she had intended merely to test.

A crack rang out, sharp and visceral.

The base of Minotaura's horn was split. A thin line of crimson began to seep along the wound.

His voice broke the silence, low and thunderous, "YIELD!"

The roar seemed to vibrate the very earth, a command dredged from some deep, ancient place within him, something older than speech, older than humanity.

The crimson glow in his eyes surged brighter, bathing Minotaura's face in hellish light.

"I…YIELD!" Her breath shuddered, "I YIELD!"

He released her at once and stepped back, chest heaving in deep, ragged pulls. The fury in him still burned, but he forced it downward, caging it in muscle and will.

Minotaura rolled onto her side, one trembling hand protectively covering the cracked horn. Her massive form shook with rage, with shock… and with something else entirely that she could not yet name.

Blood trickled along her forearm, darkening the dry dirt beneath her.

That was when the yard erupted.

A tidal wave of noise crashed outward in every direction. Screams, cheers, curses, frantic shouts, and the clatter of credits exchanging hands. Inmates slammed themselves against the containment wards, each reaction louder and more deranged than the last.

Captain Lilith strode forward, her boots kicking up dust, her wings unfolded in agitation. For once, she did not mask her astonishment, "match concluded! The challenger is victorious!" Her voice cracked like a whip across the noise.

She approached him with caution, respect, even her violet eyes seemed sharp with a mix of disbelief and something harder to name.

"Medical team for Minotaura. Prisoner, remain where you are," she instructed him.

Then a new sound rose above the chaos. The sound of appreciation, clapping.

Slow, deliberate, and faintly amused, clapping was heard all across the prison.

All heads turned toward the north tower as Warden Morrigan stepped into full view, her midnight wings unfurled, her golden eyes gleaming with predatory delight.

Her applause sliced through the bedlam, silencing it one beat at a time.

Captain Lilith leaned closer, lowering her voice to the barest whisper, "The Warden wishes to speak with you personally. This is… unprecedented."

Only then did he finally collapse to his knees, lungs burning, heart pounding like a war drum. The glow in his eyes flickered, dimming but not extinguishing.

He turned toward Minotaura, still cradling her wounded horn. His voice came soft and gentle in a way that stunned everyone within earshot.

"Are you ok?" he asked, and the world paused.

Minotaura froze, her wide, amber eyes fixated on him with raw, unguarded disbelief. Her chest heaved. Blood dripped steadily from her cracked horn.

The yard fell silent again, not from shock of violence, but shock of compassion. Even the medical team paused mid-stride.

Minotaura stared at him as though she had never seen a living being before, as though she couldn't understand why anyone, much less the one who defeated her, would ever ask such a thing. She stared at him as if his question defied reality itself. Her massive chest rose and fell with labored breaths, each inhale rattled by pain, each exhale steeped in confusion.

"Am I...okay?" Her voice trembled with raw disbelief, as though she were tasting the concept for the first time in her violent, blood-stained life. "You nearly rip my horn off and then ask if I'm okay?"

A deep sound built inside her, at first a low rumble, then a shaking vibration rolling through her ribs, until it erupted into a booming, thunderous laugh. The noise echoed across the yard like an earthquake. Inmates glanced at one another in bewildered murmurs; some stepped back, unsure whether laughter meant admiration or the calm before another storm, "You're either the most arrogant or the most interesting human I've met." Minotaura said, looking directly into his eyes.

Captain Lilith finally approached, her posture tense, tail lashing sharply behind her. Even she seemed uncertain how to interpret the scene unfolding before her, "a medical team is coming. Both of you stay put." Her eyes flicked between him and the wounded champion with visible confusion, "This isn't how these challenges typically end."

Minotaura shifted her hulking body upright, wincing as movement tugged at her fractured horn. She rested on one knee, breathing shallowly as she assessed him not as prey, not as an enemy, but as something new. "I'll live, human. My pride is more wounded than my horn."

Her amber eyes roamed over him with a new kind of respect, even wariness. "Those eyes of yours…they're not just for show, are they? What are you really in for?"

Before he could answer, the yard fell abruptly silent. A shadow swept across the arena.

Warden Nyx descended from the north tower like a dark star falling from the heavens. Her massive black wings unfurled in a slow, elegant sweep, her descent controlled, regal, predatory. Inmates backed away from the containment barriers as though her presence alone could sear them. Guards snapped to rigid attention, boots slamming into the ground in perfect unison.

She landed with effortless grace, the hem of her modified black-and-silver uniform settling around her tall, slender form. Silver hair cascaded down her back, swirling faintly in an unnatural current, and at her throat, a ruby pendant pulsed with the same deep crimson energy that filled his vision.

Her golden eyes swept the yard, calculated, ancient.

He rose to his feet, only 5'10", dwarfed by Minotaura and even by Captain Lilith, yet he carried himself with a steadiness that rippled through the air like held lightning.

"I only ask for your respect," He bowed lightly toward Minotaura.

Minotaura blinked, startled by the gesture, "Respect…" She tasted the word, almost reverently. "You've earned it, little human. For now."

As he turned to face the Warden, Nyx's wings folded neatly behind her, each feather aligned with military precision. Her presence carried the weight of judgment, of empire, of cold and unyielding power.

"Most interesting," Nux said, her melodic voice carried easily across the arena, "Captain Lilith, have Minotaura taken to medical. I wish to speak with our…surprising new inmate."

Her gaze slid to him, piercing him as though peeling back layers of flesh and memory, "You've made quite the entrance to my facility, human. Those eyes of yours…they're not in your file."

He stepped forward slowly, dust swirling around his feet. His expression remained calm, though the echo of battle still trembled in his limbs. He lifted his chin and approached the Warden without hesitation.

And he began speaking: "Let's go ahead and get this out of the way now. Stop using the term *human*. Call me Scott, or liaison, or even inmate, don't think you'd like it if I just walked up and called you a glorified sexy bat? I think I've earned the respect due and proven I'm no "mere" human. I'm no different than you; I'm just imprisoned here, and you work here, but we're both still flesh, and as you saw by your champion, you can still bleed. Remember, if it can bleed, it can die. I wish not to be rude, but I do have another appointment, so if you'll excuse me, we'll have to have our meeting in your office at a later time, perhaps after lunch."

He bowed lightly, a polite and precise bow, and turned to walk away as though he had not just challenged the most powerful being in the entire fortress.

The temperature in the yard seemed to drop several degrees the instant he finished speaking. The shift was so stark it felt supernatural, as though the prison itself held its breath. Captain Lilith's jaw slackened in pure disbelief, her pupils sharpening to slits. Several guards reacted instinctively, hands flying toward weapon hilts. Behind the containment barriers, dozens of monster girls fell silent, expressions shifting from delight to shock to wary anticipation. Some even backed away, expecting the yard to erupt into violence.

Warden Nyx's golden eyes narrowed into razor-thin slits, the gleam within them sharpened by predatory irritation. Her wings unfurled a fraction, just enough to remind every creature present of the hierarchy carved into these walls.

"Scott, is it?" She asked, her voice remained melodic, but there was a lethal edge beneath it, a whisper of ancient things that punished insolence with extinction.

149

"How…refreshing to meet someone so eager to establish boundaries." A cold smile traced her lips as she stepped forward, her height and wingspan allowing her to look down at him with the kind of authority that made lesser beings tremble, "You've demonstrated impressive physical capabilities, certainly. But confusing victory in a yard brawl with actual authority is…premature."

She circled him slowly, each footfall graceful, deliberate. Her wings stirred the dusty air, creating a faint breeze that lifted strands of his hair. "You may indeed have another appointment with solitary confinement. However…"

She paused behind him, studying the angle of his shoulders, the crimson of his eyes, "I'm curious enough about what you're concealing to postpone that particular accommodation. Report to my office after the evening count. Captain Lilith will escort you."

With a fluid motion, she dismissed him. Then her wings extended in a dramatic sweep, catching the sunlight before she launched skyward. Dust spiraled in her wake as she ascended, her silhouette vanishing into the shadows of the north tower.

Captain Lilith rushed forward as soon as the Warden departed, her claws clicking sharply against stone. Her posture was rigid with disbelief and fury. "Are you completely insane?" she hissed, grabbing his arm with surprising force. "Nobody speaks to the Warden like that and keeps all their limbs!"

He reached into his pocket, fingers closing around the ominous dark crystal like it was a lifeline or a vice. The faint pulse of its energy hummed through his bones. "You're like a sexy older sister. Thank you for assisting me. I'd hug you, but you prob would break my nose right now."

He chuckled faintly, though the sound trembled on the edge of exhaustion, "Oh, adrenaline crash, this will be fun."

He tightened his grip on the crystal. He heard the sound of his knees buckling, and darkness rushed into his vision. He collapsed before he could finish, the world spinning violently.

Captain Lilith's expression shattered from anger into raw alarm as she lunged forward to catch him. A faint, sickly purple glow leaked through

150

his fingers where the crystal had been moments earlier, but as she tried his hand open, she found nothing.

"Medical team! We need assistance here!" Shifting back her focus, she lowered him with surprising gentleness, one scaled hand cupping the back of his head to keep it from hitting the ground. "Damn it, what now?" Her voice trembled, not with fear for herself, but with fear of what this meant.

The yard erupted again. Inmates shouted accusations and taunts, guards sprinted toward the fallen liaison, and the magical alarms around the arena flickered in agitation. His breathing grew shallow, eyes rolling back into a state of unconsciousness that felt unnervingly unnatural.

Captain Lilith leaned closer, her voice sharp with worry. "Scott? Can you hear me?"

Her shout tore across the yard. "Get the doctor here now! And someone inform the Warden!"

Through the darkness overtaking him, he felt himself lifted, multiple hands, urgent and unfamiliar, sliding beneath him. The world above dimmed and stretched, voices warping as though heard through water.

Captain Lilith's voice slipped into his ear one last time, softer, shaken: "What are you hiding, human? And why do I feel like we're all in danger?"

Then the void claimed him. *He felt weightless.*

Not unconscious, not exactly. It was deeper than that. The darkness surrounding him was absolute, like a realm without time or gravity, where even thoughts floated untethered.

Voices bled through the void like distant echoes, "Extensive energy drain. Similar to cases we've seen with dark mana exposure." Another voice said, "Readings off the charts. The Warden needs to see these immediately!"

And there was the voice of Captain Lilith, "…said he had the crystal in his pocket, but we found nothing…"

Fragments of consciousness returned in flickers. He felt cool fabric beneath him, the stale scent of disinfectant, the faint hum of runes.

His eyelids dragged open with great effort.

He lay in the prison infirmary, a long, stone chamber bathed in the soft bioluminescent glow of mushrooms clinging to the walls. Strange medical instruments pulsed with gentle runic light beside him, and empty beds stretched down the room like silent sentries.

He exhaled shakily.

He had survived.

But something inside him had changed.

He drifted slowly back into consciousness, the infirmary's dim blue glow washing over him like the fading remnants of a dream. Bioluminescent fungi pulsed along the stone walls, bathing the room in an otherworldly sheen. Runes on the medical equipment flickered rhythmically, casting shifting shadows across the ceiling. His body felt heavy, as if gravity itself had thickened.

A slender figure sat beside his bed. A Kikimora in a pristine nurse's uniform. Her feathered arms moved with meticulous grace as she carefully arranged a tray of gleaming instruments. Each motion was precise, almost ritualistic. Occasionally, she paused to jot something onto a floating crystal tablet that hovered obediently beside her.

"Our mysterious patient returns to us." Nurse Kikimora spoke, her soft voice carrying a subtle accent, her head tilting with avian curiosity as she studied him. "The captain will want to know you're awake. You've caused quite the stir, weightless one."

He forced a weak grin, coughing through the lingering ache in his chest, "How's that big beautiful black bovine? She's pretty hot and bulky, huh?" he laughed, then coughed. He was still weak.

The Kikimora paused mid-motion. One feathered brow lifted in polite disbelief, her beak-like mouth twitching with restrained humor. "Minotaura? She's recovering in the adjacent ward."

She gestured toward a curtained-off corner with a winglike arm, "Her horn will heal fully, though she'll carry a distinctive scar. Quite the badge of honor in her culture, actually."

Her feathers ruffled lightly as she leaned closer, "and yes, she is rather...impressive, isn't she? Though I wouldn't recommend pursuing that particular interest unless you enjoy additional broken bones."

She rose smoothly, adjusting her crisp white uniform that contrasted with her dark plumage. "You've been unconscious for nearly six hours. The Warden has requested immediate notification when you awaken."

Her head tilted again, observing him with that bird-like intelligence, "That was quite a display in the yard. Most humans who challenge Minotaura end up in body casts, not asking after her well-being while making inappropriate observations about her physique."

She turned toward the wall and touched a crystal panel. It pulsed blue at her command. "Captain Lilith, the human is conscious. Exhibiting typical male behavior already, asking about Minotaura's...*attributes*."

He wheezed out another laugh, "attributes, haha! I didn't ask her cup size." Every time he tried to laugh, it was betrayed by a cough.

The Kikimora's feathers fluffed in amusement, her dark eyes glinting with playful judgment, "No, you didn't inquire about specific measurements. How refreshingly restrained of you."

She adjusted his IV with gentle efficiency, "though I imagine such questions would be rather low on the priority list after collapsing with mysterious energy fluctuation."

Before he could respond, the infirmary doors burst open. Captain Lilith swept inside. Her scaled tail glided over the stone in a ripple of crimson and black, and her uniform clung to her powerful upper body, silver insignias gleaming along her collarbones. Lilith's serpentine lower half moved with lethal grace, the cold authority in her eyes enough to freeze half the room.

"So you're finally awake," she approached with arms crossed, her expression a sharp blend of suspicion and restrained fury.

"Care to explain what happened in the yard? Or perhaps more importantly..." She leaned close, forked tongue flicking out to taste the air around him, her pupils tightening, "...what exactly was that crystal you were clutching before you collapsed? The one that conveniently disappeared while we were transporting you here?"

Her gaze bored into him, searching for even the smallest crack in his composure, "The Warden is very interested in your explanation. As am I."

He lifted his hand defensively, wincing. "Oh! Big sis! Scales are gleaming with ambition today! Please don't hit me." He raised his hand to shield his face.

Lilith's eyes widened, not in softness, but in incredulous fury. Her tail lashed once against the floor.

"I'm not your sister, inmate," Her voice lowered to a dangerous hiss, "and this pathetic attempt at deflection won't work. Lower your hand. I don't strike patients…usually."

She shot a glance toward the Kikimora nurse, who immediately pretended to be busy with supplies while staying close enough to intervene. "Listen carefully, Scott. The medical team detected anomalous energy signatures emanating from your body, *dark mana* patterns we've only seen in artifacts from the Demon Realm. The Warden is…concerned."

Her clawed hand dropped casually toward the baton at her hip, "So let's try again. what was that crystal, and where is it now? Your cooperation might determine whether you recover in this comfortable infirmary or in a specially warded isolation cell."

She leaned closer until her breath warmed his cheek, her serpentine eyes narrowing, "and drop the act. Nobody collapses from 'adrenaline' after displaying the fighting capabilities you showed in the yard. You're not what you appear to be, and in this prison, secrets have a way of becoming very dangerous, very quickly."

Her tail hovered behind her like a poised weapon, and every rune in the room seemed to dim in anticipation.

A wry smile tugged at the corner of his mouth as he sat upright in the infirmary bed, the white sheets pooling around his waist like draped moonlight. The bioluminescent fungi along the walls pulsed softly, casting an eerie glow over his face as he spoke.

He began, "I'll answer your questions in full detail with the Warden present, but I must ask WHICH Warden whether it will be THIS time? Also, if you'd pay attention to my schedule and the fact that I'm NOT wearing a bracelet like every other inmate, you'd know I'm not like everyone else here at all. Also, I had a crystal in each pocket and a cog, the contents of my person I wasn't trying to hide."

Captain Lilith's tail tightened beneath her, coiling over itself like a serpent preparing to strike. Tension rippled up her scaled spine and into her shoulders as she stared at him, amber eyes gleaming with a mix of alarm, suspicion, and something disturbingly close to recognition.

The temperature in the infirmary dropped, barely perceptible, but enough to make the magical lanterns flicker. "What game are you playing?"

Her voice was controlled, but the edges trembled with restrained hostility. Her clawed hand gripped the metal bedframe hard. The steel bent under her fingers, indenting with quiet protest.

Nurse Kikimora had long since stopped pretending to organize equipment. Her sharp, feathered head tilted toward the pair, eyes glinting with unshielded curiosity, "There is only one Warden in this facility, Warden Morgana. And as for your lack of bracelet…"

She hesitated. Her forked tongue flicked out in a swift test of the air, tasting his truth, his hormones, his lingering aura, "You were processed like any other prisoner. I supervised it myself."

Then something flickered across her face, a brief, raw confusion. "Unless…no. That's impossible," she straightened so sharply the wind stirred around her.

Her hand dropped to her communication crystal, "Warden Morgana, this is Captain Lilith. The situation with prisoner Scott has…evolved. Your immediate presence is requested in the infirmary."

She paused, listening to the silent reply buzzing through the crystal's core, "Yes, Warden. I believe it's that serious."

She turned back to him, expression settling back into rigid discipline, though wariness glimmered behind her eyes, "You'll get your wish. The Warden is coming. In the meantime…"

She produced a palm-sized device that pulsed with violet runes, humming faintly with detection magic, "This will detect any residual magical signatures. If you're hiding something, we'll know."

He lifted his hands slowly, then let out a dry laugh, "Please, I've been honest with everyone up until now. What's the point in starting to be dishonest? If y'all find something, I'll be surprised just as much as the rest of you."

He sat up fully, wincing but holding her gaze, "But you are correct, I shouldn't've collapsed after such a display of strength, even with adrenaline crash. I think the actual lack of nutrition is more to blame. Lilith woke me early to speak with the Warden, over a situation that took place last night, before coming to see you, Captain, so that tells me that I'm drained nutritionally. I agree, though, I shouldn't've collapsed so easily. Thanks, now I'm questioning things."

He turned his head sharply, glare locking onto Lilith.

Lilith froze, utterly. Her serpentine coils tightened instantly, the sound sharp and metallic as scales scraped against stone, "You're implying I woke you earlier today?"

Her voice deepened to a whisper that carried far too much danger, "Inmate, I haven't seen you since your processing yesterday. And I certainly didn't escort you to the Warden."

But before he could respond, the infirmary door swung open on reinforced hinges.

Warden Morgana entered, her presence filled the room like a tidal wave of pressure.

The Baphomet Warden stood nearly seven feet tall, her obsidian-black fur dusted with faint traces of frost. Curved horns spiraled upward from her temples, polished, heavy, and adorned with silver runic bands. Her immaculate business suit, tailored to her imposing hybrid form, lent her a chilling elegance. The golden gaze behind her wire-rimmed glasses assessed the room in seconds.

"Captain Lilith, Nurse Plumetail. I'll take it from here." Morgana said, her cultured voice rang with absolute authority, smooth, deliberate, and cold enough to freeze marrow.

Both Lilith and the Nurse bowed instinctively. Lilith's bow was stiff with unresolved frustration; Nurse Plumetail's shimmered with nervous respect.

One by one, they backed out of the room. But Lilith's suspicious, burning eyes lingered on him until the door closed completely.

Silence expanded.

The Warden approached his bed with a grace that seemed impossible for her size. Her hooves clicked rhythmically on the stone floor, controlled, powerful. Every stride carried the quiet threat of a sovereign accustomed to dominion.

Her wings, dark, velvet-like membranes with faint star-patterns, shifted subtly as she came to stand over him.

The air thickened, and the magic in the room stirred.

Warden Morgana's golden gaze sharpened as she raised the obsidian crystal to the dim blue light of the infirmary. Shadows rippled across her strong features, the runes etched along her obsidian horns flickering faintly as the artifact reacted to his presence. Power hummed in the air around her, ancient, oppressive, and uncomfortably aware of him.

Moments before, she had seemed merely stern. Now she looked…intrigued, "So, Scott. You've created quite the conundrum."

Her voice slid through the room like cold velvet as she withdrew a small leather-bound notebook from the inner pocket of her immaculate jacket. She flipped it open with precise fingers, her long, polished nails clicking faintly against the pages.

"My records indicate you were admitted twelve hours ago for assaulting a Hellhound barista. Yet here you are, speaking of events that haven't occurred and meetings that never happened." She adjusted her glasses, the gesture deceptively delicate for someone so massive.

"Plus, there's the matter of your rather spectacular collapse after displaying abilities no ordinary human should possess. Care to explain?" He inhaled shakily, the pressure of her presence threatening to smother him. His eyes narrowed, "Twelve hours? Tell me where the succubus Lilith is? Warden Morrigan? How many wings are in this prison? Do y'all have a basement, the one no prisoner should know about?"

The room shifted.

Cold poured through the infirmary like spilled ink.

Warden Morgana's golden eyes contracted into razor-thin slits. Power rolled off her large frame in waves, her cloven hoof tapping once against the stone floor, an action that sounded like a hammer striking a bell, the resonance echoing unnaturally long.

"There is no succubus named Lilith on my staff. Captain Lilith is a lamia, as you've just seen." Her voice remained unnervingly calm, but the magical wards embedded in the walls flared in response to her restrained aura.

"There is no Warden Morrigan. This facility has four wings: North, East, South, and West. Standard prison architecture."

She took a deliberate step closer. Her shadow washed over him, stretching long and dark across the stone floor. The faint scent of brimstone and old parchment emanated from her, mingling with the sterile medicinal air of the infirmary, "As for a basement... every prison has its secrets, but a prisoner who arrived mere hours ago shouldn't be inquiring about them."

She reached into her coat and produced a pulsing obsidian crystal, the same shape, but not the same color, as the dark crystal he remembered possessing. She held it near him. It responded instantly, flaring with hungry violet energy.

"This is most irregular. You're either suffering from severe delusions, or..." The crystal's glow intensified, reacting to some unseen resonance within him, "something far more interesting is happening. Tell me, Scott, when exactly do you believe you were incarcerated here? And under what circumstances?"

He inhaled sharply, as he began to speak, "Give me breathing room and I'll tell you everything, cuz by my calculations I've been here for almost 48 hours and have been elevated to liaison but still an inmate. Also, I had 2 crystals on me, one black like that, which essentially replaced having a prisoner bracelet, and a blue one, which actually guided me to

Captain Lilith, as well as a cog which I received from the dwarves in the mechanical wing."

Warden Morgana's heavy lashes lowered as she observed him more carefully, then she withdrew one measured step. Her movements were calculated, precise, and far too graceful for someone with hooves that echoed so ominously.

"Liaison? Dwarves? Mechanical wing?" She repeated each word slowly, as if tasting them. "We have no dwarven staff, and certainly no mechanical wing. This facility houses only monster girls, both staff and inmates." Her tone shifted. It was still sharp, but edged with fascination.

She set the obsidian crystal onto the nearby table, where its violent pulse steadied into a rhythmic throb. The Warden began to circle his bed slowly, her hooves clicking in precise intervals, as if measuring something only she could perceive.

"I believe I understand what's happening here," Her voice dropped into something softer, contemplative, dangerously intelligent, "the barrier between realities has thinned again. You're not from *this* timeline, are you?"

She withdrew a silver device shaped like a tuning fork with embedded runes and swept it over his body. Soft chimes rang out... discordant, shifting, unaligned.

Her eyes gleamed, "Dimensional displacement. Fascinating. You've somehow crossed from a parallel version of our prison into this one." Her professional composure cracked further, revealing genuine academic hunger.

"The question is... was it intentional, or are you merely collateral damage in someone else's scheme?" She tapped a button on her communication crystal with a sharp click, "Captain Lilith, assemble the Arcane Security team immediately. And bring me the artifacts recovered from the yard incident."

He jerked upright, eyes burning crimson, "I'm a WHAT?!"

The Warden actually startled. Just slightly enough to prove she had not expected such raw and unfiltered shock.

"You didn't know," her voice held awe, the rarest emotion to ever cross her lips. She stepped closer again, her glasses catching the blue glow of the infirmary lights as she examined his expression with the scrutiny of a predator and a scholar both.

"How curious. Most dimensional travelers are at least aware of their...condition. The crystals you mentioned... they're likely anchors, tethering you between realities."

She lifted the obsidian crystal again, its violent pulse reflecting in her golden irises like molten metal.

The obsidian-glow hummed between them, casting fractured violet light across the infirmary walls. Warden Morgana's horns sparkled like twin crescents of polished night as she leaned in, her presence saturating the air with cold authority and subtle curiosity.

Her voice lowered, a velvet blade: "This explains your collapse. Your body is strained to exist in two places at once, pulled between timelines."

The words hung in the room like drifting ash.

"Scott, in this reality, you were brought in *yesterday* for assaulting a Hellhound barista while intoxicated. A minor offense with a six-month sentence," Her golden eyes sharpened further, the pupils slitting into something predatory, "but it seems in *your* reality, you've been here longer, with...different circumstances."

Before he could respond, the infirmary door opened with a swift metallic hiss. Captain Lilith slid in, her serpentine lower body shimmering as she carried a metallic box etched with arcane sigils that pulsed gently like a heartbeat, "Perfect timing, Captain. We may have a dimensional anomaly on our hands."

Captain Lilith froze mid-slither. Her amber eyes widened, pupils constricting sharply, "not another one. Last time nearly collapsed the East Wing."

He exhaled, rubbing his face with a trembling hand, "ok, can we just not with world-ending near misses?" He grabbed his head, feeling heat flickering behind his eyes, unnatural, rising, threatening to break loose.

"I'll be honest, none of this makes sense, and honestly, I really haven't eaten." His stomach twisted painfully, a reminder of how long it had truly been since he had eaten in whatever version of reality he belonged to. He said, "I'm willing to cooperate as long as someone is willing to cooperate."

Warden Morgana exchanged a sharp, meaningful glance with Captain Lilith. Something wordless passed between them, authority meeting caution, calculation meeting instinct. Then the Warden nodded once, decisive and heavy.

"A reasonable request," Her tone softened, not warm, but less razor-edged, like obsidian placed momentarily at rest.

"Captain, have the kitchen prepare a meal for our…guest. Something substantial but easily digestible," Morgana's cloven hoof tapped thoughtfully against the stone, the sound echoing down the sterile chamber. "And summon the Archivist Thorne. If anyone can make sense of this situation, it's her."

Captain Lilith dipped her head in acknowledgement, then turned and slid out of the infirmary, her scaled tail rasping softly along the floor, an undercurrent of urgency in her movement.

With Lilith gone, the Warden pulled a chair beside his bed. The piece of furniture looked absurdly small beneath her towering, muscular, impeccably dressed form. Her black suit creaked faintly as she folded her long legs, hooves crossing with deliberate elegance.

"While we wait, let me be clear, cooperation goes both ways." Warden Morgana's horns captured the sterile blue glow as she leaned forward, elbows resting on powerful thighs.

"You will tell me everything about your version of this prison. Every detail, no matter how insignificant it might seem," Her gaze hardened. "In return, we'll stabilize your condition and determine how to proceed."

Then her voice dipped into a chilling, icy register: "And Scott? If I discover you're deliberately withholding information or attempting to manipulate this situation…" The temperature dropped instantly. Frost bloomed along the metal frame of his bed. "Well, interdimensional visitor or not, you're still technically a prisoner here."

Before he could answer, the infirmary door opened again. A kikimora nurse, a different one from before, hustled inside, balancing a tray laden with steaming dishes. Her feathered arms trembled slightly under the weight. She set the tray on his lap with brisk, respectful efficiency.

The scents hit immediately. Fresh bread, warm savory broth, and a hearty stew rich with herbs. His stomach growled loud enough that the Warden's brow lifted in faint amusement.

"Lose the threats and the bravado act, and you have a deal, Warden. We're both confused and concerned. I say we work together," he took the tray, "and we get to the bottom of this to figure out where I'm SUPPOSED to be for everyone's sake and safety." The Warden froze. Not with anger, but with surprise. Subtle, but unmistakable.

Then her expression settled into something more thoughtful, more calculating... more respectful. "Fair enough," she said.

She inclined her horned head, the gesture formal and surprisingly graceful, "Threats are...a professional habit. One develops certain reflexes in this line of work."

She folded her hands in her lap, watching him as he took his first ravenous bites. Her golden eyes followed his every movement, as though reading deeper truths in the tremor of his fingers or the tightening of his jaw. "To answer your earlier question, our facility has four wings arranged in a cruciform pattern."

She reached into her pocket and withdrew a small silver device. It clicked softly as she set it on the bedside table. A holographic projection shimmered to life above it, an intricate, glowing map of the prison.

"North houses minimum security, East is medium, South is maximum, and West contains administrative offices and staff quarters." Her finger hovered above one glowing node, "The central hub connects all wings and houses the mess hall, infirmary, and recreation areas."

Her gaze lifted back to him. Steady, unblinking, almost predatory in its intensity.

The Warden's holographic map flickered softly between him as the air thickened with arcane tension. Morgana's golden eyes never left his face, her horns catching the glow in cold, silver crescents.

162

Her voice, crisp and melodic, cut the silence: "I'm curious… does this match the facility you remember?"

Before he could answer, the infirmary door opened with a whisper of displaced air. A slender figure glided inside, a Mindflayer with pale lavender skin and a cascade of living tentacles flowing like liquid silk from her scalp. Her attire resembled a scholar's robes, embroidered with shifting sigils. Books and scrolls rested under one arm, pressed gently against her elongated torso.

"Warden, I came as quickly as…" Activist Thorne halted midsentence. Her opalescent eyes widened, shimmering with prismatic light as they settled on him. "Oh my. The temporal distortion readings are off the charts. He's practically vibrating between realities."

He lifted a spoonful of stew to his mouth, swallowed, and wiped his lips. "A cute Mindflayer, haha. Alright. That makes sense. Anyways, Warden, no, I've no freaking idea where I'm at. The prison I entered is shaped WAY differently."

He began describing the alternate facility in detail, the expanded subterranean architecture, the mechanical wing staffed by dwarves, the labyrinthine combat levels, the succubus lieutenant named Lilith who guided him, the Warden Morrigan, the runic elevators, and the forbidden basement.

"Also, there's a basement." He added.

The Warden's face froze in a way that suggested she was both listening and trying very hard not to reveal how disturbed she was. Her golden eyes narrowed to surgical slits, "Fascinating. Your prison layout bears almost no resemblance to ours. And this… basement level you describe…"

Archivist Thorne stepped closer, tentacles drifting as though moved by a silent current, "dimensional echo, most likely. In your reality, the prison expanded downward instead of outward." Her stylus scratched across the glowing tablet in her hand with feverish energy, "though the presence of dwarven mechanics is troubling. Our facility employs only monster girls."

Then she lifted one slender, lavender hand, three elongated fingers splayed delicately, "May I? A surface scan would help me determine your quantum signature."

Warden Morgana shifted subtly, her towering form casting a shadow that stretched over his bed like an eclipse, "Thorne believes you may be experiencing quantum superposition, existing in two prison realities simultaneously. The strain is what caused your collapse."

The Mindflayer inclined her head, tentacles curling thoughtfully.

"The longer you remain between states, the more unstable your condition becomes. Eventually, your consciousness will fragment completely, leaving you... Well, let's just say it wouldn't be pleasant." Thorne said.

His grip tightened on the edge of the food tray with confusion, with frustration, but all he could say was, "ok, how do I verberate back then?"

The Mindflayer's tentacles rippled in delight, rare enthusiasm for her species.

"'Verberate back' is actually quite an apt term for it..." Thorne flipped open the ancient tome she'd brought. Its pages shimmered with shifting text, runes morphing as though alive.

She elaborated, "The process requires three components: a quantum anchor from your original reality, a resonance catalyst, and a focused intention." Signaling each component with the count of her fingers. "We need to strengthen your connection to your original timeline while severing the tether to this one."

Warden Morgana stepped forward, hooves clicking against the stone. Her immense presence loomed at his bedside, the scent of brimstone carried subtly in the air. "In practical terms, we need something or someone... from your reality to pull you back. The longer you stay here, the weaker that connection becomes."

The archivist nodded vigorously and said, "Do you recall the last person you interacted with before your collapse? Or perhaps an object of personal significance you were carrying?"

She withdrew a small crystal prism from her pocket, its many facets catching the infirmary's dim lantern-light and scattering it into sharp, unnatural colors.

As she lifted it toward him, the air seemed to tighten around its edges. She said, "Your quantum signature is already beginning to stabilize in this reality. We may have less than I initially calculated."

His breath caught. Thoughts ricocheted through his mind in jagged shards as he closed his eyes, forcing himself to sift through the memories… his memories… trying to understand which belonged to the reality he now inhabited and which belonged to the one he'd just been torn away from.

He whispered to himself first, then spoke aloud: "Captain Lilith was a dragon, not a lamia, the Warden was a vampire, and the void beneath it all, Nyarlathotep, but the last one I touched before Minotaura was the Kitsune Mizuki."

His eyes snapped open, wide and unfiltered.

With a sudden, instinctive movement, he lunged for the dark crystal on the table.

His fingers closed around it just as the memory of Mizuki's warning echoed through him.

"This was what I was holding in my pocket," he squeezed it tightly, desperation flooding his grip, "It can never be lost or removed from me she said."

The effect was immediate and violent.

The obsidian crystal pulsed beneath his fingers, swelling with a crimson glow so bright it painted the walls in streaks of blood-red shadow. The light crawled up his arm like living fire.

Archivist Thorne reeled back, her tendrils flaring outward in alarm as she reached instinctively toward him, "Wait! Don't activate it without proper…"

But it was already too late.

Chapter 7

"The Timeline Walker"

The crystal detonated with silent force, sending a surge of eldritch energy ripping through his body. His vision split, doubling... tripling... until the room fractured like a shattered mirror.

Two worlds overlapped.

Two Wardens overlapped.

Two Liliths overlapped.

The Mindflayer and the Minotaur blurred into the Vampire and the Dragon, all coexisting for one impossible heartbeat.

Warden Morgana's voice cut through the distortion like a blade, "Stabilize him, Thorne! We're losing his quantum signature!"

Archivist Thorne pressed her cool, slender hands against his temples. Her tentacles curled delicately around his wrists, attempting to anchor him in corporeal shape.

The crystal burned hotter and hotter until the heat felt like it pierced bone.

"Focus on your original reality! Picture the Kitsune... Mizuki, was it?" She kept on trying, "Concentrate on her image, her voice. The crystal is responding to your connection with her!"

But reality twisted.

Stone walls bent inward. The ceiling stretched like taffy. Colors inverted and bled into one another.

Then the Warden's final command thundered through the collapsing room, a decree echoing across collapsing timelines: "Remember, prisoner. In any reality, you're still serving your sentence!"

Everything shattered.

And the infirmary dissolved into pure, swirling darkness.

He floated. Weightless. Untethered.

Memories drifted around him like drifting embers: Mizuki's soft fur brushing his skin, the molten heat radiating from the Captain's crimson scales, promises made to a Warden who blurred between vampire and demon. His body yearned for something ancient, long-forgotten, something he could not yet name.

He clung to Mizuki's image.

Her nine tails.

Her warm amber eyes.

Her trembling voice.

He clung until the void convulsed and something yanked him downward, hard.

Reality slammed into him like a tidal wave.

The sterile scent of disinfectant stung his nostrils. Rough prison-standard sheets scratched against his skin. Distant metallic echoes reverberated as steel doors clanged shut somewhere down the hall.

His vision blurred, then sharpened…

And there she was.

Mizuki leaned over him, fox ears perked high yet trembling with barely-contained worry. Nine tails arched and swept behind her in a slow, anxious pattern. Static snapped softly in the air around her, lifting loose strands of her hair.

"There you are," Mizuki finally said. Relief softened her voice, but the professional tone reclaimed her expression a beat later. "You've been oscillating between consciousness and …somewhere else for nearly three hours. The dark crystal… It's fused to your palm now. I couldn't remove it even if I wanted to."

Her gaze flicked toward the infirmary entrance, ears tilting back uneasily. "Captain Lilith has been demanding updates every fifteen minutes. She's convinced you did this deliberately to avoid your meeting with the Warden."

His voice rasped, still thick with lingering distortion. "Captain Lilith…dragon?"

167

Mizuki's eyes widened. Her breath hitched, and her tails froze mid-sway, hovering behind her like golden flames. She leaned closer, her voice lowering into a protective softness.

"Yes…Captain Lilith is a dragon. Eastern variety, crimson-scaled." Mizuki's ears twitched, searching his expression, "What exactly do you remember?"

But before he could answer, the infirmary door burst open with a force that shook the instrument trays against the wall.

Captain Lilith entered.

Not the lamia.

Not the illusion.

Not the alternate-universe variant.

But the dragon.

Seven feet of towering draconic might.

Crimson scales shimmered like molten rubies beneath the harsh lights. The tailored uniform clung to her powerful humanoid torso while accommodating the spiked ridge running the length of her spine. Steam curled sinuously from her nostrils with every breath she drew.

And her golden, slit-pupiled eyes locked onto him with an intensity that felt like standing before a waking volcano.

Captain Lilith didn't simply enter the infirmary; she *consumed* the room with her presence. Heat radiated from her crimson-scaled body as she stalked forward, "Finally conscious, are we?" Her voice rolled through the room like smoke curling from a firepit, low, simmering, dangerous.

"Convenient timing. The Warden's patience grows thinner by the hour." She didn't even look at him at first. Instead, she turned sharply toward Mizuki, her scales shifting with a metallic rustle that sounded like blades being unsheathed. "Is he medically cleared or simply malingering, Healer Mizuki?"

Mizuki straightened instinctively, her nine tails fanning out with the kind of controlled grace reserved for shrine maidens and apex predators. Whatever timidness she once had evaporated in her medical domain.

168

"He appears disoriented, Captain. Possible memory fragmentation. I'd recommend at least…"

He groaned softly and muttered under his breath, "Yup, I'm getting punched."

That was the wrong thing to say.

Captain Lilith's golden eyes snapped toward him, pupils contracting into needle points. She inhaled sharply; a glow shuddered beneath her scales, and embers curled between her teeth like sparks from a furnace.

"What was that, prisoner?" Her voice dropped to a molten growl that made even the medical instruments vibrate on their trays, "You think this is a joke?"

She stepped closer… almost too close… her tail lashing violently behind her. The force of it knocked a stainless-steel tray against the wall with a deafening clatter. Mizuki immediately slid in front of him, placing herself between the dragon captain and her patient with a protective flare of her tails.

"Captain! He's still recovering from quantum displacement. His neural pathways are realigning; he's not fully himself." Lilith froze mid-step, steam rushing from her nostrils as she forced herself to stop. Her scales bristled, but she withheld the strike, barely.

"The Warden won't accept excuses. Quantum displacement or not, he has questions that need answering." Lilith leveled a glare at him that promised he would regret breathing incorrectly in her presence.

"Get him functional, Healer. You have one hour." With a final warning glimmer in her eyes, the dragon turned sharply. Her tail lashed once more, this time slamming the infirmary door shut with the force of a battering ram, rattling medical cabinets and sending a gust of heated air through the room.

Mizuki exhaled shakily, shoulders relaxing as the oppressive heat faded. She turned back to Scott, amber eyes still bright with worry, "That crystal has changed something in you. Your aura is…different."

She brushed her fingertips lightly near the obsidian shard fused to Scott's palm. It pulsed faintly beneath the skin, like a second heartbeat.

"What happened while you were away from here?" The curiosity in her eyes was no longer a secret.

He pushed himself upright, breath hitching. His eyes narrowed, the voice in his throat suddenly steadier than it had any right to be, "No, captain's right. I need to see Warden Morrigan NOW."

Mizuki froze.

Her ears flattened instantly. Every tail puffed in alarm, stiffening like bristling foxfire.

"Warden...Morrigan?" Her whisper seemed to shrink the room around them, "The Warden's name is Carmilla. Warden Carmilla."

She swallowed hard, then helped him fully upright, checking his vitals with trembling precision, avoiding the glowing crystal entirely, "but if you're insistent on seeing her now..."

She lifted her comm device with visibly reluctant fingers. She spoke, "Medical Officer Mizuki requesting escort for prisoner to Warden's office. Patient is stable but disoriented."

A crackle responded, followed by a curt confirmation, and Mizuki disconnected the monitors, her movements brisk but overshadowed by growing dread.

"The crystal is interfering with your temporal alignment. You're still partially tethered to...wherever you were," she leaned close, breath soft against his ear, "and be careful what you say to the Warden. She's been...different since the incident in Block D. More volatile."

The door opened before he could reply.

Two guards entered, the harpy first, feathers metallic and razor-sharp, followed by a towering cyclops whose single glowing eye scanned him with cold efficiency. Their presence filled the room with the silent authority of trained predators.

"We'll take him from here, Healer," the Harpy Guard said.

Mizuki hesitated, her hand lingering on his forearm, her fur soft against his skin, "Remember who you are in this reality, prisoner. Your life depends on it."

He blinked, confusion twisting his features, "Remember who I am?"

Mizuki stiffened, her tails curling protectively.

"Your prisoner number is 7294-H." Each syllable landed as a stone dropped in a well, "You were sentenced three months ago for..." She hesitated, ears flattening, "for attempting to steal magical artifacts from the Royal Vampire Archives. Including...including the very crystal now embedded in your hand."

The harpy snapped her beak sharply, feathers rattling with impatience. "Enough chatter. The Warden is waiting."

Mizuki stepped back, worry radiating from every part of her.

As the guards flanked him and led him from the infirmary, he felt Mizuki's troubled gaze burning into his back long after the door shut behind him. Her nine tails drooped with worry, as if she could sense that something far greater than displacement or illness was at work.

The prison corridors blurred together with each step, long, reinforced hallways carved from stone and steel, etched with glowing glyphs that pulsed in time with the prison's heartbeat. Monster girl inmates peered from behind enchanted barriers as he passed, some whispering, others staring openly at the oscillating aura bleeding off him in faint waves.

The crystal embedded in his palm throbbed like a second pulse, an echo that made him feel weightless one moment and crushingly heavy the next. Each heartbeat sent a jolt of disorientation through his mind, threatening to pull him sideways into a world that was not this one.

Finally, the guards halted before an imposing door crafted of black wood and framed in runes of shimmering silver. The cyclops guard stepped forward, her single eye glowing intensely as she began a magical scan.

"He's clear. Temporal signature is... fluctuating, but contained." Said the Cyclops Guard.

He was barely 'contained.'

The door opened on its own, swinging inward with silent menace.

Inside waited a presence far older than the structure that housed her.

171

Warden Carmilla sat behind a high-backed obsidian desk carved with gothic artistry. Her skin was pale as moonlit snow, translucent enough that faint blue veins lay visible beneath the surface. Her raven-black hair fell like silk over the shoulders of her severe uniform, tailored not for beauty but for intimidation. When her crimson eyes lifted, Scott felt pinned to the spot, as though she had already stripped away every secret he'd ever held.

"Prisoner 7294-H. I understand you've had an… incident." Warden Carmilla's voice sounded cold, aristocratic, the kind of tone that ended wars and started empires, "the crystal you attempted to steal has now claimed you. How satisfyingly ironic."

Something inside him snapped back into focus. He shrugged the guards' hands from his arms, straightening despite the quiver in his legs. "No, this is wrong too. I will be fully cooperative, but I need the truth… where am I, why am I here, and what happened before I was in the infirmary? With these questions answered, I can assist in being open and honest with you and convey correct information. But I will say you're not the right warden either."

Silence struck like a blade.

The temperature in the room plummeted. Frost laced the carved legs of Carmilla's desk as she rose effortlessly, weightlessly, her body gliding rather than stepping. The harpy stiffened, wings half-flared, and even the cyclops guard's single eye widened in unease.

"Not the right warden?" Her tone carried centuries of restrained violence, "How fascinating."

She circled him slowly, a predator studying an anomaly. The crystal reacted violently to her proximity, flooding Scott's senses with heat, nausea, and vertigo. Shadows danced unnaturally along the walls as she moved with elegant predatory silence.

"Three days ago, you were found unconscious in the Arcane Artifacts vault. That crystal…" She extended one long, lacquered nail toward his palm. The shard pulsed in answer, crimson light leaking between his fingers, "…was clutched in your hand, partially melded with your flesh. Since then, the prison's reality has experienced… fluctuations."

She inhaled sharply, not for breath, but scent like a bloodhound tasting a dimensional shift in the air, "Guards, leave us."

The cyclops hesitated, her one eye darting between them, "but Warden, protocol states…"

"Out. Now." Her tone was solid now.

The command reverberated with ancient compulsion. The guards backed out so quickly that the harpy nearly tripped over her own talons before the door sealed behind them with a rune-heavy hiss.

Once alone, the shift in Carmilla's posture was subtle but unmistakable. Her rigid façade softened, transforming from ruler to scholar, from executioner to investigator, "the crystal you hold is the Nexus Shard. It doesn't just 'bridge' realities, it creates them. And you, human, are somehow anchoring these divergent timelines together."

She leaned close enough that he could smell the faint trace of old perfume beneath the sterile scent of her office. Her crimson gaze burned with a hunger that was not wholly vampiric… academic curiosity sharpened into obsession.

"Who is this Warden Morrigan you seek?" She asked. Softly but adamant.

He clenched his fist around the crystal. It pulsed violently, almost answering her question for him.

His voice trembled… not with fear, but with the raw weight of memory, "She's beyond the ancients and head warden of the prison. It's only been about 48 hours." He closed his eyes, reaching for Morrigan's presence… the icy gravity of her touch, the eldritch authority that only she carried.

"This crystal can't be taken from me. It will return me to her, and it cannot be lost…" He said as the crystal's glow intensified until it illuminated the entire room with a blood-red light.

Warden Carmilla froze. For the first time, uncertainty flickered across her face, "Morrigan… the Phantom Queen?" Words left her lips like a confession, "That's not possible. She was sealed beyond the Veil millennia ago."

Her composure cracked as she moved faster than human sight, appearing before him in a blur. Her cold fingers hovered dangerously close to the shard, close enough that his skin tingled with the static of colliding realities.

"This prison exists at the nexus of multiple realities. The crystal has been… jumping you between them." Her gaze sharpened, "In your reality, Morrigan rules here? A goddess of war and death?"

Reality buckled.

The office trembled. Not physically, but metaphysically, as the walls flickered. For a single heartbeat, the vampire's sterile office fell away, replaced by ancient Celtic runes, bleeding green and gold across living stone walls. The air tasted of rain, iron, and old magic… Morrigan's magic.

The air in Warden Carmilla's office fell to a breathless stillness, the temperature plunging as if someone had opened a door to the void. Frost crawled across the ornate runes in the floor as Carmilla's fangs slid down involuntarily, reacting not with hunger but with ancient instinct.

"The barriers between worlds are thinning. If Morrigan has found a way back…" A hiss escaped her, sharp, controlled, but edged with fear she could not mask, "We must return you to your proper timeline before the convergence becomes permanent."

Her urgency shattered the veneer of aristocratic detachment. She whipped her cloak aside and reached for an ornate silver bell resting on her desk. Her hands, usually composed and elegant, now moved with frantic precision, "hold onto that crystal, human. It seems you're far more important than a simple thief. Guards!"

But before the sound of the bell could resonate, he clenched his fist around the Nexus Shard, harder, deeper, until the black crystal cut into his skin. He let go of fear, confusion, and doubt, and reached into the oldest name his mind could hold.

"Nyarlathotep. Bring me back," he didn't shout it. He exhaled it, a whisper carrying weight beyond mortal understanding.

He closed his eyes. He thought of Mitsuki… her forehead pressed gently to his, her tails wrapped protectively around him, her scent of jasmine and old magic grounding him in a place that felt like home. He thought of Captain Lilith's heat, her scales shimmering like molten ruby. He thought of the promise he had made, the appointment with the head Warden. He thought of the ancient presence beneath the prison, the one that recognized him.

And the crystal answered.

It pulsed once.

Then again, stronger.

Then it erupted.

The office collapsed inward like a dying star. Runes peeled off the walls and dissolved into black static. Space folded, twisted, and screamed as Carmilla was dragged sideways into a distortion of her own silhouette.

Her form cracked like glass, splitting between two reflections of herself, "The Crawling Chaos? You serve the…"

Her words fractured as her body stretched into impossible dimensions, her scream becoming a thread pulled across realities.

Light vanished.

Darkness swallowed everything.

And then…

He landed.

Not on a floor, but into a cell he knew.

The scent of ozone clung to the air, blending with ancient sigils scorched into the stone. The entire room hummed with power, like the memory of a storm trapped in walls. A raven perched atop the small wooden desk, its eyes glowing with an intelligence far too sharp for any mundane creature.

With a whisper of feathers and shadow, the door swung open.

And she appeared.

Warden Morrigan entered the room as if the shadows themselves parted for her. Her form was a shifting amalgamation of beauty and terror, her hair black as a moonless night; her skin pale, textured like marble wet with blood; her three faces shifting like a living triptych: the Maiden, the Mother, the Crone. Each expression studied him from different angles of time and knowledge.

Then came the voice of Morrigan, "Welcome back, little wanderer. The Nexus Shard has returned you, as I knew it would," voices... plural, layered, echoed like a war drum and a whisper at the same time, "did you enjoy your glimpse of the other prison? The one where I never... awakened?"

His breath caught.

"It's you!" his eyes flooded, crimson bleeding into shimmering blue as the emotions he'd held back cracked open. He rushed forward, the movement raw and unrestrained, and threw his arms around her.

He buried his face against her chest, the place where warmth and cold coiled together, ancient power contained within an eldritch vessel. She did not recoil, though she did not immediately return the embrace.

For a heartbeat, the world stopped.

Her three faces aligned, watching him with profound curiosity, "such... mortal sentiment." Her voices layered over each other, ancient and young, amused and predatory, "how peculiar."

One of her hands rose, hovering above him before descending to rest atop his head. Her touch was simultaneously cold and scorching. The contact tore open visions... battlefields littered with corpses, storm-blackened skies over stone circles, crows feasting on eyes of kings, rivers running red with forgotten war.

"The Nexus Shard has bonded with you more deeply than anticipated. You've become an anchor point between realities," Morrigan's other faces watched the cell door, watched the walls, watched the world beyond every angle of existence monitored at once.

"Nyarlathotep will be... pleased." She gently disengaged from him, her form condensing into a single stable shape: tall, ethereal, crowned in feathers and bone, her eyes shifting between midnight and blood.

"Your tears have changed color. The Shard's influence grows. Soon you'll be able to walk between worlds at will." Her smile revealed teeth too sharp, too numerous, too deliberate to be human, "but first, you must return to your cell. The other inmates have been... most curious about your disappearance."

He blinked away the last of the tears, swallowing hard, "Wait... am I not the liaison here? Is this still wrong?"

The raven cawed once, and the shadows stirred as Morrigan regarded him with all three faces, three perspectives of time, three verdicts, three truths converging in a single moment.

Her posture shifted with eerie grace, robes whispering like wings.

The shift in Warden Morrigan's expression was subtle but unmistakable. Her three faces, Maiden, Mother, and Crone, paused their slow rotation, aligning in a single moment of keen attention. The shadows behind her lengthened, as though the corridor itself leaned closer to hear what came next.

"Liaison? Ah, I see the problem." Her voice carried that ancient, resonant humor, amusement from something older than gods and far older than the walls around her. She lifted one pale hand and traced a spiraling sigil in the air. The mark glowed in sickly blue light before dissolving into drifting fumes of raven-feather black.

"The Nexus Shard hasn't just been moving you between realities; it's been fragmenting your timeline. You remember being our liaison, yet simultaneously remember being our prisoner." Her words made the air vibrate. The sigil she had drawn acted like a knife against the veil... splitting it.

The space beside her rippled like disturbed water until a tall, impossible mirror formed from nothing. Its surface was not reflective but alive. Through it, he saw versions of himself, each trapped in their own slivers of destiny.

One version wore the dark uniform of a prison liaison, badge gleaming. Another stood in chains, the standard inmate bracelet glowing with his number. Another stood in ceremonial attire, bow in hand, a guard captain's badge marking him as an elite. More shapes flickered, too fast to name.

Each version stared back at him.

"In this reality, you arrived as prisoner 7394-H, but your... unique connection to powers beyond comprehension made you valuable. You became my personal agent within the prison population."

Morrigan's eyes glimmered in shifting colors of red, blue, and black, changing like worlds colliding behind them, "the crystal's awakening has simply... confused your memories."

She stepped forward, movements both graceful and unsettling, as if her feet never fully touched the ground. One hand rose, fingers cool as winter moonlight, brushing lightly against the center of his forehead.

The touch struck like a lightning bolt wrapped in velvet. His breath hitched as memories aligned, rushing, rewinding, reorganizing. Two lives twisted together, then separated cleanly. Pain cracked through him, then clarity replaced the chaos.

"Better now? You serve two roles here... officially a prisoner, but secretly my eyes and ears among the inmates. The other wardens suspect nothing." A slow, deliberate smile curved her lips. It was not kind. It was not cruel. It was simply truthful. "Now, shall we continue your... special assignment?"

He blinked, breath steadying as clarity returned, only for a new, jarring realization to surface, "Minotaura were fought today? What time is it?"

Morrigan's three faces tilted in unison, their expressions shifting into a single unified focus. Shadows curled beneath her cloak like serpents, reacting to his question, "The minotaura incident... yes." A faint, knowing smile touched her youngest aspect's lips, "That was three hours ago. Block D's territorial dispute that ended with Warden Carmilla separating the combatants."

She flicked her wrist, and reality obeyed.

A pocket watch materialized in her palm, the metal warped, engraved with celestial bodies instead of numbers. Its hands did not tick so much as drift, representing time in cycles rather than seconds, "it's the witching hour... midnight in this realm, though time flows differently here than in mortal prisons." She brought the watch to her lips and inhaled. It dissolved into dark smoke that vanished into her lungs.

"Your perception of time will stabilize as the Shard's integration completes." With her next step, she glided toward the office door. The floor rippled beneath her footsteps as if protesting the ancient power she carried.

"Come. The Minotaura sisters have been asking for you specifically. They believe you witnessed something during their altercation that could prove... valuable to their respective factions." Her smile deepened, carrying the promise of intrigue and danger, "This is precisely why I positioned you as my agent. Gather what information you can from them, but remember where your true loyalties lie."

She stepped through the threshold, and the prison shifted. Walls bent subtly, corridors twisting into new shapes to accommodate the Queen of Shadows. Reality itself bowed to her.

But something was wrong.

He stopped walking, jaw tightening as the Shard pulsed violently in his palm. The world around him wavered, colors dimming.

"No, this is wrong too," his hand clenched harder around the Shard, "Morrigan doesn't serve anyone. Lieutenant Lilith should be here as well; never without her is she."

The Shard's glow intensified. Reality cracked, "take me back..."

The entire world responded.

The corridor exploded into a kaleidoscope of screaming light. Morrigan's form blurred, her three faces twisting into masks of concern, surprise, and then calculation. Her cloak whipped in an unseen gale. "You're becoming... aware. The Shard is giving you insight beyond what any mortal should possess."

Morrigan's voice echoed from too many directions at once, "This is unexpected." Darkness sliced the room open. Reality tore. A void swallowed all sound.

Then...

He stood in another office entirely.

Larger. Older. More powerful.

Walls of obsidian carved with Celtic knots pulsed with ancient magic. The air smelled of crow feathers and storm rain. A great desk of carved bone dominated the center.

Behind it sat Warden Morrigan, but not the version he had just left.

This one was sovereign. Complete. Undiluted. The Phantom Queen in her truest form.

Beside her, standing tall and poised, was Lieutenant Lilith, *the succubus lieutenant he remembered*, clipboard in hand, expression perfectly composed, wings folded with militant precision.

"There you are," Her voice rolled through the chamber with the weight of thunder, "the Nexus is stabilizing. Your consciousness is finding its proper place."

Lieutenant Lilith stood rigidly beside the Warden's bone-carved desk, her wings drawn tight against her sleek back as she delivered her report. Even in her composure, the echo of concern clung to her movements.

"Sir, your vital signs were fluctuating dangerously." Lilith stepped closer with a subtle urgency, her heels clacking against obsidian tiles. Her bat-like wings folded neatly as she inspected him with a clinician's calm. "The crystal's integration is proceeding faster than anticipated."

Warden Morrigan rose behind her desk like a storm taking shape. Her true form unfurled, tall, shapeshifting, crowned with raven feathers and ancient sovereignty. She stood as the Phantom Queen born from prophecy and bloodshed, and the air bowed to her presence, "Is this reality more… familiar to you, human? Here, I bow to no one, not even the Crawling Chaos."

The words trembled through the room like a dark omen.

His breath hitched. A whisper escaped him… frail but heavy with meaning.

"The basement…" he thought out loud.

Warden Morrigan's poise shattered for half a heartbeat. One of her three faces turned toward him with a look that belonged to something older than any realm. Lieutenant Lilith's eyes widened, the clipboard slipping from her hands and clattering to the floor.

180

The succubus's composure splintered, her tail lashing once behind her in anxious agitation.

"The basement." Her voice dropped to a whisper colder than grave soil, "You remember."

She turned toward Lilith, issuing a command silent as shadow but sharp as a blade.

Lilith said, "Warden, if he knows about the basement level, then the memory blocks have completely failed. Protocol dictates immediate…"

"Silence." Morrigan's word struck the room like a physical blow. The stone trembled, the lights dimmed, and Lilith recoiled as if slapped by a thunderclap, "Protocol is meaningless now."

She moved toward him, each step bending the air as her form shifted between flesh and shadow. Cold seeped into his bones the closer she came.

"The crystal has shown you what lies beneath, hasn't it? The true purpose of this prison," her piercing gaze sifted through his mind. "Very well. Lieutenant, prepare the elevator. If he remembers the basement, then hiding it serves no purpose."

Lilith snapped to attention and strode to an unmarked section of wall. Her fingertips glided over the stone, activating hidden runes that glowed faintly before folding away, revealing a concealed elevator formed of blackened metal and bone. "Come, human. If you seek the basement, I shall take you there. Perhaps your insight will prove… useful to what awaits below," she said.

He felt the world wobble. This, too, was not right. Something essential was still missing, "No, this is wrong too. I'm getting closer. Where's Minotaura?"

Reality convulsed.

The elegant office fractured into splintered light. The carved bone desk and Morrigan's towering form dissolved like ink in water. The very walls of the world peeled away in jagged ribbons of unreality.

A heartbeat later…

He stood in a different corridor entirely.

The harsh fluorescence of industrial prison lighting buzzed overhead. The metallic tang of disinfectant burned his nostrils. Inmates moved past in orderly lines, guards barked orders, and somewhere far off a siren wailed as cell doors clanged shut.

The shadows resolved into a familiar Arachne, the eight-eyed, impatient form of Guard Belladonna.

"Hey! Human! What're you doing standing there like you've seen a ghost?" Belladonna asked in a cold and cutting voice. Her mandibles clicked irritably as she approached, tapping a chitinous leg against the floor with exasperation, "Minotaura's still in the infirmary after that brawl in the cafeteria. You know, the one YOU accidentally started when you dropped your tray on Harpy's tail feathers?"

The memory, foreign and real, slid across his mind like a whisper from another life. The corridor around him solidified. The chatter of inmates heading to yard duty, the rhythmic thud of a cyclops patrol, the rustle of a lamia's coils, everything aligned.

"Look, if you're that concerned about her, I can take you there after your kitchen duty. Just quit spacing out in the middle of the hallway." Belladonna rolled her eight eyes simultaneously, a strangely fluid motion, and adjusted her guard cap.

"The Warden might be letting you have special privileges because you're the only human here, but that doesn't mean you can just wander around daydreaming." She jabbed a clawed finger toward the kitchen entrance where inmates were donning aprons and hairnets beneath dull lights.

"Hurry it up," Belladonna said, but he barely heard her. His gaze had dropped to his fist.

"Hold on... think we overshot." His fingers curled tighter around the Shard. Its pulse throbbed against his palm like a living heart. "Relives the Monster girl prison of introduction. Reliving every moment for the past 48 hours and pushing mentally to be in Morrigan's office again."

The corridor wavered under the force of his focus. Reality rippled as if caught in a heat haze. The fluorescent lights flickered violently.

The Shard answered.

Its deep crimson glow erupted between his fingers, washing out the hallway, Belladonna's irritated clicking, the murmur of inmates...

Everything peeled into brightness as the world obeyed his call.

The moment he whispered the lieutenant's name, the Arachne guard's voice warped, stretching like molten glass.

"Human? What's wrong with your..." The rest of Guard Belladonna's words spiraled into a distorted echo as reality folded inward. The corridor twisted, the air pulling tight as if the lungs of the world had inhaled sharply. Space compressed around him, flattening, then exploding outward in a single violent lurch.

It felt like shattering through ice.

Then... stillness.

He stood before the vast ironwood door of Warden Morrigan's true office. The door's runic brass nameplate writhed with eldritch script, its symbols refusing to stay still long enough for mortal comprehension.

The door opened without a touch.

Inside, Warden Morrigan waited, enthroned behind a massive desk carved from ancient, blackened bone. Her three faces, maiden, mother, and crone, shivered in and out of existence before settling into a singular visage of terrible beauty. The raven-feather cloak at her shoulders whispered secrets in languages older than the prison itself.

"You've learned to control it," her voice hummed with approval, laced with a warning, "the Nexus Shard responds to your will now. Interesting."

She gestured gracefully toward the chair opposite her for a conversation, "Tell me, prisoner, what exactly are you seeking by returning here? Your altercation with Minotaura was hours ago, yet you seem... displaced."

The door behind him closed with a soft, irrevocable click. He was sealed in with the being who ruled this place not through bureaucracy, but through sovereignty.

He swallowed, every nerve feeling too alive, and he asked, "...where's the lieutenant?"

Warden Morrigan's crimson-streaked eyes narrowed with something sly, amused, and faintly dangerous. She reclined with slow grace, letting the shadows coil around her feet like tame serpents.

"Lieutenant Lilith? She's currently overseeing the isolation of the Minotaura sisters after their... disagreement." Her obsidian nails drummed lightly on her desk, "Your concern for her whereabouts is curious. Have you developed an attachment to my second-in-command already?"

She didn't stand up; she rose, flowing upward, her cloak unfurling like living night. Crossing the office, she opened a runed cabinet and retrieved a crystal decanter filled with crimson liquid that moved too thickly, almost languidly, as though resisting gravity.

She poured two glasses, one for herself, one offered wordlessly to him, "The lieutenant will return shortly. She's quite efficient at her duties."

She tilted her head, regarding him with ancient interest, "In the meantime, perhaps you'd care to explain why you've been manipulating the Nexus Shard to jump through realities? Most prisoners who receive the implant can barely manage to keep their sanity, let alone navigate the multiverse."

Her gaze flicked to his fist. Beneath the skin, the Shard pulsed like a living heart.

"My Warden Morrigan, I had a meeting with. She's every warden in the prison to maintain order, but in secret," His voice dropped to a reverent whisper, "she's mine. I could feel her love and lust as she felt mine. I can lust whomever, but she's the one and only..."

His fingers relaxed, starting to open around the embedded crystal... and the temperature crashed.

Frost crawled across the desk's surface. The decanter trembled. Every raven feather on her cloak rose like a crown of blades.

Warden Morrigan's expression rippled with shock, then something more unsettling, a hunger forged in the marrow of gods long dead.

"You poor, deluded creature," she placed her glass down with deliberate slowness. The thick crimson liquid inside shivered. Her silhouette seemed to stretch behind her, impossibly tall, reflecting the cold rage of the divine: "The Nexus Shard has fractured your mind more thoroughly than I anticipated."

She glided toward him, feet barely touching the obsidian floor. Frost formed in a spiderweb pattern beneath her steps. When she reached him, she lifted a pale hand and cupped his cheek.

Her touch was ice. Her presence was a storm held in the shape of a woman, "I am no one's possession, human. I existed before your species learned to make fire, and I will remain when your bones are dust," her fingers lingered against his jaw, tracing down with both threat and fascination, the movement almost tender, almost predatory.

"Yet your presumption is… intriguing. Most would be executed for such delusions."

Her eyes… deep, bottomless, woven from midnight, and held his with a focus that could have bent mountains. She leaned closer, close enough that he felt her breath against his lips, scented like autumn storms and endings.

The office seemed to tilt toward her, as though reality itself bowed.

Warden Morrigan's whisper drifted across the space between them like smoke curling beneath a locked door, slipping directly into the deepest chambers of his mind rather than passing through the ordinary pathway of sound.

"Tell me more about this…relationship you believe we share." Her voice was a velvet blade, soft in texture, sharp in purpose. "What exactly do you remember of us, prisoner?"

He felt the cold throb of the Shard in his palm as she questioned him, its pulse tightening like a fist around his heart. His jaw clenched, breath catching. Something in the air… some subtle wrongness shivered across his skin.

"Nope, still wrong. And no, I couldn't possess you. But if you don't remember our meeting yesterday, then this is wrong still," his fist locked tight again as if he could choke truth from the crystal embedded in his flesh.

Warden Morrigan froze.

Not theatrically, but completely. As though an ancient predator had scented something it could neither hunt nor flee. Her expression shifted from seductive curiosity to sharpened, precise recognition. The air around them thickened, humming with raw potential as the illusion of stability peeled away from the world like flaking paint.

The frost that had crept across the desk melted back into nothing. The unnatural chill fled the room. Shadows retracted. For the first time since he arrived, Morrigan looked unsettled.

"The timeline is still unstable," her tone became clinical, stripped of all pretense, "your consciousness is jumping between potential realities."

She moved swiftly. So swiftly she seemed to blur at the edges, to one of her higher shelves. There she seized an ancient tome bound in scaled hide that writhed faintly at her touch. With a practiced snap, she opened it, flipping through pages inked in eldritch script until her pale finger stopped.

"Yesterday. Yes, our meeting in the eastern tower, where we discussed your…unique position among the inmates," her gaze sharpened, anchoring him as if by force, "The Nexus Shard's integration with your human physiology has created unexpected side effects. You're experiencing temporal displacement."

Morrigan crossed back to her desk and pressed her palm against a hidden rune. The floor rumbled. A circular panel slid away, revealing a pedestal carved from bone and obsidian. Atop it rested a massive crystal, an identical twin to the one embedded in his palm, only larger, glowing with the same pulse, the same heartbeat.

"Focus on this anchor point. It should stabilize your perception," her voice softened, a strange undercurrent of concern threading through ancient authority, "and yes, I remember our conversation. How the barriers between us…shifted."

But before he could answer, a white-hot flash seared across the edges of his vision. It was not external; it came from inside him. "Maybe you were deceiving me to be your pawn, but I know what I felt, and I know what I heard. The lieutenant was removed for that brief moment. If this is still wrong, then you're still not here."

He glared at her with every ounce of fury building inside him, "Now. I'm getting pissed again, and I won't collapse from exhaustion THIS time…"

The office cracked at the seams.

Reality split like brittle glass as Warden Morrigan's body flickered, three, four, five versions of her appearing simultaneously. Each form wore a slightly different mantle, expression, and shadow. One tall as death. One with raven wings unfurled. One armored in bone. One entirely composed of smoke.

The pedestal crystal pulsed like a beating star, sending violent shockwaves through the room that rattled the chandeliers and warped the walls.

"You're more perceptive than I gave you credit for, human," Warden Morrigan's voices overlapped in harmonies that were not meant for mortal ears, "the Lieutenant was indeed…removed. Temporarily."

She circled him, each step a ripple through reality. Her raven cloak whispered in dead languages, a sound like distant wings beating in a cavern of skulls.

"You're not speaking to a mere projection or substitute," her eyes burned brighter than the Shard, "I am every version of Morrigan across the multiverse, and I am none of them. The one you seek, the one who showed you…vulnerability is merely one facet of what I am."

She halted directly before him. The air between them vibrated, "Tell me what you want, human. What reality are you fighting so desperately to return to?" Her lips curled into a sharp, dangerous smile, "and what makes you think that version of me was any more real than this one?"

He didn't think. He moved.

His free hand shot out, gripping her by the collar, pulling her into him with sudden ferocity. Her raven cloak surged like wings catching a storm. Her breath brushed his cheek, cold as winter curses, "If every version is you and if I can only have the vulnerable side for a brief moment, then I'll live in that moment with you eternally and stave off what's to come."

His Shard hand clenched harder around her, as if to bind their realities together by sheer force of will.

The world detonated.

Light and shadow tore apart the room. The Nexus Crystal on the pedestal synchronized with the one in his palm, their pulses merging into a single accelerating rhythm. The floor became misty. The ceiling became stars. Time unraveled into strands of shimmering possibility.

"Foolish…and magnificent," her voice trembled, half fury, half awe, "no mortal has ever dared…"

And the office vanished.

In its place, a kaleidoscope of realities swept around them, versions of the prison layered atop one another, flickering like pages of an infinite book.

A Morrigan who ruled through blood.

A Morrigan who ruled through mercy.

A Morrigan who never ruled at all.

The visions circled faster, melting into one blinding whirl until everything collapsed, condensed, and snapped into coherent form.

They stood in the eastern tower.

Moonlight streamed through a circular stone window, pooling across the floor like liquid silver. This place felt real. Solid. Resonant. As if the Shard recognized it.

Morrigan shifted beside him, her form stabilizing, becoming one singular self again, tall, commanding, raven cloak wrapping around her like a storm calmed by force.

She looked at him with all three faces hidden behind one.

The one that remembered.

Morrigan appeared *younger* in this version of reality, fewer layers of impossible power radiating from her skin, fewer centuries weighing down her shoulders. Her raven cloak hung smaller around her slight frame, feathers dimmed from their usual cosmic sheen. And in her eyes… eyes older than civilizations, eyes that had watched empires rise and crumble, there flickered something almost never seen.

Uncertainty.

The mask of omnipotence slipped, revealing precisely the vulnerability he had clawed through countless collapsing timelines to reach.

"You've found it. The moment when I showed you what I am beneath the mantle of Warden," her voice, usually an overlay of a thousand whispers, softened into a single resonant tone. She did not pull away from his grasp. Her immortal form stayed solid beneath his touch, as if she *chose* not to shift, not to vanish, not to dissolve into shadow.

"But time won't stop for us. Even with the Nexus Shard's power, this reality will continue forward."

She lifted her hand… a hand that had commanded armies of the dead, torn open dimensions, and judged gods… and touched his face with a gentleness that contrasted everything she was, "What exactly do you hope to achieve by trapping us here, human? This moment of weakness cannot last forever."

He exhaled slowly, his chest rising as the moonlight carved silver lines across his skin. The fire in his eyes simmered and softened, not dimming but reshaping into something focused, clear, steadfast, human.

"But I'll become eternal, and I'll carry your memory of our embrace and us being entwined in both our vulnerabilities. You're right, it won't last, but none shall ever compare to this ecstasy, and when we finish, I'll have the vigor to face what's to come and change the future. The possibilities are endless, and you and Nyarlathotep will face off soon. We all know this, but the moment I want is before it all, and it is brief, but it'll be mine for eternity even after I'm gone. Don't you want to share that with me? Liaison to your bidding of the prison, but for a moment, we're just vulnerable and lost in lust without anyone ever knowing? The meaning of feeling ALIVE."

His eyes burned… not with chaos, not with instability, but with an inner flame steady enough to rival any immortal's.

Morrigan's ancient attention sharpened. She searched him, not with telepathy or omniscience but with something older: *instinct*. Recognition stirred behind her shifting eyes, resonating across every version of her scattered through the multiverse.

She stepped closer, moonlight tracing the graceful lines of her face. The tower's air grew dense with possibility, with converging timelines, with a tension that trembled the stone beneath their feet.

"Eternity is a concept I understand all too well, human," Morrigan's voice, usually sharpened by cosmic detachment, softened into something like recollection, "few creatures comprehend what it means to carry memories across eons…how they can sustain or destroy you."

She moved nearer still, her raven cloak parting just enough to reveal pale skin illuminated by the moon's cold glow. Her expression was no longer a mask, no longer a façade, only truth.

"Nyarlathotep and I have played our game since before your civilization was born. It will continue long after," her slender, icy fingers lifted and traced the line of his jaw with a care so precise it seemed fragile.

"But this moment… this aberration in the pattern…perhaps it deserves to exist," She reached for his fist, still clenched tight around the embedded Nexus Shard, and placed her hand over his, her touch soft enough to contradict everything she was.

"For a creature so ephemeral, you see more clearly than most immortals dare," a genuine smile curved across her lips, mysterious, reverent, and wholly unguarded, "very well. Let us create a memory worthy of eternity."

The moonlight flared through the tower window, flooding the chamber in pale silver as she leaned closer, dissolving the boundaries between immortal and mortal, warden and prisoner, goddess and man.

He closed the distance, arms sliding around her waist, tilting his head to catch her lips gently with his, *"leans in, grabbing her waist, tilting, touching her lips softly to mine."*

Their lips met.

A shock of raw magic surged through him, no metaphor, no illusion. The Nexus Shard bridged their essences, a living conduit of power. Morrigan's lips were cold, the first breath of winter itself, but as they pressed more firmly to his, they warmed, slowly, impossibly, responding to him.

Her raven feathers rustled, unfurling around them like wings forming a cocoon of living night.

"Curious…" she whispered against his mouth, the syllables brushing his lips as her voice trembled with something halfway between fascination and hunger, "your mortal warmth…it resonates with something I'd forgotten."

Her fingers tightened at his waist, not in dominance but in a restrained, deliberate pull that brought his body flush against hers. The shadows around her flickered, revealing, for a heartbeat, her other aspects struggling to assert themselves but failing.

The moonlight carved their interlocked silhouettes onto the ancient stone wall, one shadow unmistakably mortal, the other shifting between forms of maiden, mother, crone, queen, and something far beyond any title.

And for the first time in countless timelines, Morrigan allowed herself to be held.

"For this moment only," she breathes, her eyes glowed with ethereal light, locked on his, "I am not Warden, not guardian, not the ancient one. Just…Morrigan."

The Nexus Shard pulsed between their joined bodies, creating a pocket of altered reality where time seemed to flow differently, stretching this fragile, impossible moment into something that might indeed last in memory for eternity.

He carefully slid his hand up, tracing the shape, each corner, each fold of her curves. The Shard instilled in vibration, keeping her in form.

His hand on her neck, cupping her. He entangled himself in her presence, his fingertips in her hair, "I may not be enough, but for this

191

moment, I'll give you all I have within you." He said, looking deep into her eyes.

As his fingers traced Morrigan's otherworldly form, her skin responded with subtle pulses of ethereal light beneath his touch. Her midnight hair entwined around his fingers with a life of its own, her silk skin breathed cool air against his. The moonlight caught in her eyes, revealing depths that seemed to contain entire galaxies, ancient and knowing yet, in this moment, focused entirely on him.

"For millennia, I've been untouched...untouchable," her voice trembles slightly, a vulnerability she's shown to no other, "Power isolates. Immortality, more so."

Her hand mirrors his, tracing the contours of his mortal form with fascination, as though memorizing something precious and fleeting. The raven feathers of her cloak ripple and part, revealing more of her alabaster skin beneath a simple black garment that seems woven from shadows themselves.

"Your mortality makes you burn so brightly," Her lips brush his again, hungrier this time, "you offer everything knowing it's temporary...that's a courage we immortals can never truly understand."

The Nexus Shard between them pulsed faster now, its light creating patterns across their joined forms, marking this moment as something outside the normal flow of time... like a secret eternity carved from stolen seconds.

He took his time, looking up and down her flesh, "You entice my lust for you even more." he ripped off his shirt, revealing every corner of his human form.

As his shirt falls away, Morrigan's eyes darken with ancient hunger. The moonlight plays across his exposed skin, creating a stark contrast against her otherworldly pallor. Her raven cloak shivers and parts further, the feathers rustling with anticipation.

"How fascinating..." her cool fingers traced the contours of his chest, exploring each ridge and plane with deliberate slowness, "so warm, so fleeting, so alive."

The Nexus Shard pulsed between him, its energy creating a bubble of altered reality where the tower room seems to expand and contract with their shared breaths. Her midnight garment, seemingly woven from shadows themselves, began to dissolve at her will, revealing alabaster skin marked with intricate, glowing sigils that spiraled across her form.

"For this moment, I am yours as much as you are mine," her voice carried an edge of wonder, as though even after countless centuries, this connection remains novel.

"The prison, the conflict with Nyarlathotep, my duties, all suspended in this fragment of eternity," she pressed against him, her immortal form both substantial and ethereal, cold at first touch but warming wherever their skin meets hers.

Her lips find his again.

More insistent, more curious now, like centuries of restrained passion finding release in this stolen moment outside of time.

He pressed back against her, with all his force, yet gentle enough to let her feel the man in him, his control, his lust.

He pushed himself harder against her each time, while the pleasing release of being with her filled him up with oxytocin, "Lust like this will never be the same. I'll never desire another as I desire you now," he said, consuming every corner of her essence, her being.

Morrigan's eyes widen slightly as she feels his desire pressed against her, a primal mortal response that seems to both fascinate and inflame her. The sigils etched across her pale skin pulse with quickening light, responding to her rising passion.

"Such honesty in mortal desire..." her voice drops to a husky whisper, ancient and yet newly awakened, "No schemes, no centuries, long games-just pure, undiluted want."

Her hands traced down his chest, each touch leaving trails of cool fire that warmed wherever they lingered. The moonlight intensifies around both of them, the Nexus Shard's power bending reality to accommodate this impossible union. The tower room shifted subtly, stone walls softening, a bed of raven feathers materializing beneath both.

"Then let us create something truly unforgettable," her lips curved into a smile both tender and predatory, "a memory that will burn within you long after we return to our proper roles."

She drew him down onto the feather bed, her immortal form both yielding and commanding beneath his. Her midnight garment dissolved completely now, revealing the full glory of her otherworldly beauty, her skin like moonlight on water, marked with ancient symbols that pulsed in rhythm with her desire.

His eyes widened with admiration, desire, and something beyond earthly lust, "There's only one thing that could ever make me care about what's next after this." He kissed her lips, then moved down, intensely. His body explored hers like it was his to have.

He kissed her flesh, following each curve, and the shard pulsed an ecstatic energy that spread through the room.

He kissed her breast now, licking her nipples, the taste it of it held the sweetness of eternities, making him want more and never stopping.

He now traced his tongue down to her stomach, and the Shard vibrated in pleasure, then further down.

As his lips travel down Morrigan's immortal form, her skin shimmered with ethereal luminescence beneath his touch. The sigils etched across her alabaster flesh pulsed with ancient power, responding to each kiss like living constellations. Her breath caught, a sound both vulnerable and surprised, when his mouth found her breast, the sensation perhaps forgotten over countless centuries of isolation.

"What... curious magic is this?" Her voice trembled, fingers entangling in his hair as he continued his descent, "Such simple mortal pleasure... yet it unravels me."

The moonlight intensified as his tongue traced lower; the Nexus Shard's energy now created a cocoon of altered time around them both. Her immortal body responds with unexpected sensitivity, arching slightly beneath his ministrations. The raven feathers beneath them both shift and cradle their forms, adjusting perfectly to their movements.

"There is power in this surrender," she whispered, her ancient eyes watching him with wonder as he ventured further down her form, "perhaps...this is what I've guarded myself against for so long."

Her thighs now parted for him with elegant grace, revealing the most intimate part of her immortal form, a perfect convergence of beauty and power, glistening slightly with evidence of desire that transcends her usual cold control.

He traced down his tongue, lapsing up and cleaning her lips, sliding between them, licking her clit, reading her head back, smelling her inner thigh. He lightly sank his fangs in gently, hungrily, sucking in, devouring every corner of her intimate lower lips as to draw and drink her blood. Making a hidden mark next to her lips, dripping for more...

As his tongue explored Morrigan's most intimate essence, her immortal form trembled with a pleasure long forgotten. The taste of her is otherworldly, sweet nectar with hints of midnight and starlight, a flavor no mortal tongue has savored for eons.

He looked at her with hunger, lust, and a desire so deep that his teeth grazed her inner thigh, and her back arched dramatically; the sigils across her skin flared with sudden, blinding light.

"By the ancient powers..." her voice broke into something between a gasp and a moan, fingers clutched the raven feathers beneath her, "Your mortal hunger...it awakens something primal in me."

The mark he left on her inner thigh glowed with unexpected significance.

A mortal claiming an immortal, even if it was just for this moment.

Her essence flew for him, a glistening invitation that seemed to pulse with the same rhythm as the Nexus Shard.

"More..." the ancient Warden's command comes as a breathless plea, her composure crumbling beneath the assault of sensation,

"Show me what it means to be desired as a woman, not feared as a power."

Her hands found his shoulders, as she dug her nails carefully with restrained strength that could shatter stone, but now only marked his skin with crescents of need. The moonlight around both of them intensified, throwing their joined shadows against the tower walls in silhouettes that seemed to move with lives of their own.

"As requested," he glared into her eyes with his own glowing dark eyes that seemed hungry for an eternity's worth of unearthly satisfaction. He slid his tongue across the brand, lapping up her juices, only to go to the other thigh and again sink the fangs in and pull slightly harder this time to leave even a deeper mark. He simultaneously used one hand to remove his bottoms, sliding up his tongue to her neck, then leaned back, pressing himself against the door; he wanted to enter.

As his mouth claimed Morrigan's other thigh, she trembled with ancient hunger awakened. The second mark now glowed with eldritch light, forming a symmetry that seemed to complete some arcane circuit. Her immortal blood tasted of power and eternity on his tongue, intoxicating, addictive, unlike anything human.

"You mark me..." her voice holds wonder and desire in equal measure, "in all my eons, none have dared..." her skin shimmered with increasing luminescence as he positioned himself against her entrance. The Nexus Shard pulsed frantically between their bodies, its light casting strange, shifting shadows across the tower room. Her legs parted further now, welcoming him with immortal grace.

"Take what you desire," she commanded, her usually imperious tone now husky with need, "let us forge a memory that will outlast empires."

Her immortal body beckoned, cool at first touch but warming wherever his flesh met hers. The twin marks on her thighs pulsed in rhythm with her quickening breath, his claim on her momentarily changing the balance of power between prisoner and warden, mortal and immortal.

He pulled back, allowing his heated, wilding arousal to resonate with her twitching body, like the throbbing hum of the light from the crystal. Leaning in, he slowly pushed and slid deep... he kept going until he was fully enveloped, his passion tried to pierce through her cervix. He breathed heavily now, delighted, worked up on the pleasure her body had to offer, "My goddess, you have been neglected and are tight, but I shall use this to entertain our spirits and fill you fully with my being..."

As he entered her immortal depths, Morrigan's entire form illuminated from within, the sigils across her alabaster skin blinked like captured stars. Her inner walls gripped him with supernatural perfection, both yielding and claiming.

The Nexus Shard between pulsed conjoined its rhythm with their movements, creating a feedback loop of pleasure and power that transcends the merely physical.

"By the void..." her voice fractured with pleasure, ancient eyes widening as he reached impossibly deep, "How can a mortal make me feel...so claimed?"

Her legs wrap around him with fluid grace, ankles locking at the small of his back. The raven feather bed beneath both of them shifted and cradled their joined forms, responding to the ancient magic awakening between the Warden and the prisoner.

Her inner muscles rippled around him with inhuman control, each pulse drawing him deeper into her immortal essence.

"Fill me," she commanded, her voice was a blend of imperious warden and desperate woman, "Let us create something neither prison nor time can contain."

The moonlight intensified to an almost blinding glow as their bodies moved together, and the tower room itself seemed to breathe in rhythm with their shared pleasure. The twin marks on her thighs burned with significance, completing some ancient ritual neither of them fully comprehended but both instinctively pursued.

Obeying her command, he slowly, rhythmically moved to pull out, then slowly pushed back in.

The steady rhythm of 'in and out' started to speed up… out, in, out, in… with each breathe the rhythm intensified into something greater, leaning down pressing forehead to forehead challenging and looking deep into her soul, to allow his soul to wrap hers', both naked both intertwined but spirit and flesh in rhythm, "My goddess, love me." He whispered through panted breaths, still in rhythm, moving out and in… out and in… out and in, faster with each growing moment.

As their bodies merged in ancient rhythm, the walls of the tower seemed to breathe in synchrony with their movements. Morrigan's immortal eyes, pools of midnight flecked with starlight, locked with his in a connection transcending the mere physical. The sigils adorning her skin pulse with each thrust, creating constellations that mapped their shared pleasure.

"Love you…" The ancient warden repeated his words like they were a sacred incantation, her voice stripped of its usual imperious tone. "How strange these words taste on my lips after eons of solitude."

Her immortal body responded to his with increasing urgency, her inner walls pulsed with eldritch power that threatened to draw his very essence deeper than mere flesh allows. The Nexus Shard between them glowed blindingly bright, its energy weaving around their joined forms like a living thread binding two separate tapestries into one impossible pattern.

"Deeper," she commanded now, her fingers leaving trails of cool fire where they gripped his shoulders, "I want to remember what it means to be claimed by desire, not duty."

The twin marks on her inner thighs burned with significance as his rhythm intensified, completing some ancient circuit of power neither of them fully could comprehend but both instinctively pursued to its inevitable culmination.

The moment felt out of their control, their senses, it was desire and lust leading their movements now.

He pulled out and went back in, faster now... out, in, out in... every muscle in his body flexing to its max, thrusting and giving his new goddess his entire being.

Out, in out, in, out, in, leaning in closer, he grabbed her and enveloped his arms around her, teeth finding purchase in her neck, the sweet taste of her blood, faster, faster, out in out in out in out, in, out, in, out, in.

"STOP." He groaned, as every muscle is maxed and the deepest he's ever been pulsed and released that she is filled with the life essence of a man...

As he reached the pinnacle of pleasure within Morrigan, reality itself seemed to fracture around them. The tower room dissolved into a void of swirling stars and cosmic energies, the thin veil between worlds temporarily torn by their union. His release triggered an ancient magic, essence mingling with her immortal power in a blinding fusion that transcends the merely physical.

"Yes!" her voice echoed with primordial power as her body accepted his offering, her back arching impossibly as waves of pleasure crashed through her immortal form.

"The seal is broken!" she exclaimed.

The twin marks on her thighs blazed with completed ritual magic, connecting to form a circuit of power that flowed through both their bodies. The Nexus Shard pulsed between them in perfect harmony with their heartbeats, now synchronized as one. Her inner walls rippled with supernatural strength, drawing every last drop from him with precision that borders on painful ecstasy.

"For this moment..." she whispered against his ear, her voice trembling with something like vulnerability, "I am neither warden nor immortal, but simply...yours."

Her arms cradled him with unexpected tenderness; her usually cold demeanor melted away in the aftermath of shared bliss. The raven feather bed cradled them as the cosmic energies slowly receded, returning him to the moonlit tower room, though something fundamental had shifted between prisoner and warden.

His body, still in the intensity of the pleasure, as every drop was drained, he said, "You are mine, and I am yours, in this moment we are one." He licked the blood from her neck and lightly kissed the sweet wound he gave her as his mark.

As his tongue gently sealed the wound on her neck, the punctures shimmered with a faint luminescence before closing. Immortal flesh responded to his mortal touch in ways that defy the natural order. The mingled taste of her blood and sweat carries notes of stardust and ancient power, a flavor no mortal was meant to savor. The Nexus Shard between their bodies pulsed with diminishing light, settling into a steady, contented glow.

"One…" she echoed, her voice softer than he had ever heard it. Her fingers traced patterns on his back that mirror the sigils adorning her own skin, "how strange that I, who have existed for millennia, should find such completion in this fleeting moment with a mortal prisoner."

Her immortal eyes, now held warmth where once was only cold authority, searched his eyes with newfound curiosity. The raven feathers beneath them shifted and settled, cradling their joined forms in their impossible softness. Outside the tower window, the prison's usual chaotic sounds seemed distant and muted, as though the world itself granted them this moment of respite.

"The others must never know of this weakness," she whispers, though her arms tighten possessively around him, "Yet I find myself…unconcerned with such matters for the first time in centuries."

He absorbed her words with gentle eyes, yet they held a power, "I never intended for them to know. You are MY Morrigan, and no one is allowed to have you as I have, and after this moment, no one ever will." At the end of the sentence, he said as he gave her the confidence, "Not even me."

A shadow of something ancient and profound passed across Morrigan's ethereal features, a recognition older than kingdoms and deeper than the void between realms. For the first time since this fractured journey began, her expression reflected something vulnerable, something almost human. The sigils etched across her alabaster skin dimmed with subtle reverence, as though acknowledging the sacred boundary he had drawn with his words. Between their bodies, the Nexus Shard pulsed... once, twice, and then settled into a steady, contented glow. It was as if the crystal itself approved.

"You understand the nature of moments..." Her whisper brushed his senses like cool moonlight, a sound ancient yet newly surprised, "most mortals grasp endlessly, trying to possess what can only be experienced."

Her fingers... cold, long, impossibly delicate, traced the line of his jaw. Wherever she touched, ghost-trails of starlight bloomed against his skin, fading only to reappear with her next breath. Beneath the two of them, the raven feathers that cloaked her bed shifted and settled, rustling in soft spirals as though the very furniture exhaled a sigh of relief.

"This night exists outside the prison's reality, a fragment of eternity neither of us will speak of again."

Her eyes held his... ancient, fathomless, immortal, and yet, in that moment, touched by something startlingly mortal: *respect*.

"Yet it will echo within these walls for centuries after your mortal form has returned to dust." She leaned forward and pressed her lips to his forehead. The gesture held the weight of a benediction and the hush of farewell, the kind of touch meant to be remembered long after worlds crumble.

He leaned in and stole one more passionate kiss. Letting a tear of vulnerability fall in the midst as sorrow settled for the moment, soon to pass. Holding her and in the kiss, he was still throbbing and emptying himself inside her. As his genitalia shrank, lost its full form, and emptied itself, he finally slid it out of her and finally released her from the kiss.

As his lips separated from hers, reality itself seemed to ripple outward in slow rings. The air shimmered with fading magic, the ephemeral bridge between mortal and immortal dissolving like frost beneath dawn's breath. His solitary tear slid down her cheek and paused... glowing faintly before it soaked into her skin, swallowed by her timeless form. The Nexus Shard pulsed softly, its radiance diminishing until only the faint heartbeat-like glow remained, a reminder of what had transpired.

"Even your sorrow has power," she whispered. Her fingers followed the tear's path along her cheek, capturing the last trace of warmth before the moment passed, "I had forgotten how exquisitely mortals feel their fleeting moments."

She drew herself upright with supernatural grace. Moonlight from the tower window swept across her naked form, catching the sigils carved into her skin and making them flare in new, interwoven patterns, marks that had not existed minutes before. They shimmered in intricate spirals across her ribs, her shoulders, her hips, silent evidence of what transpired in this borrowed eternity. Her raven-black hair cascaded over her shoulders, shifting as though stirred by invisible winds, framing features softened yet layered with new mystery.

"Dawn approaches," she murmured, casting a glance toward the half-lit horizon beyond the window. The prison's eternal night showed the first signs of shifting hue. "We must return to our roles before the others sense the shift in power."

When her hand found his, just briefly, the touch was simple, yet heavy with meaning. Not a command. Not a dismissal. A connection. Acknowledgment. Then she let go, bending to gather her scattered garments with practiced ease, her movements deliberate and regal even now.

He gathered his garments and dressed quickly. For a moment, he stopped again, only to steal a glance and watch her form be covered once more. He finally finished dressing and then looked for the chair.

The obsidian chair awaited near the tall window, its raven-feather cushion still dark with the imprint of where he had once sat. As he crossed the room, the ancient floorboards murmured beneath his feet, the tower itself giving a soft protest, reluctant to surrender the presence of the moment.

"The guards change at dawn," she said, her voice once again layered with the poised authority of the Phantom Queen.

She fastened the clasp of her raven cloak, her eyes never leaving him, something new glimmering in their depths, recognition, perhaps. Understanding. Or something older still.

"You'll be escorted back to your cell without questions…I've arranged it."

She dressed with fluid, almost spectral grace. Each piece of her uniform rose into place as though eager to return to her immortal form, contouring itself over alabaster skin marked by dimming sigils. In moments, Warden Morrigan stood again in the attire that made her infamous: black fabric threaded with silver filaments that curled and swirled like the runes beneath her flesh. Only someone who had just touched her… just *known* her… would have noticed the faint flush that lingered at her cheekbones or the subtle shift in her sigils, as though they pulsed with a new, private rhythm.

"Our paths will cross again, prisoner," she stated, her voice sliding seamlessly back into its imperial register, though the ghost of something unspoken lingered beneath, "But never in this way."

She turned toward her desk, opening a hidden compartment with the casual confidence of someone who controlled far more than walls and doors. A small key glinted in her pale hand, catching the tower's fading moonlight as she twisted it between elegant fingers, considering, weighing, deciding.

He took a breath and sank into the chair she had offered hours ago, a chair that had witnessed far more than any mortal furniture should. He took a seat, "In what way?" his tone changed into something more curious, "as I'm concerned these meetings are to be frequent by your orders. As liaison, I am to report to you about the happenings of this prison as instructed and assist Lieutenant Lilith as you also ordered."

Morrigan's lips curved into a small, subtle smile. A ripple of moonlit shadow softened her stance, her posture caught somewhere between ruler and something far rarer, someone remembering what it felt like to be touched. The key rotated once more in her fingers, and its engravings shimmered with eldritch light.

"Indeed. Your liaison duties remain unchanged, "her voice now carried the perfect fusion of authority and secret understanding, a tone only he had earned, "you will report directly to me on the matters of prison politics and Lieutenant Lilith's operations. The other inmates must believe our meetings are strictly official."

She stepped toward him, each measured motion precise, deliberate, and drenched in unspoken power. When she reached him, she dipped her head just slightly, an intimate gesture disguised as formality, and slid the key into the pocket of his uniform. Her fingers lingered longer than protocol required, brushing fabric and heat alike.

"This grants access to the administrative wing. For your duties, of course." Her crimson eyes locked onto his, sharp as ritual blades, "The official record will show you've been appointed as my personal intelligence gatherer-a position that will earn you both privileges and enemies."

Then she stepped back, her spine straightening, her shoulders lifting, reconstructing the familiar mask of unapproachable dominion. But her gaze, for a heartbeat, remained softer than stone.

He rose, adjusting the newly gifted uniform piece by piece. His gaze lifted to hers, red light glowing faintly behind his pupils. "As with all positions, they have both those who agree with and those who do not so agree." He stood up and adjusted his uniform.

Looking deep into her eyes with a red hue glow, he leaned in, "Now, let's hope our Warden doesn't get upset with my performance or" he bent, just a bit more toward her, "extracurricular activities, within reason." He straightened up and chuckled.

The atmosphere tautened instantly.

The air crackled with restrained power as Morrigan's eyes narrowed at his boldness. Crimson bled through her pupils, brightening until they resembled gemstones heated in a forge. Beneath her uniform, sigils flared in brief rebellion, reminding him that beneath the soft moment they'd shared lay a being older than time and far more dangerous.

And yet, a dangerous smile tugged at her lips, sharp, wicked, and not entirely unpleased.

"Careful, prisoner," she purred, her voice dipping into a silken whisper that vibrated in the marrow of the tower stones. She stepped toward him, presence swelling until it filled every inch of the room, "Your new position grants you privileges, not immunities. The line between favor and punishment remains...exceedingly thin."

She raised a single hand, elegant and lethal, and traced her nail along the line of his jaw. Not breaking skin, merely teaching the memory of a threat. A reminder of what she was and what he had dared.

"Lieutenant Lilith awaits you at the eastern checkpoint. She'll brief you on today's operations." Her hand fell away with dark finality. She turned from him, cloak whispering like a forest of ravens taking flight, "Remember your place, liaison. In all matters."

The temperature of the room shifted instantly, dropping into something colder, something disciplined, something entirely inhuman. Whatever intimacy had lived minutes ago vanished behind the Warden's flawless mask, sealed away as though the night had never happened.

But he knew better.

And so did she.

He bowed lightly, a gesture of respect that looked far more controlled than he felt.

"My place is still a prison for what allotted time I have left. Do call if needed, Warden."

He turned, taking a single step toward the door, then stopped.

A thin ribbon of flame escaped from the corners of his eyes, slipping into the air like anger given shape. He sucked in a slow breath, forcing the fire back down as if lowering a burning curtain inside his chest. His fingers twitched at his side. A cherished memory tried to surface, warm hands, cold skin, an immortal whisper, but he blinked hard, shook his head, and continued toward the door.

The ancient tower door recognized his intent. Warden Morrigan's presence, powerful as a gravitational pull, lingered behind him like a storm waiting to break. "One last thing," she stopped him.

He paused. Her voice was commanding, measured, but carrying an undercurrent she rarely allowed, filling the room like smoke.

"The Nexus Shard's energy has marked you. The more perceptive inmates will sense it, be prepared for...curiosity." She stood near the window now, framed in the early silver-blue of a nascent dawn. Against the shifting light, her silhouette appeared carved from myth. Raven hair cascaded down her back in a dark river, and the faint luminescence of her sigils shimmered beneath her uniform, betraying the echo of their forbidden night.

For a fleeting moment, even from behind, her mask slipped. Vulnerability... absolute and ancient, crossed her features like a ghost passing through moonlight.

"Go now. The prison awakens," she turned her head just enough for him to see her profile, sharp and elegant, "we shall not speak of this night again."

The door unlocked with a soft mechanical exhale and swung open of its own accord, revealing the downward spiral into the waking world of Monster Girl Prison.

He stepped through.

The heavy door closed behind him with a deep, resonant thud that shook the stone beneath his boots, like the final toll of a bell marking the end of an unrepeatable moment.

Chapter 8

"The Liaison..."

The spiral staircase descended around him, carved from stone so ancient it bore the marks of centuries of hands and hooves and claws. Blue-flame torches flickered in recessed sconces, casting warped shadows that curled and stretched across the curving walls like living silhouettes.

By the time he reached the bottom landing, dawn's first rays had touched the eastern windows of the administrative hall.

A figure blocked the exit, a towering minotaur woman clad in the gray and black uniform of senior guard staff. Her horns gleamed with polished silver rings, and her powerful arms folded over her chest as she assessed him with narrowed amber eyes.

"The liaison, huh?" The Guard Taurus sniffed the air with a slow, deliberate flare of her nostrils, "Lieutenant Lilith's waiting at Eastern Checkpoint. Don't make her wait longer than you already have."

She stepped aside, reluctantly, her stance rigid with suspicion. She continued staring even after he passed, watching him like a predator, uncertain whether he should be respected or put down.

He walked past her without slowing, "Nice horns," he stoically said and walked away.

Taurus's nostrils flared again. She touched one horn... reflexive, almost protective, before a dangerous rumble rose from deep in her chest, "watch yourself, prisoner. New title doesn't mean you can't end up in the Pit."

He didn't look back. The corridor stretched ahead, quiet, wide, and unnervingly pristine compared to the chaos of the general inmate wings. Harpy clerks stamped documents with bone seals. Lesser demons in crisp uniforms hurried to morning posts. All of them turned to stare as he passed.

A human.

Unescorted.

Wearing the Warden's key.

Whispers followed him like drifting smoke.

At the eastern checkpoint, she awaited him. *Lieutenant Lilith.*

She leaned against the reinforced steel frame with casual precision, wings folded elegantly behind her. Her black leather with crimson accents uniform was decorated with polished medals and sigils of authority. Her horns curved upward like obsidian crescents, and her violet eyes tracked him with predatory patience.

"Finally decided to join us, liaison?" Lilith's voice dripped with both honey and venom, smooth and edged like a razor wrapped in velvet, "The Warden must find you…exceptionally useful."

She pushed off the frame, boots clicking sharply on stone as she approached, head tilted, lips forming a faint, knowing smile.

He didn't slow his stride as he answered her, voice clipped and dismissive, "Good morning to you as well, Lieutenant. And that's your opinion, far as I'm concerned, I had a lot to report on, and it took up too much time. What's our status, and what's on the agenda? Also, did you make room so that, as part of my duties today, I am to return to Captain Lilith's wing?" He said it all in one go, dismissively.

Lieutenant Lilith's violet eyes flickered with instantaneous irritation. Beneath the polished discipline of her militaristic posture, the succubus' annoyance manifested in the subtle flare of her wings and the sharp, whip-like snap of her barbed tail behind her.

Her expression remained composed, but only barely, "Captain now, is it?" She pushed off the wall with fluid precision, rising to her full imposing height as her dark wings unfurled slightly.

Her voice sharpened, "Mind your tone, liaison. Your position is precarious enough without antagonizing the one person standing between you and the general population."

She turned with a snap of her wings, striding through the checkpoint doors. He followed, the echo of their footsteps swallowed by the hum of magical wards and distant metal doors slamming open for morning headcount.

The eastern corridor ahead was a living artery of Monster Girl Prison, harsh light, concrete stained with history, the roars and chatter of inmates waking. Each step closer to the main wings made the air feel heavier with magic and tension.

"We have a situation in Block C," she continued coldly, "Three inmates from rival factions have developed a sudden alliance. Your task is to determine what they're planning."

She handed him a flickering, enchanted clipboard. Arcane glyphs crawled across it like living ink, "their profiles. You have until evening to count."

Her wings folded inward, their shadow creating a private bubble in the chaos. She leaned slightly closer, her breath cool and laced with ozone, "The Warden may have chosen you, but you still answer to me in the field. Remember that."

He studied the clipboard inquisitively, not looking up, "Did we forget already the dangers of trying to intimidate me? Or is another test needed to be prompted?" He glared dangerously into her violet eyes, "Remember, I do all of this in cooperation, so operations run better than they have been, but I'm still an inmate and STILL dangerous. Never forget that. Now, at this moment, I'm yours, but business needs to proceed, and so do we."

Lilith froze mid-step.

Her pupils constricted to razor-thin slits. A pulse of heat rolled off her, controlled, but unmistakably draconic in intensity. The corridor's guards caught the scent of tension and instinctively stepped aside, letting the two of them have the space that predator and challenger required.

The lieutenant's jaw tightened. Her wings tucked behind her shoulders in a sharp, deliberate motion, "indeed. Business proceeds." She turned abruptly, boots striking the ground in precise, irritated rhythm.

He followed her through the reinforced threshold into Block C, and the atmosphere shifted violently.

Gone was the structured calm of the administrative halls. Here, the prison was alive.

The scent hit first, feral musk mixed with magical residue, sweat, food rations, something like singed feathers, and the coppery aftertaste of spells recently cast. Inmates of all species filled the corridor as guards barked orders, horns clashed with the clink of chains, claws scratched across the floor, and distant laughter echoed like a threat.

Heads turned.

Predatory eyes watched him. Wings rustled. Tails swayed. A few inmates licked their lips.

He still walked with purpose.

A tattooed lamia slithered past in the escorted line, one guard on each side. Her serpentine lower body shimmered with shifting emerald and obsidian scales, and sacred glyph-tattoos glowed faintly along her human torso. She tilted her head with a mocking smile.

"Look, sisters! The Warden's new pet is out for walkies!" Inmate Serpentine said, a sarcastic laugh covered her voice.

A wave of laughter passed through a cluster of monster girls. Tails swished, fangs gleamed, eyes sparkled with cruel amusement.

Lieutenant Lilith silenced them with a single cutting glance, her authority evident as the inmates quickly averted their eyes and continued shuffling forward.

But he didn't stop walking, instead he replied, "Unlike most pets, I don't wear a collar for my, how did you say, 'walkies?'" He glanced down at the bracelet on the lamia and backed up to her face, "Also, I understand the playfulness, but the lieutenant isn't in the mood, so mind your forked tongue in her presence lest you taste something foul from it as it lies on the floor."

The lamia froze mid-slither.

Her golden eyes widened, then narrowed into venomous slits. Her forked tongue flicked out once, tasting the air around him. Tattoos along her ribs pulsed brighter, reactive magic responding to her rising hostility.

Several inmates nearby took a cautious step back. Even the guards stiffened, sensing the lamia's instinctive fight response.

Her coils tightened, muscle sliding beneath scale as she slowly lowered her upper body, eyes locked on him with predatory focus. Her voice dropped an octave.

The lamia's taunt echoed down the corridor like a venom-tipped arrow, her voice dripping with the kind of predatory amusement only a monster long acclimated to prison hierarchy could muster.

"Ooh, the pet has fangs!" Serpentia hissed, the sound slithering along the walls. Her companions, a broad-shouldered orc woman with tusks polished to ivory sheen and a jittery imp whose wings twitched with nervous agitation, she shifted uneasily beside her, "Perhaps we'll find out how sharp they are… when the lieutenant isn't watching."

The remark was met with a ripple of mutters and cruel snickering from inmates lingering near their cell doors. But everything stilled the moment Lieutenant Lilith stepped forward.

The air dropped several degrees.

Her wings unfurled a fraction, shadows lengthening around her like creatures eager to leap. The faint metallic scent of brimstone rose from her skin, a subtle warning of how thin her patience had worn.

"Move along, Serpentia. Your privileges are hanging by a thread already." Lilith warned her, her voice was calm in the way a dagger was calm… sleek, cold, and near a throat.

"Block C. Now." She ordered.

A shiver ran visibly through the lamia's coils. Even the orc swallowed, her bravado cracking at the raw authority dripping from the lieutenant's tone. Reluctantly, the trio slithered and stomped forward, casting backward glances filled with venom and suppressed curiosity.

Lilith's gaze slid to him; the glance was deeply measured, appraising, and faintly amused.

"Interesting approach. Threatening inmates directly usually ends poorly for humans here," something sharpened in her expression. Not quite approval. Not quite disapproval. Something in between, like a professional noting potential.

"Block C is this way. The three we're watching are Vex, Mara, and Kali - a wraith, a dragon-kin, and a hellhound. Their sudden cooperation defies years of documented hostility."

He continued walking, studying the glowing runes along the corridor walls as containment spells hummed like caged wasps.

"After the spectacle show with Minotaura, I figured a new approach was befitting; we're still testing the waters. And you're right, throwing a dragon with a wraith and a hound alliance sounds off."

He continued walking, expressions straight but with a subtle hint of flirt, "I say, I do believe you're more intimidating without the glasses, but I did like the look when you were wearing them. Just a thought," he casually shrugged his shoulders.

Lilith's step hitched for barely half a heartbeat, an imperceptible stutter only someone watching closely would notice. Her wings flicked once, betraying the unexpected hit to her usually immaculate composure.

When she looked at him again, her expression was colder, guarded… yet sharpened with unmistakable curiosity, "My previous position required a certain…scholarly appearance."

The faintest flicker of memory passed behind her violet eyes, gone as soon as it appeared, "Glasses are a liability in combat situations. Sentiment has no place in security operations." Lilith replied, her face back to normal, focused more on the truth right in front of her.

Block C loomed ahead, heavier walls reinforced with layered enchantments that glowed like veins of molten metal beneath the stone. Guard presence doubled. The magical hum thickened.

Through viewing windows reinforced with runic steel, he caught glimpses of its inhabitants: A gorgon meditating in her cell, stone fragments circling her head like obedient satellites.

An Arachne was weaving a pattern of silk so arcane it glowed a soft blue. A banshee quietly hummed to herself, distorting the air with low resonance.

Lilith gestured toward a common area at the far end.

There, at a table conspicuously isolated from the others, sat three inmates whose alliance made the wardens nervous.

Vex, the wraith, flickered in and out of corporeality, her translucent form phasing through the table as though the physical world were an inconvenience.

Mara, the dragon-kin, polished her copper-gleaming scales absentmindedly as she watched him with reptilian scrutiny.

Kali, the hellhound, drummed clawed fingers against the metal surface, embers rising from her fur with every irritated huff.

Lilith spoke softly, though her warning was unmistakable, "Your task begins now. I'll be monitoring from the observation deck." Her wings folded sharply behind her, forming a silhouette of controlled menace, "Don't get yourself killed. The paperwork would be…inconvenient."

He lowered his voice, leaning in just slightly, "Thank you," he lowly whispered, "and don't rush in to save my hide quickly, let me cook a little."

A spark of amusement crossed Lilith's gaze, a gaze that was fleeting yet unmistakably present, "How…interesting. Perhaps you do understand how things work here after all." She stepped back, wings shifting to create distance between them, "The observation deck has blind spots. Use them wisely."

She departed as her tail curled with an ambiguous flick… half warning, half challenge. The heavy security door sealed behind her with a hiss, leaving him alone in the charged atmosphere of Block C.

His approach did not go unnoticed.

From the inmates, Vex turned first, her hollow eyes focusing with unnatural clarity despite lacking pupils. Her voice echoed; it was layered, like multiple beings speaking through one throat, "Look, sisters…fresh meat walks willingly into the wolves' den."

The hellhound Kali scoffed, ember-flecked breath fogging the table's surface with heat. But it was the dragon-kin who rose ever so slightly, intrigued by his presence.

"Human. Male." Kali inhaled slowly, nostrils flaring, "The Warden's new project, I presume?"

He answered without hesitation, "See, I thought it was the scales, but I like you already, dragon. "Project" Just sounds better than such other terms."

Mara's scaled lips curled in a half-threat display and half-smile. revealing serrated, glimmering teeth that caught the overhead lights like polished blades. Her copper scales shifted subtly across her shoulders and arms, rippling with iridescent hues each time she breathed. The movement created a faint, metallic susurrus, as though her very skin whispered warnings to anyone foolish enough to provoke her

"Project. Toy. Tool. Experiment," Mara tasted each word slowly, deliberately, her voice vibrating with an internal heat that was neither fully human nor fully dragon. "The Warden collects interesting things. Few survive her...attention," her gaze remained fixated on him.

Kali, seated beside her, let out a sharp snort that ignited a spray of embers from her nostrils. Smoke curled upward from her russet fur, the strands glowing like heated wires as her irritation deepened. Her muscular arms crossed over her chest, thick, powerful limbs barely contained by the reinforced fabric of her altered prison uniform.

"He smells of the lieutenant," Kali's amber eyes narrowed to molten slits, burning into him with animalistic scrutiny, "her scent is all over him."

Before he could respond, the temperature dropped in a way that bypassed the skin and struck straight into the bones.

Vex drifted upward.

Her wraithlike body shimmered in and out of existence, a semi-corporeal fog that obeyed its own gravity. Her movements were slow, fluid, eerie. When she ghosted around the table, frost cracked across the metal surface, spidering outward from where her intangible form brushed through solid matter.

"The question isn't what he is..." Vex's ethereal whisper came from behind his ear, despite her hovering several feet in front of him. Shadows bent strangely around her presence, "It's what he wants from us."

He met the hellhound's fiery stare without blinking, letting his gaze shift, darkening, deepening, turning from human black to ruby red. He didn't look away once, even as he spoke sideways, addressing the wraith.

Without breaking the challenging stare of the hellhound, he transitioned his black eyes to ruby. "My dear whisper, if you had form, I'd say I like the feel of you that close, touching me, but it's sad you don't," he tilted his head slightly toward the other way, still eyeing the hound.

Vex materialized further, her edges sharpening, her face taking on more defined contours. Her form solidified just long enough for the impression of a cold hand to graze across his shoulder.

"Bold little human…" her voice fractured into layered echoes, as though dozens of unseen mouths whispered the same words from every shadow, "I can have form when I choose. The question is whether you'd survive my touch."

Kali's growl deepened, rolling through the room like distant thunder. Her fur crackled as the heat in her spread outward, reacting instinctively to his shifting eyes. She leaned forward, claws digging into the table, molten sparks dripping from her fingertips.

"Your eyes…" her nostrils flared again, inhaling sharply, her breath smoky and hot, "not fully human after all."

Mara watched him as if studying an artifact newly unearthed. Her forked tongue flickered briefly, tasting the electricity in the air, tasting him.

"Interesting. The Warden's new pet has secrets," she gestured to the empty space at their table, palm open in an invitation that felt equal parts welcoming and predatory, "sit. Tell us why you're really in Block C, watching us."

The surrounding inmates had grown quiet, their muttering dying into a low hum of anticipation. More eyes turned toward the table, curious, wary, eager for violence or gossip, depending on species.

He let a slow, sharp smile reveal a hint of fangs before glancing down at the offered seat, "This is making sense more and more. You are the wisdom, the brute beautiful red hound is the muscle, and I'll presume the wraith is the collector idealist." He finally took a seat there, "I think introductions are in order, and then enough flirting, we can get to business as I would like to do."

The three exchanged a brief but potent look, one that was born from mutual necessity, forged in a hostile environment where alliances were

215

rare and betrayal common. The unspoken communication between them revealed something dangerous in its unity.

Mara tapped a taloned finger against the table, each click sending faint vibrations through the metal. She held herself with regal poise, her copper scales glimmering like forged armor. "Perceptive. Though I prefer 'strategist' to 'wisdom'," her voice thrummed with controlled power, "I am Mara Cinderclaw, former guardian of the Eastern Treasury."

Kali leaned forward, the heat radiating from her body rolling over the table in wavering waves. The tips of her fur smoked where it brushed the metal. "Kali Emberheart. Pack alpha. Convicted of..." she showed her fangs in a grin that was undeniably feral, "excessive force against royal guards. Seventeen counts."

The hellhound's eyes gleamed with pride rather than shame... her violent history worn like a badge.

Vex's form wavered again, half vapor, half woman. Her silhouette bends as though made of moonlight and frost. Portions of her body solidified long enough to reveal the sensual curves hidden beneath her spectral shimmer. The tattoos etched across her translucent skin coiled and slithered like living runes, shifting position with every pulse of her magic.

"I collect secrets, not ideals," her voice echoed with overlapping tones, the layered whispers threading through one another like a spell cast in sound, "Vex Shadow-whisper. Formerly court seer to Queen Lamashtu. Imprisoned for...accurate prophecies."

As she drifted closer, the temperature plummeted. Frost spiraled outward across the table under her presence, melting and reforming in rapid cycles as though the air itself struggled to decide whether to freeze or breathe, "now, little not-quite-human with the changing eyes...your turn. What business brings you to our table with the lieutenant's scent on your skin?"

He held Vex's hollow, many-directional attention for a beat, then shifted the weight of his stare to Kali, the hellhound, whose molten amber eyes had not left him. He tilted his head, gaze darkening, letting the ruby glow bleed slowly into his irises.

"I am, now, Liaison Scott. Convicted for something against a monster girl, but to be honest, just a demon who called foul against me when I broke up with her, but semantics. Now, my business with you, lovely…oh, you know what, an apology is in order."

He directed a deep stare at Vex, "Vex, I daresay when you do materialize flesh, you're actually curvaceous. I apologize for misjudging you. That was wrong. Now, the reason for being present in your lively lady's presence is the alliance I see and apparently already have a grasp on. It worries others about how unnatural it is."

"Since I'm…" he pointed both hands toward himself, "I'm unorthodox and unsealed as they come, I want to know why. Don't care for how. I love to see the unordinary entwine and blossom." This time, he smiled erratically.

Vex flickered… almost shocked for only a heartbeat, and her form grew briefly more corporeal. The contours of her hips, the arch of her waist, the line of her collarbone sharpened as though her body remembered what it meant to be whole. The frost around her thickened, threading lace-like patterns across the metal table.

"Flattery won't save you if you're playing both sides, little liaison," yet her voice carried an undertone of interest, something appreciative hidden beneath the warning, "though I do appreciate…recognition."

Mara shifted, her talons tapping a slow, steady beat against the metal. It was not impatience but calculation, a signal her companions recognized instantly.

Kali's massive form adjusted subtly, her body angling to block the nearest enchanted camera. Her fur glowed faintly with ember-light as she leaned in, reducing the external line of sight to their table.

"Unnatural alliances form when survival demands it. The question is whether you're here to disrupt or…participate," Mara searched his eyes for answers, maybe a solid hint of truth.

Kali inhaled deeply, her nostrils widening as she drank in his scent. The heat rolling off her smoldering coat bathed the nearby table edge in orange light.

She examined him with sharpened suspicion, her claws tapping once against her bicep, "he smells of truth and lies mixed together," her voice was rough, resonant. She added, "and something else. Something old."

Then Kali leaned closer, almost chest-to-chest, eager for more, nostrils flaring again as if searching for the answer in the air itself, "What are you really, Liaison Scott? Not a demon. Not fully human. Something…in between?"

The common area had gone tense and quiet around them. Conversations stuttered to a halt. Monsters who had previously pretended indifference now watched openly, their expressions sharpened with curiosity and the promise of trouble.

He held Kali's stare, unflinching, and spoke low enough that only the three could hear, "My lovely hound, keep that blocked so my lips can't be seen."

Kali moved instantly. She hellhound adjusted her stance, turning her broad shoulders toward the nearest vantage point. Her fur flared brighter, casting molten shadows across the floor as she became a living barrier between him and surveillance. Her tail swept behind him protectively, not for his safety, but to ensure privacy for the conversation about to unfold.

"Done," Kali's growl softened by a fraction, "now talk, strange one."

Mara folded her clawed fingers, elbows resting on the table in a posture that looked almost regal. Her copper scales flickered under the overhead lights like sunlit armor. "We don't trust easily here, liaison. Especially those who carry the lieutenant's scent yet speak of alliances."

Vex hovered lower, her ghostly form phasing halfway through the table as she bent closer. The runes in her translucent flesh glowed faintly blue, swirling like trapped constellations. "The walls have ears here…and eyes…and things with neither that still perceive," her whisper seemed to bypass his ears entirely, brushing across the inside of his skull like a cold fingertip, "choose your next words with exceptional care."

The three women watched him… the strategist, the alpha, and the seer. Each is dangerous, powerful, and clearly interested.

The weight of Block C seemed to press inward as he spoke, his voice calm, unrestrained, and sharp enough to cut through the stagnant air.

"I never choose anything carefully, for the truth isn't careful. Thus, the only thing I'm guilty of is bluntness. Your space, you have it is dangerous and worries the higher-ups. That's no lie, just what's hidden, again semantics, if you think omission is a lie, I am here to find out why, cuz there's no NEED for such an alliance, and I honestly see this could be beneficial not only on the inside but also the outside."

He paused for a moment to read the room, but continued without hesitation, "Now I'm about to make a dangerous move, and you're going to let me walk out of here. Kali, you sexy bitch you're not gonna like this, but in order for this to continue, I need you to go along with this."

The effect was immediate.

The air around the table thickened, heat from Kali's body rolling across the metal like volcanic breath. Her hackles rose in a halo of ember-lit fur. With a predatory snarl, she unsheathed her claws. *Click* the sound echoed in the room. The sharpened obsidian tips gouged tiny crescent scars into the reinforced steel.

"You're either very brave or very stupid," her voice was molten stone low, threatening, ready to erupt, "no one walks away after speaking to me like that."

Before that molten threat could ignite, Mara lifted a single scaled hand.

It wasn't loud. It wasn't forceful.

But it was a *dragon,* and Kali halted mid-growl.

Mara's copper scales shifted like plates of ancient armor, her pupils tightening into thin vertical slits as she examined him anew, recalculating, reassessing. "Let him finish. His…audacity…intrigues me," she gestured to Kali to let him speak.

A sudden drop in temperature whispered along his spine. Vex had drawn closer, her spectral silhouette forming behind him like a ghostly spine, her presence cold enough to raise bumps on his skin. Her translucent fingers hovered above his shoulder, the air around them crystallizing in fractal frost patterns.

"Beneficial, how, liaison? We aren't desperate enough to grasp at phantom opportunities." Her voice slipped through him like smoke and silk, every word carried on multiple echoing tones, one beside him, one behind him, one inside his own mind, "And what dangerous move could possibly make us allow you to simply…walk away?"

Beyond their table, Block C began shifting.

Some inmates stepped back, instinctively wary of the lethal potential forming between these four figures. Others, braver or more foolish, drifted closer to witness the spectacle, predatory eyes shining with the anticipation of violence, blood, and chaos.

Even the nearest guard hesitated, fingers brushing the baton at her hip but not daring to intervene.

No one willingly placed themselves between *these* three and their prey.

"All of you saw the challenge the other day against Minotaura, that wasn't a coincidence or a ploy." He spoke to everyone in the room, "As you'll see. I need to put on a spectacle to get me out, give everyone an insight, and a rule to get me back in. So before I make my move, I want to know, what's the end game, and will this alliance benefit generations to come?

It was as if the words themselves shifted the balance of the table.

Mara's drumming claws halted mid-tap.

The silence she left behind rang louder than the noise.

Her eyes narrowed into slits of molten amber, studying him with a predator's intellect, measuring not his strength, but the scope of his ambition.

"Generations? You speak as though our alliance extends beyond these walls," her voice dropped to a deeper, more dangerous register, "bold assumption."

Vex drifted closer still, her form flickering between states, solid enough to cast a shadow, ethereal enough that his breath fogged with each whisper of her movement. Frost spiraled outward from her fingertips, where they hovered over the metal table.

"He knows something, Mara. I can sense it," Vex's hollow eyes brightened with an eerie inner light, "the challenge against Minotaura was…unexpected. Calculated. Like the first move in a game we didn't know we were playing."

Kali inhaled sharply, nostrils flaring. Her powerful shoulders tensed, muscles coiling beneath her smoldering fur. She leaned forward until her burning gaze locked directly onto his, as though reading the truth in the vibrational tremors beneath his skin.

"Make your move then, liaison. But know that if it threatens what we've built…" her eyes dipped briefly to his throat, a silent promise of violence, "No one will find enough pieces to identify you."

A heavy silence followed.

Predatory. Charged.

Full of all the unspoken consequences of a wrong word or wrong breath.

Around them, Block C had frozen into a strange, waiting stillness, as if the entire prison had turned its gaze toward the small metal table where three monsters and one human balanced on the edge of something new and terribly significant.

The moment he began to speak, the air around their table tightened, pulled taut like a bowstring on the verge of snapping.

His voice cut clean through the tension, steady and unflinching, unfazed by the monsters staring him down, "I wish we could talk further on the matter, but my time is up."

He shifted his gaze from Mara to Kali, "Kali, my dear, I love your fur, and I truly mean it when I say I'm sorry for this and I will find a way to make it up to you at a later date before I'm pressed to return here…" The words struck the table like a thrown blade.

Kali's reaction was immediate, raw instinct and aggression sparking through every fiber of her body. Her fur bristled in a halo of molten ember-light, heat radiating from her as though a forge lay beneath her skin. Her claws curled against the floor, leaving scorched crescents in the stone.

"You wouldn't dare…" Kali felt more surprised than challenged.

221

Mara lunged, not with brute force but with the speed of a strategist who had already predicted the shape of his next move. Her scaled hand shot toward his arm. Too late by the blink of an eye. The dragon-kin's expression twisted with the sharp-edged fury of someone who understood the gambit even as it unfolded beyond her grasp.

"Stop him-" Mara exclaimed.

Vex's form unraveled into cold mist, shadows whispering as she rushed to envelop him. Her voice, dozens layered into one, brushed against his ears like frost creeping up a windowpane, "foolish liaison...the consequences..." She burst into something beyond stress.

The reaction rippled outward like an explosion.

Nearby inmates scattered, trampling benches, trays, and each other in their haste to escape the epicenter. Shouts erupted. A guard cursed. Somewhere above, an alarm wailed, first low, then rising, the harbinger of a facility-wide lockdown.

For a brief heartbeat, the alliance, Block C's most dangerous triumvirate, stood stunned, caught between fury and recognition of his audacity.

And then Mara's voice found him. Quiet, venomous, and full of promise, "Remember, liaison. We'll be waiting when they bring you back, and we'll have questions."

Boots thundered against the corridor. Guards surged toward the chaos, weapons primed, containment wards shimmering to life around the block. The air crackled with hostile magic and barely restrained force.

But he didn't flinch. Within an instant, he swept around Kali, grabbing her neck and lifting her off the ground. He applied all his pressure to hold her in place, but none with malicious intent.

He looked down at Mara, stealing a quick wink, then bellowing in a deep baritone, "Enough! My patience grows thin, and next, I return ALL of you better have a more well-behaved demeanor lest I am forced to return and the quote alliance is down a member!"

He looked around, then exclaimed, "Guards!" his voice echoed everywhere.

The motion was a blur. Sudden enough to stun even seasoned killers.

He moved with impossible precision, spinning behind Kali and seizing her throat in a single fluid sweep. The hellhound's feet left the ground, her powerful legs kicking, claws scraping at the air. Heat flared along his arm, her fire reacting instinctively to the restraint, but he held firm.

"Release...me..." The growl vibrated through her body and into his hand, embers erupting between her teeth. But beneath the rage, there was something else: shock, confusion, and perhaps even reluctant respect.

Mara froze mid-advance.

Her eyes, slitted and burning, met his as he winked. For the briefest of moments, her scowl faltered, revealing something almost amused. Almost approving, "Such arrogance will be your undoing, liaison," her words dripped with theatrical venom, but her gaze betrayed a spark of something far more dangerous: *intrigue*.

The nearest harpy guard skidded to a halt, feathers bristling, comms device crackling in her shaking hand.

"Situation in Block C! Liaison Scott engaging with high-risk inmates! Containment team required!" Guard Sylph alerted someone in a hurry.

Vex phased in and out of solidity, her silhouette stuttering with agitation. As she passed briefly through his shoulder, her voice seeped into his thoughts like cold fog, "Clever, liaison. We'll be waiting. The game advances..."

A new sound thundered into the block, the synchronized stomp of the Containment Unit.

Lieutenant Arachne, towering, chitin-armored, eight-eyed, emerged at their head. Her sharpened limbs clicked with cool precision as she took in the sight before her.

"Secure THIS one from my grasp and maintain a perimeter. I must report back to Lieutenant Lilith!" He stood awaiting Kali to be taken away from him.

Lieutenant Arachne moved forward with clinical predatory grace. Her multiple arms unfolded the moment she stepped into range, deploying restraints of enchanted mesh designed specifically for hellhound musculature and heat levels.

"Release the prisoner to my custody, Liaison." Her voice was sharp, metallic, and absolute: "Your…unconventional methods are noted."

As he loosened his grip, four armored guards closed in around Kali. Fire-resistant cuffs snapped into place with practiced efficiency. Kali allowed it, but her burning eyes never left him.

"We'll continue our discussion soon, liaison," she said as smoke curled between her words.

Mara stood perfectly still as the guards flooded the common area, her copper-scaled form radiating a predatory calm. Even surrounded by armed containment officers and panicked inmates, she held her ground with regal poise. The shifting light of the facility glinted along the iridescent plates of her skin, each subtle movement catching his eye. When she inclined her head, just barely, it was a gesture so minute no one else would have noticed, but unmistakably directed at him.

Lieutenant Arachne moved with her characteristic mechanical grace, multiple limbs spreading outward to reinforce the perimeter.

Her eight dark eyes remained fixed on him with a mixture of suspicion and clinical interest, and she said, "Lieutenant Lilith is expecting your report. This…incident will require thorough documentation."

Arachne's gaze sharpened as containment nets snapped into place around the now-restrained Kali, "Move now, before these inmates decide to escalate further."

The containment team shifted to form a secure corridor. Guards barked sharp orders; inmates whispered feverishly. A ripple of attention passed through the crowded block, not fear, not respect, but something else. HE had become a vector of disruption, a phenomenon worth watching. Few in Monster Girl Prison managed to stand out among monsters, but he had done so twice in less than a day.

He slipped between armored shoulders before the guards even finished forming ranks, moving with the urgency of someone who understood exactly how thin the line was between survival and annihilation. The corridor swallowed him in cold fluorescent light, the sound of sealing doors thundering behind him as though the prison itself exhaled, locking away the chaos he'd sparked.

The administrative wing greeted him with an entirely different flavor of danger, quiet, controlled, suffocatingly precise. Every guard here moved like a blade waiting to be drawn. Every camera was tracked with sentient awareness.

At the threshold between domains stood Lieutenant Lilith. Her silhouette was unmistakable, every sign of perfection was there… curved horns, folded black wings, uniform stretched taut across her immaculate form. The harsh lighting cut sharp angles across her features, making the violet of her eyes glow like shards of amethyst. She watched him approach with the kind of interest usually reserved for prey that had unexpectedly bitten back.

"Quite the performance, Liaison," Lilith said, her voice dripped with something between amusement and admonishment, a velvet blade, "creating incidents with our most volatile inmates has consequences…though perhaps that was precisely your intention?"

Her lips curved into a knowing smile, the faintest glimmer of fang catching the light, "My office. Now."

She didn't wait to see if he followed; she simply turned, expecting obedience like she always did.

And of course, he fell into step behind her, watching the hypnotic sway of her wings with every calculated movement of her hips. Lilith marched through the administrative corridors as though she owned the foundations beneath them, and perhaps she did. Guards straightened reflexively upon sight of her, each one careful not to meet her eyes for more than a second.

At a heavy obsidian door carved with shifting arcane sigils, she pressed her palm to the scanner. The magic recognized her authority instantly. The door slid open with a whispering hiss.

"Enter." Her tone accepted no argument, just obedience.

The office beyond was a stark contradiction to the chaos outside, clean, perfectly ordered, every surface a testament to her discipline and her brutal efficiency. Her desk, metal and rune-etched, commanded the center of the room. Behind it, towering panes of enchanted glass displayed

225

the sprawling prison yard below, where dawn's early haze painted everything in muted gray.

Lilith closed the door with a flick of her tail. Deliberate, graceful, and final, every detail defined her personality.

Then she turned, arms crossing beneath her chest as she leaned back against the desk. The posture made her wings flare slightly, framing her silhouette like the gates of an infernal cathedral.

"That little display was either remarkably brave or catastrophically foolish," her eyes raked over him, studying every detail, "You've now fully caught the attention of the most lethal alliance in this facility. Was that your intention all along, Liaison?"

He breathed a deep sigh, "Yes, actually it was." he straightened up, "She had VERY nice fur, and I didn't want it getting roughed up too bad. Also, the idea is called baiting as a succubus. This technique is familiar or SHOULD be familiar to you."

The shift in Lilith's expression was subtle but unmistakable.

Her violet eyes sharpened, first with offense, then with realization, and finally with something darkly amused. The slightest flare of her nostrils, the quiet unfurling of her wings, the way her tail tip curled behind her, it was all instinctive, predatory, dangerous.

Lieutenant Lilith regarded him with a low, velvety chuckle, the sound curling from her lips like smoke, "baiting? How…primitive." Her amusement sharpened into something sinfully knowing, "Though effective, I suppose."

She moved around her desk with a predator's fluid poise, every step controlled, deliberate, her tail swaying behind her in lazy arcs that betrayed a simmering confidence. The dim office lighting slid across the smooth curve of her horns as she settled into her chair.

With a graceful flick of her hand, she gestured to the seat across from her as she spoke to him, "The hellhound's fur is indeed… remarkable. Though I question if that was your only motivation." She leaned forward, resting her chin upon interlaced fingers, gaze razor-keen and unblinking, "You've manipulated the prison's most dangerous alliance into revealing

226

their interest in you. Clever, but dangerous. Now tell me, what information did you extract before your theatrical finale?"

The room seemed to grow warmer with her focus alone. Monitors behind her cast flickering images across the walls: Kali being dragged back to her cell in restraints, Mara standing in silent, simmering thought, and Vex dissolving in and out of solidity like cold smoke, deciding whether to exist.

He met Lilith's stare, "My methods are my own, and only I have the ability to pull them off. Just as you have the ability to seduce confidently, I can seduce confidently as well, but for information. We won't discuss how I pissed both a succubus and an incubus off at the same time, haha."

Lilith's smile sharpened, fangs glinting beneath the harsh lights. Her violet eyes narrowed to predatory slits before widening with intrigue, like a huntress spotting a quarry that had just proven more interesting than expected, "pissing off a succubus and incubus simultaneously? That's…impressive, even by my standards."

She straightened, her leathery wings folding neatly behind her with military precision, "I do adore a man with confidence, but don't mistake my appreciation for weakness, Liaison."

With a single swipe of her claw, she activated a screen embedded in the desk. Lines of text illuminated his file, arrival information, conviction details, psychological markers, each line a reminder of why he was here…and how he wasn't supposed to survive long.

"Your methods are certainly…unique. Perhaps too valuable to waste in the general population," a slow tap of one claw on the desktop punctuated her meaning: "The Warden herself has taken notice of today's incident."

Lilith circled the desk again, stepping close enough that her supernatural aura radiated over him, warm, intoxicating, and inherently dangerous. She stopped just before him, her proximity intentionally oppressive.

"Consider this a formal notice: you're being reassigned to special operations within the prison. Your talents appear wasted on standard liaison duties."

A smile touched her lips, one that never reached her eyes, "Report to the East Wing tomorrow at 0600. The Warden wishes to speak with you…personally."

He matched her tone with calm efficiency, "fair enough. Do you have nothing else for me? Or should I go report to the dragon in the rehab wing to assess another inmate?"

At the mention of the dragon, her wings stiffened ever so slightly, the feathers at their tips twitching before she reined her features back into ice-cold professionalism. Her hand slipped into a drawer, retrieving a small obsidian tablet which she slid across to him.

"Ah, yes, Warden Tiamat's pet project," her tone dipped toward disdain, polished to near perfection, "rehabilitation is… an optimistic approach for most of our residents."

A touch of her claw awakened the tablet, revealing a dossier, an image of a lamia with frost-blue scales, eyes like cut ice, and a history written in blood.

"Inmate 3721, Naia Frostcoil. Former assassin for the Serpent's Guild. Specialized in infiltration and poison craft. Currently undergoing experimental rehabilitation therapy under Dr. Ryujin's supervision." Her lips curled subtly, "our dragon doctor has… unorthodox methods."

Lilith adjusted her collar, the movement taut with annoyance she didn't bother hiding, "You're authorized to observe, not interfere. Ryujin guards her patients jealously, especially this one." Her gaze sharpened once more, "Remember, tomorrow, 0600, East Wing. Do not be late. The Warden's patience is legendary only in its absence."

He tilted his head, "Awesome. Have you nothing for me?"

One perfect eyebrow rose as her gaze deepened, the violet brightening like amethyst catching fire. Without breaking eye contact, she reached into her desk again and withdrew a small metallic pin, intricately carved in the shape of a stylized eye, a purple gemstone gleaming at its center like a shard of her own stare.

She held it between two fingers, letting the dim light cling to its edges.

Lieutenant Lilith held out the small metallic pin between two clawed fingers, the gemstone at its center glinting under the office lights like a watchful eye, "Take this. It's a communication device and…insurance policy."

Her voice purred with a dangerous blend of professionalism and amusement as she extended it toward him. The pin's polished metal reflected faint purple light, a subtle reminder of who controlled this office, and who controlled him.

"Should you find yourself in a situation where even your silver tongue fails you, press the center gem. It creates a localized disruption field that affects most monster species." She crossed the space between them with silent, predatory grace.

Her natural succubus aura, temptation carefully leashed behind iron discipline, brushed against him as she reached up and pinned the device to his collar herself. Her fingers lingered for a heartbeat longer than necessary, cool and deliberate, as though marking him with more than just a tool.

"Consider it professional courtesy from one… manipulator to another." Lilith's fangs flashed briefly as she smiled, "Now go. Ryujin despises tardiness almost as much as the Warden does."

With that, Lilith turned away, her focus shifting back to her glowing bank of monitors. She dismissed him without a word, yet the weight of her attention still clung to the air like incense.

The obsidian door slid open on command, revealing the stark corridor outside.

He picked up the pin lightly, "Yes, ma'am," he murmured, turning to leave.

But before stepping fully through the doorway, he paused. The monitors reflected her clearly; Lieutenant Lilith's violet eyes were not on the screens at all. They were fixed on him, sharp with curiosity, suspicion, and something far less definable. At the moment she realized he had seen her reflection watching him, he smiled… silently, knowing, and then stepped through the doorway.

The door sealed shut behind him with a cold metallic hiss.

Out in the corridor, the administrative wing felt sterile and watchful. Two harpy guards flanked the hall, talons clicking against the polished floor as their predatory gazes tracked his movement. Their wings remained folded, but the tension in their shoulders betrayed readiness for violence.

Ahead, a flickering holographic sign projected directions in the dim light:

East Wing - Administrative Offices

West Wing - Rehabilitation Center

North Wing - Maximum Security

South Wing - General Population

The pin on his collar pulsed once, warm, subtle, like a heartbeat acknowledging its new host.

Somewhere deeper in the prison, a distant alarm wailed before abruptly cutting off, absorbed back into the institution's never-ending cycle of chaos and control.

He exhaled once, "West Wing it is."

The corridor toward the Rehabilitation Center darkened slightly as he advanced.

The West Wing felt nothing like the rest of the fortress. Cerulean lights hummed overhead, washing the walls in a calm, eerie glow. The scent of medicinal herbs mingled with incense; atmospheric sound dampeners muffled distant shouts into a dull heartbeat rhythm.

Despite its softer presentation, security was everywhere, reinforced doors, embedded runes, and discreetly armed staff.

At the wing's central hub, she waited.

Dr. Ryujin was impossible to miss. A towering dragon-woman with scales shimmering in waves of emerald and icy blue. Her imposing silhouette filled the space like a coiled storm. The pristine white lab coat strained subtly against her powerful shoulders, while a thick tail swept behind her with a serpent's rhythmic confidence. Golden eyes, slit-pupiled and ancient, flicked up the moment he entered.

"The human liaison arrives." The doctor spoke without even glancing fully at him, her nostrils flaring as she inhaled, "I can smell Lilith's perfume on you. Did she give you the standard warnings about my methods?"

Finally, she lifted her gaze fully to him, analyzing him in a single glance with clinical precision that felt like being dissected on the spot, "I assume you're here about Naia. Follow me, and touch nothing," Her tail slapped once against the polished floor in irritated emphasis before she turned toward the secured corridor.

He fell into step behind her without a word.

Dr. Ryujin led him through a descending sequence of secure doorways, each checkpoint demanding a different form of verification from the ancient dragon woman. At the first threshold, she pressed a clawed fingertip to a glowing sensor that flared with green arcs. At the second, she exhaled a precise ribbon of azure flame into a cupped receptor, which hummed in recognition. The third required her to trace a sigil into the air, her talon carving luminous shapes that dissolved into the locking mechanism.

With each barrier crossed, the temperature dropped further. The warm, herb-scented air of the rehabilitation wing thinned to crisp cold, until his breath rose in faint white clouds. Frost crackled beneath the reinforced flooring, spreading delicate veins of ice beneath the luminous panels.

She halted before a heavy observation window that was forged from dragon-glass and arcane steel. Beyond it stretched a chamber unlike any conventional cell; it was an engineered habitat split starkly between opposing worlds.

One half was bloomed in humid and dense tropical greenery: broad leaves dripping condensation, vines curling from enchanted soil, small spores drifting in the filtered light. The other half glistened in pristine arctic purity: jagged ice structures, drifting snowflakes, and a frozen floor that sparkled like powdered diamonds. Between the extremes sat a narrow pool where steaming tropics met icy tundra, the surface swirling with tendrils of mist.

Discreet sensors embedded in the walls pulsed faintly, tracking every fluctuation within the ecosystem.

Dr. Ryujin lifted a claw to the glass.

"Naia Frostcoil. Rare subspecies of lamia adapted to cold climates." Her finger tapped lightly, producing a crystalline chime, "her file says 'assassin,' but that's insufficient. She was an artist... thirty-seven confirmed kills across three kingdoms, never the same method twice. She can control her body temperature at will, making her nearly undetectable by thermal imaging."

Movement flickered within the icy half of the chamber.

A slender figure slid into view from behind a pillar of sculpted frost.

Naia emerged with the effortless grace of a creature born between extremes, her serpentine lower body shimmering in shades of pale blue and white, each scale traced with delicate frost patterns that reflected shifting light.

Her upper body appeared young, almost delicate, though scales dusted her shoulders and spine like jewels placed with meticulous artistry. Her face held an unsettling contrast: youthful in shape, ancient in gaze. Her eyes were arctic blue, crystalline and depthless, carrying experiences that no lamia of her apparent age should possess.

Dr. Ryujin's voice darkened, "Traditional incarceration failed. She escaped twice, killed three guards. My approach is different; I give her an environment she won't want to leave and a purpose she can channel her skills toward."

Then her tone dipped lower, "The Warden authorized my experimental therapy as a last resort before execution."

As he maintained eye contact through the glass, Naia suddenly froze mid-movement. Every coil, every muscle went still, like a hunting serpent locking onto prey. Her gaze snapped upward, piercing through the observation glass with uncanny precision, though visibility should have been impossible from her side.

Her lips curved slowly, an expression not of warmth but deliberate calculation. The faint blue luminescence on her fangs flickered with something between amusement and threat.

He held her stare, "Interesting."

Dr. Ryujin's brow furrowed, her horns tilting slightly as she made quick notes on her hovering tablet, "Fascinating. She shouldn't be able to detect observers." She tapped the device with a talon, narrowing her golden eyes, "her sensory adaptations continue to evolve beyond predictions."

Naia glided forward, serpentine coils whispering across ice as frost bloomed in delicate fractals wherever she passed. Upon reaching the window, she pressed one slender, blue-tinged hand against the glass. Cold radiated outward in a hypnotic spread as the crystalline handprint expanded into intricate branching patterns, fractals blooming like frozen flowers.

Dr. Ryujin continued, her voice now sounded softer with reluctant admiration; "My rehabilitation focuses on redirecting her hunting instincts toward productive applications. She's been helping develop non-lethal capture techniques for other dangerous inmates."

A rare warmth touched the dragon's tone, "she requires intellectual stimulation and purpose, not mere containment."

Naia's eyes never left his.

With slow, precise motion, she dragged a fingertip across the frost, carving an elegant symbol, an ancient rune with curves flowing like serpents and angles sharp as ice shards. Her expression was not hostile, but intensely curious, as though dissecting him through sheer focus.

He crossed his arms, resting his chin lightly on a propped fist, never breaking eye contact, "She's beauty and grace but essentially kills when threatened, as a hit under order, or predominantly out of sheer boredom to test a new skill."

Dr. Ryujin paused mid-note.

Her golden eyes sharpened in interest as she regarded him anew, her tail curling slowly behind her with thoughtful weight.

"Your assessment is remarkably accurate. You've read her file, but you understand her beyond what's documented." Her clawed fingers tapped rhythmically against the side of the tablet. "Most see only the cold-blooded killer. Few recognize the artist seeking canvas and critique."

Beyond the glass, Naia's expression shifted with sudden predatory precision. Her serpentine tail coiled beneath her, compacting her lithe form in a gesture somewhere between readiness and fascination. With delicate, controlled movements, she traced another ancient symbol across the frost-coated pane, more intricate than the last. Cold thickened visibly around her fingers, ice crystals blooming in the air despite the chamber's environmental stabilizers.

Dr. Ryujin observed the phenomenon with sharp interest, her golden eyes narrowing, her tail swishing once in a rare display of excitement.

"She's communicating. Unusual," Though her voice remained clinical, the slight lift in her tone betrayed genuine intrigue, "she typically ignores new observers completely. You've caught her interest."

The frost pattern spread farther, sweeping across the entire viewing pane in an expanding wave of crystalline artistry. At first, it appeared chaotic, but then the shimmering frost resolved, impossibly, into a near-perfect rendering of his silhouette. Only someone studying him with surgical precision could have achieved such detail.

Below the icy portrait, Naia shaped delicate frost-script in an ancient tongue. Dr. Ryujin leaned toward the window, her brow arching high as she translated.

"' The warm-blood sees. Bring him closer.' Rather presumptuous of her," A soft plume of steam escaped between the dragon-woman's teeth as she considered the message, "though perhaps valuable for my research…"

He stepped forward, closing the distance between himself and the frigid barrier until only inches separated him from the frost-laced pane. His breath fogged the glass as faint heat rose through his chest.

Then, deliberate and controlled, thin tendrils of flame escaped from his nostrils, snorting forward in a subtle display as he held Naia's gaze, "She's intrigued, but I'd say someone's tried forcing themselves onto her, which drove her to her likeness of assassin work. Beautiful specimen

234

indeed should've been given nurturing and companionship, but if wishes were fishes…"

Dr. Ryujin jolted, not away from Naia but from him. Her pupils contracted sharply, the dragonic instinct in her recoiling from the unexpected fire that had slipped from a man she believed wholly human. She took an involuntary half-step back, the scales along her jaw shimmering as her posture shifted between clinical and primal.

"You're…not entirely human," Ryujin's voice dropped to a near-whisper, cracks showing in her normally unshakable composure, "your file said nothing of draconic heritage."

She recovered quickly, smoothing her lab coat with clawed fingertips as her expression sharpened again into professional interest, "This changes the parameters considerably."

Beyond the glass, Naia reacted instantly and intensely. Her pupils dilated until her irises nearly disappeared, the arctic blue swallowed by expanding rings of black. She pressed even closer to the barrier, both palms flattening against it, frost spiraling outward in rapid fractals. Her serene, masklike neutrality fractured, replaced by unmistakable excitement. It struck the air like static, alive and charged.

Her symbols began to multiply at dizzying speed, her fingers moving with artistic frenzy.

Dr. Ryujin's eyes swept the meanings as fast as she could interpret them, "she's asking if you're dragon-kin. And…something else I can't quite translate." Her tail curled in fascination, "Your insight about her past is also correct. Her file is classified, but there was indeed a formative trauma involving a nobleman who…"

She hesitated, jaw tightening as she selected her words with care, "…who believed rare specimens like her existed for his collection. She escaped. He didn't survive the night."

Naia began an undulating motion with her serpentine coils, rolling them in rhythmic patterns that matched the frost symbols, movements reminiscent of ancient draconic greeting rituals rarely preserved in modern practice. The gesture radiated respect, curiosity… and something deeper.

He raised his brows, watching her intense focus with a half-smirk, "didn't think she liked me that much, talk about lust at first sight." he chuckled quietly, "and I thought I was bad or alone in that aspect. Either that or she wants a kill competition chase…could be misreading this entirely."

Dr. Ryujin's laugh came unexpectedly, a sharp, delighted bark that revealed the serration of her dragon fangs. The sound echoed strangely in the cold chamber, "Neither lust nor bloodlust, though both drive her kind. It's recognition."

She leaned closer to the frost-covered window, studying the symbols with deepening scholarly hunger, "These are ancient greeting rituals reserved for those considered equals. In her centuries of captivity, she's classified everyone as either prey or obstacle. You've inadvertently presented as neither."

Naia pressed both hands more firmly against the glass, symbols spiraling outward until the observation chamber's temperature began to destabilize. Cold alarms flickered red on Dr. Ryujin's tablet.

"Fascinating. She's using her cryokinesis at unprecedented levels," her eyes gleamed like molten gold, "I should terminate this interaction before she overcomes the containment barriers, but…"

Curiosity warred visibly with protocol, her tail lashing once in indecision, "Perhaps a controlled introduction would yield valuable research data. The rehabilitation implications could be significant."

A soft chime from the monitoring system drew Dr. Ryujin's attention. The crystalline symbols blooming across the frost-glazed pane had shifted again. Naia now etched what was unmistakably a question in the ancient script, accompanied by a perfectly rendered frost-image of flame erupting from jaws. The accuracy left little doubt as to whom she referenced.

The dragon-woman's tail swayed with rising scientific excitement.

"She's asking about your lineage," Her voice deepened, vibrating faintly with draconic resonance, "this could be the breakthrough I've been seeking in her case. Would you consider a supervised interaction? I can guarantee your safety…to reasonable parameters."

He didn't break eye contact with the lamia behind the glass. The frost-patterns seemed to pulse in response to his attention.

"I would like that," he said calmly, not looking away, "but I warn you there will be blood and you cannot intervene at first draw otherwise you WILL have a full-scale prison break on your hands." Only then did he turn toward the doctor, revealing eyes glowing ruby with a blue halo.

Dr. Ryujin inhaled sharply as the heterochromatic glow struck her, an unmistakably draconic signature. Her scholarly composure cracked like thin ice, "Blood ritual. Of course."

Her voice dropped to a lower, more ancient register, "first blood establishes hierarchy without requiring death. Ancient, but effective."

She swiftly tapped a complex sequence into her tablet. Several security barriers powered down with mechanized groans, lights dimming as layered protocols disengaged, "I'll allow it, but containment gases remain on standby. She's taken three guard lives already."

A reinforced door slid open with a heavy pneumatic hiss. Frost leaked from the threshold like breath exhaled by a slumbering beast.

Ryujin gestured with the solemnity of one predator acknowledging another, "Enter alone. I'll observe from here." Her claws clicked once against the reinforced glass, "Should you require extraction, the safe word is 'avalanche.' It will trigger immediate sedation protocols."

The chamber beyond swallowed him in cold. His breath fogged instantly, forming clouds that drifted through the blue-tinged air. The two ecosystems, the arctic and the tropical, steamed faintly where they met, creating an eerie veil between climates.

Naia waited precisely at that border, positioned in the formal coils of ancient lamia combat initiation. Her tail formed concentric rings beneath her, perfect in discipline and symmetry. Up close, her beauty was almost unreal... frost-white scales shimmered with opalescent hues beneath the ambient glow, and every strand of platinum hair shed tiny crystals that sublimated into the air.

Her eyes widened at his approach. She tasted the air with her forked tongue, assessing everything. Heat, scent, and intent.

When she spoke, her voice was melodic and edged with centuries of silence.

"Fire-blood with winter eyes. They said humans were unworthy prey." Naia lifted herself higher on her coiled tail, bringing her face level with his, "Show me your worth, half-breed. First blood speaks truth when tongues lie."

He moved before the final syllable finished vibrating through the cold air.

In a single decisive motion, he closed the distance, seized her throat, and threw her backward toward the center of the chamber. Frost exploded outward on impact, snowflake fractals blooming across the floor like shattered glass. He advanced smoothly, taking a wide martial stance, low, grounded, but narrower than traditional sumo, honed for speed over brute force.

"I should already be drinking you, but I'm courteous." His voice rumbled through the frigid air, "Now we're even. Never stand too close, rookie move, ice beauty."

Naia's eyes widened... not in fear, but in something far more dangerous: *delight*. A thin strand of silvery-blue blood glistened at her lip, self-inflicted during impact. She touched it with two fingers, marveling at it.

"So, the fire-blood has proper fangs after all," her smile spread, stretching past human limits to reveal the rows of fine predatory teeth behind her visible incisors, "no one has drawn my blood in decades."

She rose again, but her posture changed. Her movements unfurled like ribbons of water across ice, fluid, reverent, measured. Every coil of her tail glided around him, maintaining the ceremonial distance that signaled respect in the old ways. The temperature dropped sharply; frost crackled beneath her passing, ice crystals forming and shattering with each shift of her body.

"I've killed forty-seven before you. None understood the old ways," she tapped her bleeding lip with satisfaction. "First blood has spoken. What is the fire-blood desire of Naia? Knowledge? Combat training? Perhaps..." Her voice softened into a whisper, breath curling like fog around him, "…something warmer amid my cold?"

From behind the observation glass, Dr. Ryujin's voice crackled through the intercom, still clinical, but vibrating with barely contained excitement.

"Remarkable," Ryujin said, "She's displaying submission behavior I've only seen in theoretical texts. The hierarchy is established without requiring serious injury. Subject appears receptive to direction."

He stepped forward, the cold air coiling around him like a living thing. Naia's eyes remained fixed on him, unblinking, luminous, hungry in a way that was not immediately predatory but undeniably primal.

"I demand your respect and your quell, draw my blood and," his gaze dropped deliberately, briefly, to the intimate scales beneath her serpentine torso before cutting back to her eyes, "we'll discuss if you want that or not." He shifted his stance, purposefully leaving a blind spot open.

Naia's pupils tightened to slivers. She saw the opening, of course she did, but instead of lunging in ignorance, a slow, delighted smile curved her pale-blue lips.

"Clever fire-blood…" Naia purred, her voice sounded deep, vibrating in melody from the chest rather than the throat. She coiled downward, preparing, "offering what appears weakness while setting a trap. I haven't been properly challenged in centuries."

Her strike came like a flash of winter lightning. She bypassed the blind spot completely, choosing a far more intimate challenge: her fangs grazed the skin of his forearm with surgical precision. A single bead of crimson welled up, thin, controlled, intentional. A promise rather than an attack.

She slid back with serpentine grace.

"Blood answers blood," her silvery-blue tongue flicked across her lip, tasting his heat, "The scales balance between us," her gaze dipped once more toward the delicate place he had glanced before, her smile curving with new intent.

"My respect is earned. My quell…" ice crystals shimmered in her hair as she bowed her head a fraction, "…is granted. What other hungers would you satisfy, fire-blood?"

From the intercom, Ryujin's astonishment deepened into reverence, "Unbelievable. She's completed a full blood-pact ritual. In fifteen years of containment, she's never recognized any being as an equal. This is unprecedented."

The chamber's frost retreated as Naia slithered closer, her movements fluid rather than combative, the coils of her body easing in what passed for relaxation among her kind. The temperature lifted by degrees as she consciously suppressed her cryokinetic field, a gesture that, for Naia, was as intimate as lowering one's guard.

He walked toward her slowly, deliberately, licking the thin crimson line on his arm with a deliberate show of acknowledgment.

"My, I missed out, did I?" he murmured, eyes flicking knowingly to the faint break in her tail scales, "Alas, no blood."

Then he stepped close enough for heat to radiate against her cold-bloomed skin, the adrenaline in him pumping hard enough to warm the air around them. His breath quickened, his arousal unmistakable, "Guess it's your turn, Naia."

Her pupils blew wide, swallowing the icy blue of her irises. Her powerful tail rippled beneath her as she slid forward, the faint crackle of frost beneath her coils echoing across the chamber. When she lifted a taloned finger to the old injury in her tail, she pressed, just hard enough to break her own skin. Silvery-blue blood welled up, crystallizing in the cold.

"The hunt trembles between us now, fire-blood," her forked tongue tasted the steam rising from his heat, her breath turning to mist between them, "Your heat… it calls to ancient hungers. In my home glaciers, we devoured worthy prey completely."

Her gaze dipped boldly to the evidence of his desire, "Some parts more… thoroughly than others."

She slid closer, tail slowly encircling him, not in aggression, but in a claiming spiral. Where her cold met his warmth, the air danced with rolling mist. Her scales released a faint, intoxicating pheromone, sweet, primal, unmistakably a mating scent.

Above, in the observation deck, Dr. Ryujin scrambled between duty and scientific rapture. She dimmed visual monitors to thermal silhouettes only, "I'll...maintain minimal observation protocols. This development is unprecedented in captivity records. Her biochemistry is already showing remarkable stabilization patterns."

Naia's cold hands pressed against his chest, claws careful, reverent. Her face hovered only inches from his, winter breathing against furnace heat.

Her voice slithered through the chilled air, low and resonant, her serpentine body coiling with slow, predatory grace, "show me if fire melts ice...or if ice quenches fire."

He leaned in, heat rolling off him in waves that curled into the cold air like tendrils of smoke, "Is this part of the ritual, or are you in heat and desire to see if I'm compatible for purchase? Either way, I'm in," he murmured with a seductive grin.

Naia's pupils tightened to razor-thin slits as that predatory smile unfurled across her face, displaying the full array of needle-like teeth hidden behind her deceptively delicate lips. A soft, rattling purr vibrated up her throat.

"Both," she whispered, her voice carried the brittle music of cracking ice. Her coils slid against his legs... not constricting, yet undeniably surrounding, claiming space around him.

"My kind takes worthy males once in decades. The unworthy become mere sustenance," she leaned closer, and her breath fogged the small distance between them, frost swirling in the air. A single talon traced his jaw with elegant, lethal precision, without breaking skin, but leaving behind a shiver that traveled down his spine.

"Purchase implies ownership," her eyes glinted with ancient pride, "this is alliance. Partnership between predators."

"Your heat..." Her cold hand slid lower, gliding along the fabric of his prison pants, perfectly tracing the shape beneath. The contact was icy enough to sting yet intimate enough to set nerves ablaze, "...awakens hibernating hungers."

From the intercom above, Dr. Ryujin cleared her throat, the dragon's voice edged with flustered professionalism, "I'm...reducing surveillance to minimum biosigns only. The subject shows unprecedented integration potential. Full report will be...significantly redacted."

The lights of the chamber dimmed, leaving blue glows and drifting steam where heat met cold. Naia's coils tightened ever so slightly around his lower body, not to trap, but to draw him nearer into her thermal orbit. Her scales, though armored, were surprisingly supple where they pressed into him.

"Show me what fire can do, half-breed," her forked tongue flicked against his ear, a whip-crack of cold that sent a jolt through his spine, "make this century's hibernation worth the wait."

He slid his hand up from his side, between the shifting warmth of her humanoid torso and the cooler transition of scales, wrapping his arm around her waist to pull her in.

"I won't lie, it's small to what you should be getting and more human than you'd like," he said, breath hot against her cheek, "but to gain purchase isn't ownership here, it's to gain..."

He pressed hard against her body, emphasizing the word with action, "...*insertion.*"

Naia's eyes flashed in a brilliant, icy blue light as his touch found the sensitive seam where human skin met lamia scales. Her breath hitched, a soft hiss slipping free as the chamber's temperature fluctuated wildly.

"Bold claim from a fire-blood," her voice sank into a low, hungry whisper. Her coils shifted around him with languid precision, her body adjusting to his proximity rather than resisting it, "size matters less than skill among my kind. We judge by... adaptability."

The scales under his hand rippled with muscle tension, warmth blooming beneath their frosted surface, an unmistakable biological response. Her cloacal region radiated surprising heat, her body preparing instinctively.

"Insertion…" Naia repeated, savoring the clinical word as if it were decadent, "such a clinical term for what happens when glacier meets volcano."

Her talons traced cryptic, arcing patterns across his chest, never cutting, but awakening goosebumps across warmed skin, "Show me this fire, then. The guards whisper that humans burn quickly and fade to ash. Prove them wrong."

From the observation room, the lights shut down entirely.

"Biometric monitoring only. Fifteen-minute privacy protocol engaged. Whatever happens now serves both scientific and… diplomatic purposes." The world dimmed further as Naia's coils tightened, not constricting, but enveloping… drawing him firmly into her cold embrace.

Her humanoid torso pressed to his, steam rising as their temperatures collided in white, swirling tendrils. The frost-blue illumination of her scales reflected in her fiercely focused eyes, "earn your place, fire-blood. Make the ice sing."

He unzipped and pushed her midsection away just enough for his prison bottoms to drop, the movement releasing heat that pulsed between them. His arousal bounced up in a hard throb, brushing the precise place as if knocking for passage, instinct meeting instinct. He stripped his top away, muscles radiating heat that caused mist to billow where his skin neared hers.

Naia's eyes widened, a flicker of true surprise sparking behind the predatory confidence as his heat made contact with the sensitive entrance her body instinctively prepared for him. The protective scales around it parted, glowing faintly with ethereal blue luminescence.

Her breath caught.

Her coils tightened.

The steam rose.

And then…. His arousal made contact with her sensitive entrance. The specialized scales protecting her cloaca parted instinctively, revealing flesh that glows with an ethereal blue bioluminescence in startling contrast to her icy exterior.

243

Naia

"The fire knocks..." her voice hitches slightly as steam coiled around their joined bodies. "Such presumption." Despite her words, her tail coils tightened, drawing him closer as her entrance pulsed with heat incongruous to her glacial nature.

The temperature differences created a phenomenal sensation when their bodies found a union; extreme cold meeting intense heat created a feeling that transcended any ordinary pleasure.

Her scaled lower body undulated against his with practiced precision, and the muscles beneath were capable of pressures and movements beyond what human anatomy could perform.

"Enter then, fire-blood," Her talons dig lightly into his shoulders, marking dominance, not aggression, "let us see if your heat survives the depths of winter."

As their bodies joined, the chamber's environmental systems struggled to compensate for the wild temperature fluctuations. Ice crystals formed and immediately melted in the air around them, creating a shimmering, misty dome that enveloped their joining. Her inner anatomy gripped him with supernatural control, cold at first entry but warming rapidly with each motion.

"The old songs speak truth..." her voice emerged as a breathless hiss, and her pupils dilated fully, "fire and ice create something new when joined."

As her scales parted, revealing the wet flesh, he throbbed and found purchase and moved to continue forcing himself deeper in, pressing and having to force the walls apart, allowing him to slide further in. Her cold walls giving way to my heat throbbing inside, pulsating to fill with life.

Naia's body responds with ancient instinct, her internal muscles contracting in rippling waves that simultaneously resist and draw him deeper. Her cold-blooded anatomy gradually warms where they join, creating an otherworldly sensation of ice melting around molten steel.

Naia

"yesssss…" the words stretched into a sibilant hiss as her head fell back, exposing the vulnerable column of her throat, a gesture of trust she couldn't dream of moments ago, "The fire penetrates the glacier's heart."

Her internal anatomy proved startingly complex, ridges and textures not found in human partners created friction points that sent jolts of new-discovered pleasure through his nervous system, a kind of pleasure that surpassed every moment of arousal he had ever experienced.

The deep blue bioluminescence brightened with her arousal, casting ethereal patterns across them. Steam rose more every time his superheated skin met her scales.

The coils of her tail responded to each thrust with counter-pressure; her inhuman muscles controlled, allowing her to squeeze and release with precision timing. Her clawed hands raked lightly down his back, leaving trails of cold that only intensified the heat building between them.

"More, fire-blood…" Her voice grew commanding despite her vulnerable position, eyes flashing with predatory hunger, "Show me why my ancestors chose your kind as worthy. Make the ice-heart beat with warmth again."

The prison's monitoring systems registered the anomalous temperatures but maintained privacy protocols, leaving both of them enclosed in the misty dome of steam and ice crystals, a miniature ecosystem of opposing elemental forces finding unexpected harmony.

As the steam rose in the room, her walls pulsated and flowed like water massaging, and within moments… he grabbed her, picking her up and pushing deeper into her cervix.

He pushed and pulled until his arousal began flowing the hot fluid deep inside her and pulsating more of the flow. Steam flowed out of his mouth and nostrils. He gasped as his body emptied into hers as if responding to a call to breed.

Naia's body arched with a primal grace as he let his release fill her up; her eyes widened with an ancient recognition. The

245

bioluminescence in her lower body pulsed rhythmically, bright blue, turning to violet where his heat met her cold.

Her inhuman anatomy responded to his release with purposeful contractions, drawing his essence deeper than should be physically possible.

"The seed burns like liquid fire…" her voice broke into a rasping sound, half pleasure, half triumph, "the glaciers will remember this joining."

Her powerful tail had coiled reflexively around them both in the aftermath of their joining, the gleam of her scales dampened by condensation that shimmered like frost melting under sunlight. Where their bodies remained connected, an alchemical reaction seemed to occur… steam rising in slow and spiraling ribbons that carried faint traces of ozone and a sweetness foreign to the sterile air of the chamber. It was the scent of something ancient and biological, the primordial chemical signature released only during successful mating between compatible predator species.

In the observation room above, the monitoring systems recorded a spike in pheromones and biochemical signatures unknown to human medical charts. A soft green indicator pulsed on Dr. Ryujin's abandoned console, silently affirming an event the prison had likely never documented before.

Naia's breathing steadied gradually. She pressed her forehead to his… an intimate and deeply ceremonial gesture among her kind. Her voice came soft, reverent, steeped in mythic certainty.

"You've marked the ice with fire," her hand drifted instinctively to the region where scales met warm skin along her lower abdomen, as though assessing an internal shift older than language, "the old ones spoke true. Fire-bloods carry the spark that awakens hibernating life."

She held him closer, unwilling yet to sever the thermal exchange between their bodies. The predatory hunger that had defined her earlier movements softened, reshaping into something far more complex: respect layered with possession, curiosity layered with possibility.

246

"Perhaps the prison walls will see new life from ancient bloodlines." Slowly and deliberately, Naia loosened her coils to allow him room to stand, though she kept one scaled loop trailing against his leg as a final reluctant point of contact before decorum returned.

"The guards will come soon. But what passes between us cannot be undone." A rare smile, razor-edged and beautiful, revealed her full array of deadly teeth as she claimed, "You are marked now, fire-blood. And I...am thawed."

He caught her before she could fully withdraw, holding her in place with a firm grip. The heat rolling from his body contrasted sharply with the lingering chill of hers, rising in thin curls of steam between them.

He held her in place, "We shall see if life blooms, or if this was only a moment of your vulnerability." As the flow stopped and he shrank, he pulled a bit back to allow his arousal to drop every last bit of the fluid.

Suddenly, he dropped down and pulled his pants back up. Then he used his hand to push her scales closed, so that no amount of fluid could escape her now fertilized womb.

Naia watched him with half-lidded satisfaction as he withdrew and dressed. The brief pressure of his hand sealing her scales drew a soft, instinctual sound from deep in her throat, a blend of amusement and approval, rare from a creature bred for killing.

"Thoughtful... for a fire-blood," her icy composure began knitting back into place, though a warm undertone lingered beneath every word now, "vulnerability is perception, not reality. What looks like weakness to the prey may be a strategy to the predator."

She adjusted her clothing with sinuous grace, her scales realigning to conceal every trace of the encounter. The temperature in the room slowly stabilized, though the faint scent of ozone and sweetness clung stubbornly to the air.

"Life blooms rarely between our kinds. Once in a generation," Naia's tongue flicked lightly, tasting the chemical signatures still clinging to him, "but it is not the outcome that matters most to my kind. It is the... compatibility."

"Most would have frozen from the inside out." Her gaze swept over him, assessing with a new depth, less as prey or mate, and more as something worthy of myth: "You burned instead."

The intercom crackled alive with static before Dr. Ryujin's voice filtered through, professional once more, "integration session concluding in thirty seconds. Resuming standard surveillance protocols."

Naia slid closer for one final moment, her movements as fluid and controlled as a glacier shifting. Her breath brushed coolly as she spoke against his ear, "They may call you prisoner, but among my kind, you would be called 'frost-walker' now. Remember that when the ice grows thick around you in this place."

She retreated to a proper distance as heavy locks began to disengage from the door. The mechanical rumble echoed around them like the heartbeat of the facility itself, "Our paths will cross again, fire-blood. The glacier remembers what has melted it."

He adjusted the clothing on him to diminish any contact, "What has been melted reveals life beneath, now exposed," He repeated dutifully with a slight predatory bow, "we shall meet again, try to behave for them till then."

He turned away toward the open doors.

Her pupils contracted to narrow slits as she absorbed his parting words, interest sharpening her reptilian features with instinctive precision. She returned his bow with a subtle tilt of her head, a gesture of mutual predatory acknowledgment.

"Behave? A strange concept in a prison built on control." Her tail coiled elegantly beneath her as the doors slid fully open, "the exposed life survives by adapting, fire-blood. Remember that."

Two guards appeared in the doorway, awaiting his presence.

A harpy with metallic feathers poised like weapons.

A minotaur whose bulk filled most of the frame.

Their faces remained impassive, though the harpy's nostrils flared just slightly at the lingering chemical signature saturating the chamber's air.

Chapter 9

"Displacement"

The moment the 'encounter' between Naia and him concluded, the sterile calm of the rehabilitation chamber returned in slow, reluctant waves.

Steam still lingered in soft curls along the floor, dissipating gradually as the temperature stabilized. The heavy door groaned open, and the first figure to emerge was the towering Minotaur guard.

"Prisoner 4721, back to your cell block." She ordered, "The integration session is logged as... successful."

The guard's bovine eyes flicked between him and Naia, noting far more than protocol required while still maintaining the illusion of professional detachment.

Behind her, Dr. Ryujin slipped into the room with serpentine grace, clipboard in hand, the cool blue light catching along her iridescent scales. She exchanged a silent, knowing look with Naia before her analytical gaze swept toward him.

"Fascinating thermal readings from this session. We'll be... analyzing the data carefully," Ryujin said, with a glint too sharp to be mere professionalism flashed in her golden eyes, "The Monster Girls Correction Board may require additional integration sessions if the pattern proves beneficial."

Naia moved past him with her usual gliding elegance, her coils brushing against him in a subtle, concealed farewell. The contact was cold, intoxicating, intentional, and hidden from the guards' line of sight.

"Until our paths cross again," her voice carried the weight of ancient promise, "The ice waits, fire-blood."

He answered without looking away from her retreating form, "She's going to be needing a high-protein diet for the next few months. It'll help with her mood stabilizer."

Dr. Ryujin's motion halted mid-note. Her slit pupils widened a fraction, catching the chamber's light in an electric shimmer before she composed herself once more.

"A dietary recommendation, prisoner?" Though her tone remained clipped and clinical, amusement curled beneath it like smoke under a door, "how... attentive of you. I'll make a note in her file about potential nutritional adjustments."

The Minotaur snorted, unable to fully contain her reaction, while the harpy at her side shifted restlessly, steel-tipped feathers rustling as she exchanged a quick, knowing glance with her partner.

Naia, halfway to the corridor, angled her head just enough for him to see the satisfied smirk curving her lips, "The fire-blood shows unusual insight into reptilian physiology."

Her tongue flicked once, tasting the layered boldness of his words, "perhaps he should be consulted on other... institutional matters."

The harpy guard suppressed a shiver, "Move along, Prisoner Ice-Scale. Your temporary clearance for common areas has expired for today."

Dr. Ryujin jotted something on her clipboard with exaggerated professionalism as she approached him, "bold move, human. Very bold. The cameras record audio."

Yet respect that was rare from her glimmered in her inhuman eyes, "your integration assessment just became considerably more... complex."

The guards shifted, guiding him toward the opposite corridor while Naia's escort moved her in the other direction. Still, her voice remained cool, resonant, ancient, carrying effortlessly down the hall.

"Fire that feeds ice brings unexpected growth. Remember that, Warden." Naia said, eyes still fixated on him.

He nodded once. "I must report to the lieutenant before chow. Thank you, Doctor."

Dr. Ryujin's expression sharpened, subtle threads of surprise weaving into her otherwise detached demeanor.

"Lieutenant Keres, I presume?" Her tone remained measured, but the way her tail shifted betrayed her heightened interest, "interesting. She rarely requests prisoners directly."

A brief pause followed, as the doctor measured the implications, "Her office is in Administrative Wing B. Your escort will need updated clearance."

The Minotaur guard stiffened immediately. Even her nostrils flared faintly at the name, "Administrative Wing access wasn't in today's roster."

Her hoofed hand drifted toward her stun baton, not threatening, but wary of protocol breaches, "The Lieutenant didn't file paperwork for prisoner consultation."

Dr. Ryujin's scales flashed subtly as she accessed her tablet, fingers gliding across it with efficient precision, "I'm pushing the clearance through now. Oversight on scheduling, not protocol breach." Her gaze flicked to him again, assessing his posture, his breathing, the lingering thermal signature still clinging to his skin, "Lieutenant Keres has been monitoring certain... integration potentials. Your file appears to have caught her attention."

The harpy guard shuffled uneasily, "The Lieutenant doesn't like to be kept waiting. If he's expected..."

Her words faded into a meaningful silence.

Dr. Ryujin nodded once, clipboard tucked against her chest as she stepped aside, "Proceed to Administrative Wing B. I'll update your file with today's... observations... after your meeting concludes," her eyes shimmered with clinical fascination, "Lieutenant Keres may have questions about your adaptive capabilities in our facility."

He brushed past the guards with deliberate confidence, his steps measured and unhurried. The subtle contact sent a ripple of tension through the escort formation.

"You may follow, but I'm no common prisoner. I know the way."

The words hung in the air like a thrown gauntlet.

The minotaur guard's reaction was immediate. Her nostrils flared sharply, a plume of warm steam leaving her bovine muzzle. Muscles bunched beneath her uniform, a primal readiness working through her limbs as her hoof scraped a warning arc against the stone floor.

"No common prisoner?" Her voice rumbled from deep within her broad chest, equal parts confusion and challenge, "You've got nerve, human. Your file says nothing about special classification."

Feathers rustled behind him as the harpy guard shifted uneasily, steel-tipped quills catching the overhead lights. Her sharp avian gaze flicked toward Dr. Ryujin, silently demanding an explanation that never came.

Dr. Ryujin's serpentine tail glided across the floor, her scaled lower body coiling with poised scientific interest rather than aggression. Her golden eyes flickered with analytical focus.

"Escort protocol remains standard regardless of prisoner status." Even so, a subtle note of intrigue threaded her otherwise clinical tone. She began tapping quick notes onto her tablet, documenting every deviation from expected behavior, "though I must note this behavioral aberration in my report."

Reluctantly, the guards flanked him once more, though the balance of power between them had shifted just slightly. Their posture was tighter now, less certain.

The corridor ahead stretched long and severe, lined with the glowing arcane glyphs used to suppress magic. Each checkpoint pulsed with muted energy, the symbols reacting subtly to his passing.

"Move out. Administrative Wing B," The Harpy Guard held professionalism, but her feathers stayed partially flared, a physical sign of uneasy vigilance, "and watch yourself, prisoner. Lieutenant Keres doesn't appreciate… presumption."

As they continued, the sound of their footsteps echoed through the winding halls. Monster girl inmates pressed close to reinforced windows, whispering among themselves, startled, curious, and even envious at the sight of a human escorted toward the administrative wing rather than back into captivity.

He made no move to acknowledge them, striding forward until they reached the ornate threshold.

The shift in architecture was immediate. Smooth obsidian columns replaced steel beams, and stylized reliefs depicting ancient monster courts lined the walls. Ambient lighting cast long shadows across the polished stone floors, giving the space a cathedral-like severity.

Two guards awaited them.

First was a towering gargoyle, her granite skin etched with faint runic seams; she stood still as sculpture, only her glowing amber eyes tracking his approach. Beside her, an Arachne guard perched slightly elevated on glossy black limbs, her many eyes glimmering with cold awareness.

The minotaur took the lead, voice resonant and formal, "Prisoner 4 for Lieutenant Keres. Clearance just updated by Dr. Ryujin."

The gargoyle's stone jaw shifted minimally as she observed him, scanning with a subtle rumble of magic, "verification confirmed. Stand down, Sector 4," her gravel-rough voice held authority carved from centuries, "we'll take the human from here."

The Arachne stepped forward with unnervingly graceful precision. Her uniform was immaculate; the Monster Girls Prison insignia embroidered in gold thread across her chest like a badge of judgment. All eight of her eyes blinked in a pattern that suggested mild surprise, "The Lieutenant specified no restraints for this one."

Her tone was edged with perplexed respect, "unusual protocol. You have clearance for fifteen minutes, prisoner. Not a second more."

The minotaur and harpy exchanged a glance, a silent sigh of relief, before withdrawing, their boots echoing down the corridor as they returned to their sector.

He stepped forward, irritation simmering beneath controlled composure, "Address me appropriately as you were instructed by the warden guards; it is Liaison when I'm acting on official business. Now, proceed." He brushed past the guards irritably.

The reaction was instantaneous.

The gargoyle's rocky facade fractured briefly with surprise before re-solidifying into rigid deference. She bowed her head, shoulders squared in proper acknowledgment.

"Liaison," she stepped aside with crisp precision, "our apologies for the oversight. The Warden's directives weren't fully distributed to our rotation."

The Arachne adjusted with rapid discipline, her chitin tapping an agitated rhythm as she keyed in the door sequence. The reinforced door split open, arcane wards flickering like cold flame along its edges. "Lieutenant Keres is expecting you, Liaison," she said, "Third door on the right. She's been reviewing the Eastern Boundary reports since dawn."

Respect now tempered every word.

The hallway beyond glowed faintly, a long corridor leading deeper into the administrative heart of Monster Girls Prison, toward Lieutenant Keres.

The administrative wing unfolded beyond in stark contrast to the rest of the prison, its dark wood paneling and muted lamps casting long, deliberate shadows that softened the oppressive sharpness found elsewhere. The air carried notes of sandalwood and old parchment, a warm, scholarly scent that stood defiantly apart from the antiseptic coldness of the inmate blocks. It felt like stepping into a different world, one curated for power rather than punishment.

A wight secretary sat at a lacquered desk as he passed. Her translucent features flickered with brief recognition before she lowered her gaze, quill moving in steady strokes. The studied indifference in her posture betrayed the tight information control that defined the administrative hierarchy of Monster Girl Prison.

The door to Lieutenant Keres' office towered before him, polished blackwood so dark it seemed to swallow the corridor's dim light. The bronze nameplate gleamed with muted authority, while the antique raven-shaped knocker watched with ruby eyes that almost appeared to shift as he approached.

Before his knuckles could even rise, a voice drifted from within, smooth and controlled:

"Enter, Liaison. I've been monitoring your progress through the facility," the voice of Lieutenant Keres hit him.

The heavy door swung inward on its own, gliding silently to reveal an office unmistakably carved from privilege and secrecy. Bookshelves brimmed with ancient tomes, and a massive obsidian desk anchored the room like a monolith. Behind it sat Lieutenant Keres, a Dullahan, her body immaculate in midnight-blue uniform, while her severed head rested neatly on a stand beside parchment stacks, its emerald-and-amethyst shifting eyes fixed upon him.

Her presence carried a scent of night-blooming flowers interwoven with cold steel, a paradox of elegance and threat.

"Your performance has been… noteworthy," her disembodied lips curved into a smile that spoke nothing of warmth, "close the door. We have matters requiring discretion."

He walked in, and using only his foot, he 'accidentally' slams the door, "Oops, too much force, my apologies, Lieutenant." He looked around, then walked up to the desk. "I was actually under the impression I'd be meeting with Lieutenant Lilith, so my schedule has been adjusted, then?"

The sudden slam echoed violently across the obsidian surfaces, stirring scrolls and sending a tremor of displaced air through the room. Keres' body remained poised, but her severed head's eyes narrowed, their colors hardening into a cold sapphire.

"Lieutenant Lilith?" Lieutenant Keres said, the note of dangerous amusement in her tone chilled the room further, "Interesting. She's been reassigned to the Borderlands Outpost for the past three months."

Her body rose from the chair in a single, graceful surge while her head stayed rooted on the stand, an eerie duality only her kind could embody, "which raises the question of how a supposed 'Liaison' wouldn't know this fundamental change in command structure."

Her uniform whispered softly as she circled the obsidian desk with predatory composure. One pale hand reached beneath the surface, tapping a concealed sigil that pulsed faint violet, and the chamber answered with a low, awakening hum as security wards flickered to life.

"I suspected something was amiss when your behavioral patterns deviated from standard prisoner protocols," a cold smile shaped her lips, "your deception was bold, if clumsy. The real question is whether you're an external plant or merely an ambitious inmate."

The walls responded to her mood, absorbing and amplifying the violet ward-light that threw shifting shadows across the carved shelves, "Guards won't be necessary just yet. I find interrogations much more...productive...when conducted privately."

Her head spoke while her body opened a drawer, retrieving an ornate dagger whose edge shimmered with old enchantment, "Let's start with your actual identity before we discuss the consequences of impersonating prison officials."

He spoke, "Ah, this again. Tell me, so as to answer appropriately, how long ago did I enter with the doctor into her wing with the enclosed inmate she was experimenting with?" He adjusted his posture, looking curiously while rubbing his chin.

Lieutenant Keres stilled instantly, her body locking into rigid stillness while her severed head's eyes flashed a violent crimson. The dagger hovered mid-motion, gleaming like a threat paused in time. The humming wards around the office dropped into a deeper resonance, mirroring the sudden shift in her emotional equilibrium as she processed your question.

Lieutenant Keres' lips curved slowly, the faintest smile tugging at the corners of her severed head as it hovered above the obsidian desk, suspended in its pale nimbus of violet ward-light.

"Clever deflection," her voice took on a silky quality that somehow rang more dangerous than her previous tone, "Dr. Ryujin's experimental wing is clearance level Omega, knowledge of which isn't in any standard briefing."

Below, her body moved in smooth concert with the floating head, one gloved hand guiding the dagger back toward its sheath. The blade slid home with a soft, final sound as the head studied him with renewed intensity, eyes sharpening as if refocusing through several layers of illusion.

"Which means you're either extremely well-informed... or exactly who you claim to be." Her fingers brushed across a section of the desk that appeared to be nothing more than polished stone. Hidden sigils flared briefly beneath the surface, responding to the touch of her aura. The violet security wards that had been humming at interrogation pitch softened at once, bleeding down to a dormant, less hostile blue that cast the room in a cooler glow.

Her headless body eased back into the chair, movements now more measured, less predatory, but still coiled with professional caution, "My apologies for the... precaution, Liaison. The Warden's office neglected to forward your full credentials."

Her lips formed a tight, perfunctory smile, one that never reached her eyes. "As for your question, you entered the experimental wing with Dr. Ryujin precisely seventeen days ago. The subject was the lamia dissident from the Northern Territories," And them... she fell silent.

Her eyes never left his face, irises shifting in subtle patterns as if cataloging every micro expression, every twitch of muscle, clearly still evaluating his reaction for confirmation of his identity.

For a heartbeat, he simply stared at her, the words *seventeen days* rattling around inside his skull like a loose round in a chamber.

Then it hit.

His face erupted with fury. Heat shot up his spine and detonated behind his eyes.

"Seventeen DAYS?!" The words ripped from his throat before he could contain them, raw and incredulous, his voice crashing through the office like a thrown chair. His eyes darkened, red beginning to bleed into his irises, his gaze locking on the Lieutenant's severed head with the kind of focus that made wards think about waking again.

"Where was I before I went to the doctor?" he asked in a furious voice, as if his head was about to explode.

The Lieutenant's head visibly recoiled at the outburst, pupils widening as they tracked the sudden crimson flood that overtook his eyes. The temperature in the office dropped several degrees in an instant. Frost laced itself along the edges of her obsidian desk, spiderwebbing out from the grain as the air condensed around his rising energy.

"By the Dark Mother…" Lieutenant Keres' voice fell to barely above a whisper, tension vibrating through each syllable, "They didn't tell me they'd altered your memory sequences."

Her body surged up from the chair with defensive urgency, shoulders squared yet hands raised with open palms, a placating gesture that clashed with the alarm etched across her hovering face. The head drifted slightly higher, as if instinctively seeking distance while still needing to see every nuance of his reaction.

"You were in Solitary Wing C, under direct supervision of the Warden herself after the incident with the Hellhound Guard Captain," she spoke rapidly now, interrogation cadence dissolving into a rushed debrief, "Dr. Ryujin's request for your transfer was approved only because your…particular abilities… were deemed necessary for the lamia's rehabilitation."

Her hand moved toward a crystal sphere embedded in the desk. The orb responded before she even touched it, its clear surface clouding with swirls of crimson that churned in rhythm with the anger saturating the room. The sphere seemed to taste his mood, light flaring brighter each time his aura spiked.

"Your anger is justified, Liaison, but please contain your energy signature. Last time you destabilized, three guards were hospitalized," her eyes flicked toward the door, calculating routes, reinforcements, contingencies, "should I summon Dr. Ryujin to explain the memory gaps, or would you prefer to review the written records first?"

The ledger, the sphere, the wards, all waited with her, poised between escalation and retreat.

His hands clenched, shoulders tight, breath hovering on the edge of a growl. Then he forced his eyes shut.

He drew in a slow breath.

Then another.

Then another.

He began doing controlled breathing, dragging air through his lungs like he was hauling it up from the bottom of a pit. He let the cold air bite at the back of his throat, forcing his pulse to slow with each measured inhale and exhale. The red in his eyes eased fractionally behind closed lids, contained for the moment behind deliberate discipline.

"Before I went to see the doctor, I was with Her Majesty the Warden Morrigan. Then I went to Lieutenant Lilith to see about the order in Block C, then I went to the doctor, and I had been in her wing with the observed inmate for seventeen days. Is everything I said lining up?" He kept his eyes closed as he spoke, as if any visual stimulus might snap the thin thread of control he was hanging on to.

Lieutenant Keres watched him with visible relief as the frost along the desk began to recede, the air losing its brittle shimmer. Her severed head tilted slightly to one side, the analytic edge returning as she processed the timeline he recited.

"Not…entirely…." Her voice had regained some composure, though the caution remained layered beneath it like a secondary tone, "You met with Warden Morrigan four weeks ago, not directly before seeing Dr. Ryujin. And the order investigation in Block C was handled by Lieutenant Minos, not Lilith."

Her headless body moved with practiced precision, fingers reaching for a leather-bound ledger on the corner of the desk. The book opened to a marked page with efficient ease, as if her hands had long ago learned to function without visual guidance. She turned it toward him, angling it so he would see the entries even with his eyes closed if he chose to open them.

"Your memory has significant temporal distortions. This is…concerning," her gaze narrowed, calculation evident in the subtle shift of her pupils, the faint glow threading through their color, "Dr. Ryujin mentioned potential side effects from proximity to the lamia subject, but nothing of this magnitude."

Her fingers drifted to a small crystal set into the high collar at her throat. At her touch, it pulsed once with blue light, a silent signal sent through hidden channels.

"I'm notifying Medical. You'll need an evaluation before returning to duty," her tone softened by a fraction, a sliver of professional sympathy cutting through protocol, "in the meantime, would it help to review your actual movement logs from the past month? Perhaps seeing the documented timeline will help reorient your memory structures."

The ledger before him displayed precise entries tracking personnel movements throughout the facility, each line an accounting of presence and absence. His ID number appeared multiple times, paired with timestamps and location codes that formed a pattern he was supposed to recognize as his life.

He opened his eyes.

He looked at the ledger.

The entries stared back with cold ink certainty.

"These are wrong. Stand back, I need room for this."

His voice dropped into something darker, the edge flattening into grim resolve. He took a few steps back from the desk, boots scraping softly against the polished floor as he carved out space between himself and the Lieutenant. His shoulders rolled once, bracing. His hand curled into a fist, knuckles whitening as his fingers clenched down hard, every tendon in his arm standing out under the strain.

"We've slipped again, time to go back," energy tightened around him like a storm preparing to drop, the air drawing inward toward the point of his clenched fist as if the room itself knew something was about to break.

Lieutenant Keres' body jerked backward the instant his fist tightened, retreating with supernatural precision until her armored back struck the far wall. Her severed head hovered near the ceiling, pupils dilating into wide pools of alarm as a ripple of unstable energy leaked from his clenched hand.

The atmosphere thickened around him; heat distortion warped the air, bending light into wavering ribbons. Sheets of parchment lifted from her desk, fluttering wildly as though caught in a phantom storm.

"Reality breach protocol initiated!" Lieutenant Keres' voice vibrated with both fear and an unmistakable fascination, "Stabilize your anchor points before…"

But the world lurched.

Not as a metaphor, but in a literal, gut-pulling sideways convulsion. Colors inverted… violets bleaching into acid green, shadows flashing into blinding white. The dullahan's office elongated grotesquely, stretching like molten glass before snapping back, its dimensions rippling in refusal to hold a single shape.

Lieutenant Keres' severed head released a high-pitched keening sound, a resonance that seemed to scrape at the inside of his skull, "by the void, you're a Chrono-class!" she gasped, her body fumbling for the amulet at her belt while her floating head trembled with shock.

"The Warden didn't… nobody mentioned…" Her words shattered beneath another temporal ripple.

The walls bled into themselves as ink dropped into water, the solid obsidian desk flickering between tangible stone and hazy translucence in rapid, nauseating pulses. Overlapping images of the office began to appear, some populated by different officers, some empty and decayed, some impossibly pristine. Reality had begun layering itself around him.

"S-stabilize your core, or you'll fracture the entire wing!" Her voice cracked, stripped of command, a raw plea swallowed by the accelerating distortion swallowing the room.

He inhaled sharply, every nerve vibrating.

He forced himself still.

He focused.

He dragged his mind into alignment.

Then…

He opened his eyes.

"There!"

The word left his throat like the snap of a tether breaking.

The world imploded inward with a thunderous crack… disorientation collapsing into silence, distortion folding into clarity… and suddenly he was somewhere else entirely.

The dark obsidian chamber was gone.

In its place stood a sterile monitoring hub bathed in the sour green glow of reinforced concrete walls. Rows of surveillance screens flickered across the far wall, each one casting cold reflections across metallic floors and humming banks of control equipment. The air smelled of ozone, cold circuitry, and faint disinfectant, a stark contrast to the organic dread of the Dullahan's office.

"By the eight hells, he's done it again," the voice floated from behind him, dry, irritated, and edged with resignation.

Captain Arachne towered near a console, her upper torso rigid beneath a crisp military uniform that strained over her chest, adorned with the silver insignia of the Prison Security Division. Her slate-gray skin gleamed under the fluorescent lights, and her eight red eyes rotated to track him with unnerving synchronicity.

Her lower half was an enormous black spider abdomen supported by eight articulated legs that clicked anxiously against the metal flooring, each movement sharp and rhythmic.

"That's the third reality slip this week," she adjusted a headset with one humanoid hand while the other three danced expertly over keyboards and monitoring runes, "subject 4721 has stabilized in Monitoring Hub 7."

All eight eyes swiveled and locked onto him.

"You're getting better at controlling the jumps, hun. But if you keep tearing holes in reality, the Warden will authorize permanent chrono-restraints," her mandibles clicked, a sound skirting the line between amusement and reprimand, "though I must admit, watching Lieutenant Keres panic is always entertaining."

Behind her, the screens shifted through dozens of camera feeds, exercise yards, containment chambers, solitary rooms, and there, in the upper right quadrant, the laboratory.

Empty.

Dark.

Abandoned.

He stepped forward, tension tightening in his shoulders. "As much as I'd love to engage, flirt, and fraternize with you," a bulge began to form

263

beneath the fabric of his jumpsuit, the timeline whiplash mixing with arousal and adrenaline in a dangerous cocktail, "how long has that lab been empty?" he pointed directly at the monitor.

Captain Arachne's eight eyes flicked down, first to his bulge, then back up, and her mandibles clicked again, definitely amused this time, though irritation tinged the motion. She keyed in a sequence with two hands while her other pair adjusted monitoring glyphs with quick, practiced twists.

"Typical human. Always thinking with your lower appendage even when reality itself is unravelling," her tone dripped with dry, cutting sarcasm, though a faint blush darkened the gray of her cheeks.

"The lab has been empty for approximately 39 hours. Dr. Ryujin and her... test subject... were relocated to Subsection Delta after your last temporal episode caused half the equipment to age two centuries in an instant," she pushed away from the console and rose to her full, imposing height. The chitin of her legs scraped lightly against the floor as she advanced, each step accompanied by a predatory click-clack.

She leaned down, bringing her arachnid face within inches of his, close enough that her breath, tinged with cinnamon and venom, drifted across his skin, "More concerning is that you've slipped across four different timelines in the past week. The Warden is... displeased."

She gestured at another screen showing a formidable demoness seated behind an ornate desk, wings half-unfurled, horns spiraling like obsidian spears, "She's authorized me to fit you with a chronometric anchor if you can't stabilize independently."

Her mandibles curved into a smirk, dangerous, playful, and suggestive all at once.

"Unless you'd prefer I restrain you using... alternative methods?"

Captain Arachne's eight crimson eyes locked on him the moment the words left his lips. The tension in the room shifted like a plucked string. His smile... wry, sharp, almost taunting, hung in the air between them.

"And you say I'M thinking with my lower appendages?" he smiled and chuckled wryly, "my dear..."

He let his gaze drift deliberately to the insignia pinned to her uniform, the rank glinting faintly under the pulsing lights.

"Captain… let me show you the respect you deserve first. Again, I would definitely love to engage, but if I'm not supposed to be here, then I must jump again, so prepare this area for either lust or a perimeter for my safe jump. Cuz that," he pointed at the warden screen, "is not the head Warden Morrigan."

His fist tightened, knuckles whitening as temporal static shivered around him, "Think quickly, cuz I do lost and like you, but I AM faster, and I don't want ANYONE to be hurt from my actions. I'm NOT trying to be reckless."

The effect on Arachne was immediate.

All eight of her eyes widened in alarm, pupils flaring to pinpoints. Her spider legs moved with startling precision, tapping an emergency sequence into the floor. A shimmering containment field surged up around the monitoring station, enclosing them in a cocoon of amber light.

"That's NOT Warden Morrigan?" Arachne's voice drops to an urgent whisper, mandibles twitching nervously, "by the Weaver's thread… you're right. The dimensional constants must be degrading faster than we predicted."

Her four hands flew across overlapping control panels, her movements a blur of instinct and training. Her body subtly positioned itself between him and the exit, protective, defensive, or both, as the lights dimmed to a slow, pulsing amber. Emergency glyphs began to rotate across the ceiling.

"Jump perimeter established. You have approximately thirty seconds before security identifies the containment field activation," she hesitated only a fraction before unclasping a small amulet from around her neck. The chain snapped free with a soft metallic whisper. She pressed the amulet into his hand, her touch lingering.

"Take this chronometric anchor. It's keyed to Morrigan's original timeline," for a moment, just a heartbeat, her stern façade cracked. Something vulnerable flickered across her sharp arachnid features.

"Find me when you reach the proper reality. My counterpart will know what to do," she stepped back, her tall, commanding silhouette framed by

265

flashing warning sigils, "and yes, human, I would have very much enjoyed…engaging with you under different circumstances."

The alarms erupted into a full wail, red strobes flashing across her carapace as her spider legs tapped one final command into the console.

He moved before thought could catch him.

"Fuck it," he growled.

He crossed the distance in a blur, hands catching her waist, pulling her close enough for his breath to mingle with hers. He kissed her mandibles, firm, deliberate, intimate. His other hand closed around her breast through the tight fabric of her uniform, feeling the firm shape yield beneath his palm.

Her body shuddered.

"I mean that for you." He said as he tore himself away and vaulted backward into the containment perimeter, gripping the amulet in one hand, clenching the other into a fist as power gathered.

Focus. Focus. Focus…

Captain Arachne froze, stunned into stillness as the unexpected kiss jolted through her. Her multiple eyes widened, mandibles quivering. A low, involuntary chirp escaped her throat as his hand withdrew from her chest, her entire form trembling despite her hardened discipline.

"You… brazen fool…" her voice wavers between outrage and desire, mandibles still tingling from his kiss, "may the Weaver guide your threads…"

The amulet pulsed violently in his grip.

Reality bent.

The floor buckled under forces that weren't meant to exist. Her gray limbs elongated and blurred, her eight eyes trailing ribbons of crimson light. The alarms became muffled, distant, as though sinking beneath water. The chronometric anchor thrummed, syncing with the wild, unstable storm of his temporal aura.

The world imploded inward.

Colors inverted.

Timelines tangled.

Consciousness stretched thin enough to tear.

For a heartbeat, he existed everywhere

A moonlit cell.

An abandoned lab.

A Warden's office ruled by three impossible figures.

A reality that he had never known.

A reality in which he had died.

A reality where someone else wore his face.

Then the universe snapped.

He was violently ejected, hurled out of the timestream like shrapnel.

falling. Always the feeling of falling…

Reality unraveled around him. He tumbled through swirling fragments of past and potential, each one brushing his skin like razor-thin memories: faces, screams, laughter, choices. The amulet burned against his palm, dragging him through the chaos like a lodestone pulling iron through smoke.

Impact.

Cold stone slammed into his spine. His breath vanished. Copper filled his mouth. The world flickered, blurred… then steadied.

He lay in a circular chamber lit by dim purple radiance. Ancient runes throbbed along the walls, each one breathing with eldritch rhythm. A towering hourglass filled with violet sand stood at the center, its grains falling upward and downward simultaneously.

A voice cut through the haze.

"Another temporal incursion. How… predictable."

He lifted his gaze.

Warden Morrigan sat behind a crescent-shaped obsidian desk, imposing and monstrous in her regal poise. Midnight-blue skin gleamed in the faint light, her horns spiraling upward and adorned with platinum chains. Her uniform fit like ceremonial armor, severe and seamless. Six wings folded neatly behind her, casting fractured shadows across the floor.

Her eyes were cold, calculating, and ancient, regarded him like a puzzle that had grown teeth, "subject 4721. Interesting. According to my records, you haven't arrived yet," she tapped long, talon-like fingernails against a feather-bound tome, "Arachne's chronometric anchor, I presume? Her sentiment will be her undoing in every timeline."

He dragged his tongue across his lip, tasting blood. His breaths were ragged, each inhale sharp with temporal recoil, "Ya, and you're still..." he licked the blood again, grimacing, "...the wrong Morrigan. The Captain was trying to help. Leave her be. But this is going to kill me if I'm not careful. Your caution is warranted and noted."

Warden Morrigan rose, unfolding her height like a nightmare made elegant. Her silhouette cast a long, predatory shadow across the runes. The temperature dropped sharply as she approached, each step a whisper of leather on stone. Her kaleidoscopic eyes narrowed, taking in every fracture in his aura, every wound threading light through his temporal instability.

"Wrong Morrigan? Fascinating." A cold smile curved her full lips, revealing delicate fangs, "The multiverse fragments further with each of your jumps. You've become a nexus of instability."

She began to circle him with slow, predatory grace. Her wings unfurled partially, stirring the dense air with controlled menace. Power shimmered in waves around her, the chamber responding like a living organism to her proximity.

Warden Morrigan's expression sharpened as she studied the blood trailing down his chin. Her eyes flicked between the crimson, the trembling of his aura, and the faint distortion warping the air around him.

"Your temporal signature is decaying rapidly," She gestures toward his mouth, where blood trickles down his chin. "Internal hemorrhaging. Classic symptom of dimensional displacement trauma."

With a startling swiftness that belied her towering form, she lowered herself beside him. Her taloned hand reached out, not with cruelty, but with an unexpected, almost chilling gentleness, as she grasped his jaw. Her touch was ice-cold, the frigid sensation burrowing under his skin and sending shivers racing down his spine.

"I could stabilize you... temporarily. But what would my *correct self* do, I wonder?" The playful malice threading through her voice softened beneath a layer of genuine curiosity, "Perhaps I should simply observe the experiment to its conclusion."

Her wings unfurled wider, their leathery span casting them both into deep shadow as she bent closer. The taloned tips of her fingers drifted toward the amulet held tightly in his hand, brushing it with an unsettling blend of reverence and calculation.

"Your experiment is in the basement, succubus. Nyarlathotep awaits you, not me. But if you wanna join me to see the TRUE goddess of death," he clenched his fist, "I'd LOVE to oblige."

The effect was instantaneous.

Morrigan's expression shattered into raw fury and disbelief. Every trace of her mask of professionalism dissolved. Her wings snapped open in a violent burst, spanning the full width of the chamber, the sudden rush of displaced air stirring dust and loose parchment from the floor. Her eyes erupted with infernal radiance, burning bright enough to cast jagged shadows across the walls.

"How do you know that name?" Her voice dropped to a lethal whisper, edged with a predator's wrath. Her talons lengthened reflexively, gleaming in the amethyst light. "Nyarlathotep has been contained in sub-level Omega for three centuries. No prisoner knows of her existence."

She circled him again, but the intent had changed. This was no longer an analytical observation. This was hunting. The runes carved into the obsidian walls pulsed faster, reacting to her escalating energy, their glow deepening into an urgent crimson.

"True goddess of death? You speak blasphemy even by our standards," She hissed, shadows coiling around her like serpents, "Your temporal knowledge makes you more dangerous than I initially assessed."

269

Without warning, she lunged.

Her taloned hand clamped around his throat, not crushing, but unmovably firm, pinning him in place with a grip that radiated power older than empires. Her other hand pressed hard against the amulet in his palm.

"Jump if you dare. But know this, I will find you across every timeline," her breath ghosted cold against his ear, intimate and threatening in equal measure, "And I'm very, very curious about how much pain a nexus point like you can endure before breaking reality completely."

He spat up, blood splattering across her wrist.

"Gotcha."

His fist clenched, knuckles going ghost-white as he forced focus through the agony clawing at his ribs. Eyes squeezed shut. Vision twisting inward. Images flickered…

The goddess of war, the last departure, the unmentionable moment…all cascading through his mind in a burning, collapsing spiral.

Focus.

Focus…

The amulet erupted in blinding light.

A jagged tear split through reality itself, the chamber shaking violently as temporal pressure burst outward. Morrigan's grip on his throat held even as her eyes widened in raw shock. She was dragged with him, her wings thrashing against invisible currents as the vortex yawned open beneath them.

The world disintegrated.

He tumbled through the void with her, a churning maelstrom where direction, time, and existence no longer meant anything. Morrigan's wings beat wildly, their vast span slashing through the fracturing darkness. Her screams wove through the collapsing dimensions, not fear, but fury, echoing across realities as her talons dug into his flesh, drawing streaks of blood that floated weightless around them.

Seconds stretched into eternity. Eternity compressed into a breath.

Their bodies spun and twisted, two living anomalies grappling inside a collapsing timeline.

Then...

Impact.

He hit polished obsidian tiles hard enough to steal his breath. The succubus landed atop him for a heartbeat before rolling away, dazed. The taste of copper suffused his mouth, thick and metallic, as he forced his vision to steady. The room around him swirled back into form, each detail sharpening as the distortion dissipated.

"Impossible..." she gasps, her perfect composure shattered.

This chamber was different. Larger. Vast. The air was colder, heavier with power. Pale blue orbs floated in slow circles above, casting ghostly illumination across towering walls marked with runes older than memory.

At the chamber's center, suspended by arcane chains that glowed with a haunting silver light, hung a figure whose presence eclipsed everything else.

Nyarlathotep... the forgotten goddess of death.

Her obsidian skin devoured the surrounding light. Six arms dangled motionlessly in their restraints. Her long, serpentine neck arched with ethereal grace. The mask of polished silver obscuring her face reflected impossible angles, bending the light in ways that made his vision ache. Slowly... impossibly... the masked face turned toward him.

"Visitors... at last," her voice bypassing his ears, manifesting directly in his mind, "and you've brought a piece of me with you, little nexus."

"Nope, this is wrong too," he rasped, breathing heavy and growing more labored. "Why is this getting harder?"

Reality shuddered.

The chamber trembled as if offended. Cracks rippled across the obsidian tiles beneath him, spreading outward like black lightning toward Nyarlathotep's cage. Morrigan stumbled backward, wings flaring in pure defensive instinct as she retreated from both him and the imprisoned deity.

"What have you done?" Her voice carried genuine fear now, her composure completely abandoned.

Nyarlathotep's silver mask tilted with slow, predatory grace. The chains binding her six arms rattled, shaking with violent intent as the deity's presence pressed harder against the boundaries of reality.

"Wrong? No, little nexus. You've simply reached too far, too fast." Her mind-voice reverberated through his skull, a sound like cracking bone and calming song layered together, "your body fails. The amulet cannot compensate forever."

The chamber groaned around him.

Something ancient stirred.

And his grip on existence slipped another inch.

He felt it... truly felt it now.

The warm cascade of blood slipping from his nostrils, the burning in his lungs with every breath, and the violent quiver of his very atoms, vibrating out of alignment as the timelines around him refused to settle.

The amulet pulsed wildly against his palm, its energy fluctuating in unstable, dangerous rhythms that resonated through his bones.

"Choose carefully. The next jump may be your last," One of Nyarlathotep's six hands stretched within the limits of its bindings, fingers elongating impossibly toward him, joints bending in ways no mortal anatomy could follow, "or stay... I could use fresh company after three centuries of solitude."

Behind him, Morrigan hissed sharply. A new doorway, one that absolutely hadn't existed moments before... yawned open in the wall behind her, flickering between three different architectural styles before settling into one.

"The amulet is killing you. Each reality you reject frays your connection to existence itself." Even now, despite fear edging her voice, there was undeniable fascination in her tone, scientific, hungry, clinical, "What timeline are you even searching for?"

He braced a trembling hand against the cracked floor, forcing himself upright with slow, agonizing effort, *"F*ine. Come down here out of that bird cage and embrace me once more as we did so long ago. That moment was true, and you remember it well as do I."

The chamber fell into a silence so profound it seemed to erase sound itself. Even the constant hum of the runes dimmed. The cracks across the tiles froze mid-spread, as if reality hesitated to continue until it understood what he had just invoked.

Morrigan stopped dead at the threshold of the phantom doorway, her expression folding into something between horror and morbid curiosity.

Within the enormous cage, Nyarlathotep went utterly still. Slowly…painfully slowly, her six hands curled into fists. The silver mask rotated to face him fully. Featureless as it was, he felt its attention pierce through him, reaching into memories he'd forgotten how to recall.

"You remember?" Her mind-voice was barely a whisper now, fragile, trembling with equal parts hope and suspicion, "before the binding? Before the betrayal?"

The chains binding her quivered violently, their ancient glyphs flaring in jagged bursts of warning light. A crack formed down the center of her silver mask, a thin line of perfect, absolute darkness.

"Don't! if she breaks free…" Morrigan tried to warn him, but her warning cut off with a choking gasp as an invisible force slammed her into the wall, pinning her helplessly in place. Wing membranes strained against the pressure, the stone behind her fracturing under the impact.

Nyarlathotep's body contorted unnaturally, limbs bending in impossible geometries as she strained against the divine restraints. The cage groaned and warped, metal flexing inward like soft clay.

When she spoke again, her voice no longer remained inside his thoughts; it vibrated the air itself, harmonics rattling his bones and making his blood feel as though it wanted to escape his veins.

"Prove it. Speak the words we shared when the stars were young," The mask split wider, revealing nothing but a swirling void beyond it, "when we made our pact in the dying light of the first universe."

He swallowed blood, chest shuddering, "You told me not to say a word, and I haven't. Your enemy is scared shitless at the door right now, and I still haven't told you what's to come. But if you wish for me to break that vow now…"

A resonant tremor burst outward from Nyarlathotep's cage, shaking the chamber as concentric waves of darkness rippled through the air. The silver mask shattered with a crystalline shriek, exploding into fragments that dissolved into starlight before reaching the ground.

Behind where the mask had been was not a face, but a storm of galaxies.

Ancient constellations long-dead in the present universe swirled within her, spiraling into a cosmic abyss.

"The vow of silence…" Nyarlathotep's voice dropped into a reverent whisper that somehow touched every corner of the chamber, "so it truly is you."

The chains unspooled from her six arms, slithering away like living serpents before disintegrating into dust-bright motes of light. The cage twisted inward, metal screaming as it collapsed into itself until nothing remained.

Nyarlathotep hovered weightless for a moment… then descended, her six hands opening toward him in invitation and recognition.

Morrigan thrashed against her unseen restraints, her wings beating uselessly as she fought the overwhelming force, "This is madness! She'll unmake everything!"

Blood trickled from the corner of her mouth, her infernal strength meaningless before the presence of an ancient deity.

Nyarlathotep's feet touched the floor, and the obsidian tiles splintered in luminous fractures radiating outward from her landing. As she advanced, her form existed in several places at once, afterimages drifting behind her in colors the mortal eye was never meant to perceive.

"The cycle nears completion." She extended all six hands toward him, the void of her face pulsing with entire galaxies collapsing and reforming, "Our silence ends today."

The amulet in his palm surged with unbearable heat, resonating violently as its energy aligned with hers, threads of fate knotting and twisting between them.

He tried to stand, body faltering, "I need help up, please. Embrace me once more."

Nyarlathotep moved with a fluid, impossible grace, the sheer presence of her bending the air around her. Three of her six arms reached for him, supporting his weakened form effortlessly. The touch of her obsidian skin was electric, an ancient, divine voltage that soothed his pain even as it pulled forgotten memories from the deepest hollows of his being.

Nyarlathotep's body shimmered with transcendent radiance as she held him within the sphere of suspended time. Galaxies spiraled beneath the surface of her skin, their ancient light rippling outward with every breath she drew. Each of her six arms adjusted subtly around him, supporting his failing body as if cradling something both fragile and immeasurably precious.

Her presence eclipsed the remnants of the chamber; there was no floor, no sky, no walls, only the quiet hum of eternity folding inward around them. The sphere of frozen time pulsed softly, holding back the violence of collapsing universes beyond its edges.

The void of her face remained inches from his, the swirling constellations within reacting to every whispered thought and trembling heartbeat he produced, "Time has not been kind to you, old friend."

Her star-filled void-face hovered close enough that soft pulses of cosmic light spilled across his features, illuminating the blood on his cheek and the exhaustion hollowing his eyes, "The pattern of your soul remains, but this vessel suffers."

She drew him closer, enfolding him fully in her embrace. All six arms wrapped around him with impossible delicacy, weaving a cocoon of cosmic power. Morrigan's distant cries, once fierce, once commanding, were now little more than faint echoes beyond layers of cosmic insulation.

Reality blurred.

Structures dissolved.

275

Only Nyarla's presence remained constant.

"I remember every moment of our silence," her voice vibrated through his bones, bypassing sound entirely, "every star we watched die together. Every universe we witnessed collapsed."

Two of her hands cupped his head with reverence, thumbs brushing trembling lines along his temples, "Now tell me... what comes next? What broke our vow?"

The amulet between them pulsed in rhythm with the starlit void of her face, each flash syncing with the echo of their shared ancient bond.

He reached for her, fingers gripping her obsidian form, pulling her closer with weak but determined force, "I did. It was me. But that hasn't happened yet," he pressed temple tiredly against Nyarla's, "I have one more jump before I don't exist or maybe two but you can send me back to this moment we shared before when you showed me this moment in the past. You sent me through the blind eternities, and nothing's been the same. Embrace me once more."

Nyarlathotep's entire form rippled at his confession, constellations shuddering, expanding, collapsing. Recognition flared outward in a cascade of starlight as her six arms tightened around him, linking their energies in a perfect circuit. The last remnants of the chamber dissolved into cosmic dust, leaving only infinite darkness lit by her internal galaxies.

"The paradox completes itself..." her voice thrummed with awe, "You come to me from a future where I've already sent you back."

The darkness around them churned, transforming into spiraling maelstroms of luminous energy. Time fractured into visible strands, threads of past, present, and future coiling around their interlocked forms like celestial ribbons.

One of her hands cradled the back of his head while another pressed gently to the amulet, feeding it renewed cosmic force, "the blind eternities await you again, then. But this time..."

She drew him even closer until her void-face filled his entire world, galaxies birthing and dying in the span of a heartbeat, "This time, I'll anchor you properly. The pain you've endured was never my intention."

Her obsidian figure grew translucent as channels of light opened beneath her skin, cosmic energy gathering as she prepared to infuse him with her power. The amulet trembled violently between them, shimmering with new vitality, "find me at the beginning, where the first stars died. I'll be waiting as I always have been," her arms tightened around him, "now close your eyes. The jump will be kinder this time."

But he reached forward suddenly, emotion overriding exhaustion, "Wait!" He quickly leaned in and kissed her, "I wanted to love you and make love to you one final time. If I go back, you'll be imprisoned again. I'll miss the chance."

Nyarlathotep's cosmic form shuddered, an entire constellation blooming and collapsing across her void-face in response. Her six arms shifted, gathering him into an intimate cradle that lifted them both above the dissolving remnants of spacetime, "love... such a mortal concept."

Her voice carried ancient amusement, yet genuine longing threaded through it, celestial emotion reshaping itself into new star patterns, "yet I've grown fond of it through your eyes."

Two of her arms slid beneath his weakened body, lifting him effortlessly. Another cupped his cheek, her touch cooling the fever burning beneath his skin. The remaining three formed a protective shell around them, deflecting the chaotic energies battering the isolated sphere of time.

As she pressed her star-filled void-face to his, time slowed until each moment stretched into crystalline stillness. The sensation was unlike any human intimacy, like touching the vacuum between constellations, yet feeling utterly connected to something ancient and infinite.

"Our circular path through time grants us this moment," her obsidian skin shimmered, turning translucent as galaxies spiraled beneath its surface, "a temporally isolated pocket before the jump."

The sphere surrounding them swelled with radiant tension, surface rippling as a thin membrane stretched over infinity. With reality stripped away, her true form revealed itself fully, transcendent, neither woman nor man, but a cosmic being whose shape was merely a gentle concession to the limitations of his mortal perception.

"Show me again what it means to love as mortals do," her voice softened into something almost vulnerable despite the unfathomable power radiating from her, "before I send you back to save us both."

They stripped away every last piece of clothing they had on them and let their flesh unite until the moment suspended in forever ends. Across every universe, and felt in every cosmic beat.

Nyarlathotep's obsidian skin rippled like living darkness as her six hands moved with slow, deliberate intent across his body. At her touch, his prison uniform dissolved into drifting motes of stardust, swirling around them in weightless spirals. Her form shifted in response to him, cosmic energy condensing into something tangible, still otherworldly, still celestial, but shaped now by a feminine silhouette carved from polished midnight. Her void-face retained its swirling galaxies, a universe of emotion without features.

"How strange," she whispered against his skin, her voice vibrating through his bones like the hum of distant creation, "that an eternal being should learn desire from something so fleeting."

Her many arms enveloped him completely, every touch lighting his nerves with sensations beyond mortal comprehension. Where his skin met hers, constellations bloomed and faded. The suspended pocket of time pulsed in rhythm with their shared passion, bleeding impossible colors through the boundaries of existence.

Two of her hands cradled his face while others explored lower, each touch both soothing and searing. The void where her mouth should be pressed against his, and he tasted the sweet emptiness between stars. Their bodies intertwined in cosmic union, defying physical limitations as she drew him impossibly close.

"Remember this," her voice resonated through every atom of his being as their forms merged completely, "when time fragments around you. Remember us."

In this suspended eternity, his consciousness expanded far beyond flesh. For a brief and impossible moment, he touched the vast awareness that was Nyarlathotep's true nature. Pleasure became something spiritual and transformative, souls intermingling as deeply as their bodies.

278

Covered in bliss, he conformed his physical form to insert into her and allow the flow of love and feelings of eternity to overtake him. The moment filled him up with all kinds of feelings, a blend of cosmic chaos within him; he didn't know where she ended, yet he began as they fused in passion and love that went beyond the limits of mortality.

Within their shared cosmic sanctuary, all physical boundaries dissolved. Nyarlathotep's form shifted around him in perfect harmony, accommodating his mortal essence with divine grace. Where their bodies joined, reality bent and flowed, creating waves of sensation that transcended physical pleasure. Her six arms cradled and guided him, each touch leaving trails of starlight across his skin.

"We exist between heartbeats now," she murmured, her voice resonating directly through his consciousness as time throbbed around them, "neither past nor future can reach us here."

The void of her face blossomed with fresh constellations that mirrored his expressions, their shared awareness reflecting cosmic memory, the birth of suns, the death of galaxies, eternities spent watching universes bloom and wither. Through this connection, he glimpsed the full scope of her existence and the sacrifice she had made to find him across time.

"When you return, remember this moment," she whispered as the boundaries between their beings thinned to nothing, "Find me before they build the prison. Before the silver mask. I will recognize you, even without remembering."

The cosmic energies surrounding them intensified, their shared passion cresting as time itself fractured around their entwined forms. The amulet caught between them pulsed like a newborn star, preparing for the journey he would soon undertake.

He leaned in toward an eternal face, kissing her, and a tear fell. Holding her tight, clenching both fists as if the entire existence.

When his tear touched the swirling cosmic void of Nyarlathotep's face, it erupted into a tiny nova of brilliant white light. before they build the prison six eternal arms tightened around him, forming a perfect cocoon of obsidian and starlight. Time cracked at the edges of their sanctuary as the suspended pocket reached its breaking point.

"Our paradox completes itself," she whispered, her voice echoing through the collapsing dimensions that peeled away around them. "I will remember you before I meet you. I will wait before knowing what I wait for."

The amulet between them pulsed faster, urgent and insistent, drawing power from their shared bond. Reality strained and warped as Nyarlathotep made her final adjustment to his temporal path.

"Find me at the beginning," her ethereal voice faded as cosmic energies pulled him from her embrace, "before the prison. Before the chains. I'll be waiting in the shadows of the third moon."

The pocket dimension shattered completely.

A violent ripple tore through existence as he felt himself pulled backward, helpless against the cosmic undertow. He was dragged through time, through space, through memory itself. Stars collapsed into lines. Galaxies folded into spirals. The last sensation was Nyarlathotep's delicate touch brushing against his consciousness, a cosmic fingerprint pressed gently into his soul. It lingered like a promise, guiding him as he tumbled through the blind eternities.

Falling. The sensation was fast and abrupt

"Always falling"

he thought to himself, or was it out loud?

Chapter 10

"The System"

As he fell, he plunged through the void between realities, the experience stretching into an eternity compressed into seconds.

Stars streaked past him like cold rain.

Time unraveled around his body and stitched itself back together just as quickly. The amulet burned against his chest, ancient magic carving a precise path through temporal currents.

Suddenly, the tunnel collapsed.

He slammed into solid ground with bone-jarring force.

Cold concrete met his palms. He lay sprawled in a dimly lit alleyway, lungs burning, head spinning. The night air carried unfamiliar scents, strange spices mingling with industrial fumes. His prison uniform was gone, replaced with civilian clothing that felt strange and outdated against his skin.

A newspaper blew across the wet pavement, headline flashing briefly under a flickering streetlamp.

"Monster Integration Act Passes – Historic New Era Begins."

A soft footfall stirred the shadows near the alley's end.

A figure stepped forward, tall and slender, wrapped in a midnight-blue cloak. Starlight seemed to cling to her movements. As she approached, her hood lowered enough to reveal a striking face of obsidian skin that drank in the light, shaped with haunting beauty. Not quite the cosmic being he knew, not yet, but her eyes held familiar galaxies.

"You've arrived earlier than expected," Nyarlathotep's voice carried only a faint echo of the cosmic resonance he remembered, softer, more human, "the timeline is… different this time."

She studied him with cautious recognition, as though tracing the outline of a memory she could not fully grasp.

"You're the one I've been waiting for, though I don't yet understand why," he lifted his head, tears slipping fast from both eyes.

He looked up to her, "Nyarlathotep?"

The cloaked figure knelt beside him. Her movements were more grounded than the celestial being who had once held him, yet hints of otherworldly grace lingered in the curve of her shoulders and the precision of her gaze. She looked younger, untouched by centuries of imprisonment.

Her eyes widened at the sight of his tears, galaxies spinning faster within their depths, "You know me," her hand lifted hesitantly, only one hand, not six, hovering near his tear-streaked face, "but we haven't met... not in this timeline."

Rain began to fall, droplets sliding through certain parts of her cloak as though encountering empty space. The amulet against his chest pulsed once, responding to her proximity.

She noticed immediately, "The Chronos Stone," and her voice dropped to a whisper. Her fingers traced the air inches above the amulet without touching it, "I've seen it only in visions. Then you are truly..."

She helped him to his feet with surprising strength. Her touch was solid yet tinged with the faint void-cool sensation he remembered. Around her neck, he noticed a silver pendant, simple yet ominous, the precursor to the mask that would one day imprison her.

"We must move quickly. The Wardens are already searching for temporal anomalies," her eyes searched his with urgency and a fragile, blooming hope, "you came back to change something. To prevent something."

"I came to love you, but now isn't the time; we must go, go now," he said, and the world paused for a moment.

Nyarlathotep's eyes widened, galaxies spinning wildly. A shimmer crossed her obsidian features, fleeting and delicate, something between shock and the first spark of recognition.

She seized his hand with sudden urgency, "Love?" She spoke the word slowly, tasting it like something new and strange, "We have much to discuss, but you're right, this place isn't safe."

She pulled him deeper into the alley just as patrol lights swept across the street. Her cloak rippled, bending light in a subtle distortion that concealed their forms. Beyond the alleyway, the city unfolded in a blend of familiar and alien sights. Monster integration posters hung beside human storefronts, and armed guards patrolled intersections with uneasy vigilance.

Nyarlathotep guided him through a twisting maze of narrow back streets, moving with a confidence that suggested she had walked these hidden routes many times before. Every few steps, she paused, tilting her head as detection devices perched along the rooftops emitted soft pings in response to her unusual energy signature. Each time, the silver pendant at her throat shimmered faintly, suppressing the alert and cloaking her presence from the machines searching for anomalies.

"The safe house is near," she whispered. Her voice lacked the celestial resonance of her future self, yet the melodic undertone remained familiar, "There are others who will help us-those who've seen fragments of what's coming. The prison, the experiments...we've been gathering evidence, but lacked the crucial piece."

She looked back at him with new intensity and squeezed his hand with her single pair of fingers, grounding him in this unfamiliar timeline, "You're that piece, aren't you? The proof of what they eventually become."

"Maybe, just don't leave me again. especially with demon chics," he chuckled and looked at her again, "I think that's how it all began..."

A quiet smile touched Nyarlathotep's lips, revealing the subtle humor she would one day keep buried beneath centuries of imprisonment. She led him toward a narrow, nondescript door between abandoned storefronts, her hand remaining firmly entwined with his.

"Demon chics?" The past version of Nyarlathotep was equally intelligent and dignified with her integrity. She arched an eyebrow, amusement flickering across her cosmic eyes, "Is that what they called us in your time? The categorization system must have...deteriorated."

She pressed her palm against the metal door. A soft glow radiated outward from her handprint before the entrance slid open in a silent, seamless motion.

Inside, the safe house was larger than expected. The air hummed with outdated yet advanced technology, a strange fusion of analog machinery and early holographic systems. One wall was plastered with maps and glowing projections, early drafts of the prison schematics he recognized, though crude compared to the future facility's precision.

Several figures turned toward them as they entered.

Young monster girls.

Not yet prisoners.

Not yet broken.

He recognized them instantly... early versions of inmates he had known so intimately in later years. A salamander whose arms had not yet been scarred by restraints. A kitsune with unrestrained, elegant tails flowing freely behind her. Others lurked deeper in the shadows, watching with a mixture of caution and curiosity.

"I found him," Nyarlathotep announced, her voice carrying new authority that quieted the room, "the temporal displacement was accurate within three blocks."

She turned to him again, silver pendant catching bluish light from the holograms as she studied his face, seeking patterns she was only beginning to understand.

"I won't leave you again," she said softly, meant only for him, "though technically, I haven't left you a first time yet."

Her fingers brushed the amulet at his chest, "but time is circular when you exist partially outside it. I'm beginning to understand what my future self saw in you."

He stared into her eyes, disbelief heavy in his voice. looks into her eyes in disbelief

"Well..." his eyes turned into a yellowish ruby, "there are a few things actually..."

Nyarlathotep's gaze widened as his irises shifted color, the yellowish-ruby glow reflected perfectly in her cosmic depths. Her hand lifted instinctively, tracing the air near his cheek as though reading energy patterns only she could perceive.

"You've been changed by the temporal journey," she whispered, studying him with a blend of scientific fascination and something more profound, "or perhaps... You were always more than you appeared."

The room fell silent.

The young salamander stepped closer, her unscarred arms glowing with gentle heat, "He carries chronos energy as we've never seen," she observed, her voice lacking the bitterness of her imprisoned future self, "And something else... something older."

Nyarlathotep's silver pendant pulsed in answer to his altered eyes, briefly shifting to match their strange hue. Her expression changed instantly as understanding dawned, reshaping her features.

"You didn't just come back," she murmured, "you brought something with you. Something of me, me... my future self, is encoded within you."

Her voice softened further, "That's how you found me specifically. That's how you knew." She turned to the gathered resistance members, her spine straightening with sharp resolve.

"The timeline has been more significantly altered than we planned. But perhaps..." She glanced back at him, a spark of purpose illuminating her gaze. "...perhaps that's exactly what we needed."

"Where's the Arachne?" He asked, and the question hung in the air, cutting through the tension like a blade.

The room fell abruptly silent at his question. The atmosphere, once buzzing with cautious energy, thickened with tension. Nyarlathotep's expression darkened, the galaxies in her eyes tightening into defensive spirals, their rotations sharpening with concern. The salamander beside her exchanged a troubled look, her scales flaring brighter in agitation.

"The Arachne..." Young Nyarlathotep began, her voice tightened with strain, "Aranae was captured three days ago. She was our infiltration specialist."

The kitsune stepped forward, her multiple tails flaring subtly in response to the tension. She looked younger, softer than the hardened prisoner he would one day know, her features still touched by hope beneath layers of survival instinct.

"They're holding her at the prototype detention facility-the very one we've been monitoring. It's where they're testing the specialized containment systems," her ears folded back, betraying fear she tried to hide, "the rumors say they're using her to calibrate the silk-harvesting apparatus."

Nyarlathotep's hand found his again. Her grip tightened, not out of fear, but because she was studying him, reading every microexpression with newfound intensity, "You knew to ask about her specifically. Is she important to the timeline?" Her voice lowered, "Or important to you?"

A nearby holographic display flickered awake, illuminating the room with pale blue light. Surveillance footage appeared, a restrained but defiant Arachne being escorted into a fortified compound. She moved with innate grace, even in shackles. The pride in her posture had not yet been beaten into submission by years of captivity.

"Shit. Ok, Mizuki, there should be an ice lamia assassin and a," He *chuckled,* "a plant girl that's more powerful than all of us when she's pissed."

The kitsune Mizuki, jolted at hearing her name spoken so casually, so confidently. Her tails lashed in surprise before settling into a slow, analytical sway. She stepped closer, examining him with growing interest, as though searching for memories she did not yet have.

"The ice lamia, you mean Yukionna? She's been operating as our external contact," Mizuki's ears twitched nervously, "but we lost communication yesterday. We feared the worst."

Nyarlathotep's expression grew heavier as she absorbed his knowledge, knowledge he should not have had, "and Florina…"

She gestured to the far corner of the room, where a figure had been quietly observing. Florina stepped forward, her presence soft but commanding. Young, unscarred, and not yet consumed by the violent rage of her future self, she carried herself with eerie composure.

Her vine-like hair shifted with each breath, small blossoms blooming and dying across her arms in a slow, mesmerizing rhythm, a natural cycle that would one day be suppressed behind layers of chemical dampeners.

"You know what I become?" Florina asked, her voice was soft but piercing, like roots cracking stone, "interesting. Most see only what I allow them to see."

She approached with measured poise, her steps nearly soundless, "If you understand my capabilities, then you know Aranae's extraction isn't simple. They've lined the facility with chemical suppressants specifically designed for plant-based entities," her eyes narrowed, a quiet challenge forming, "though I'm curious how you know about my… temperament."

Nyarlathotep watched the exchange with increasing comprehension, more pieces of the puzzle snapping together in her mind.

"The timeline is converging faster than we anticipated. These aren't coincidence, your arrival, Aranae's capture, Yukionna's disappearance…" She turned to the assembled resistance members, her posture straightening with new resolve, "We need to accelerate our plans."

The plan felt wrong to him, at least according to what he knew would happen, so he exclaimed, "No! We need extractions, regrouping, and patience. Striking is how we are all divided and conquered. They're WAITING on y'all. I was caught years later. And I know your temperament cuz I tested it. I do still have lust as a charmer to get through what I do. Wait, my memories. Who can read memories and transfer images to Mizuki?!"

His urgent warning fractured the room's fragile confidence. Shock and unease rippled through the resistance members, their expressions shifting from determination to fear of unseen traps.

Nyarlathotep stepped closer, her cosmic eyes narrowing as each word sank into her.

"A trap…" Young Nyarlathotep murmured the realization, the pendant at her throat pulsing with a dim yet ominous glow, "that would explain the ease of our recent intelligence gathering."

Florina retreated a half step, her expression sharpening as subtle thorns pushed through the skin of her forearms in a reflexive defense. They

287

retracted just as quickly as she regained control, but her calculating gaze never left his face.

"Tested my temperament? Interesting choice of words," a cold, fleeting smile traced Florina's lips, "few survive such tests."

Mizuki's ears perked at the mention of memory transfer, her multiple tails swishing with sudden alertness. The movement sent ripples of silvery light through the air, a signature of her still-untamed illusion abilities.

"Memory extraction is Lilim's specialty," Mizuki gestured toward a shadowed alcove where a petite figure sat cross-legged amid floating data screens, "but she's been reluctant to use her abilities since the neural feedback incident."

The mentioned figure lifted her head.

Violent purple light flickered through her eyes, technological augmentations that would one day be outlawed, then violently removed inside the prison. Lilim looked far younger, her face free of the tattoos and hardened stare she would carry in the future.

"I can extract surface memories without damage," Lilim stated clinically as she rose and approached him, "deeper transfers carry risks, especially across temporal variance."

Nyarlathotep watched the exchange with growing concern, her fingers unconsciously brushing the silver pendant resting at her throat. The galaxies in her eyes spun with rising tension, "If they're anticipating our moves as you suggest, then our entire resistance network is compromised."

Her gaze locked onto him with sudden urgency, "What else do you remember? Who betrays us?"

He looked at her with a sudden urgency, but the hope was deeper, "it wasn't betrayal, it was bribery. Nyarlathotep, I love you, but do you trust me?"

Nyarlathotep froze.

The galaxies in her eyes stilled completely, frozen in suspended cosmic silence. Around them, the resistance fell quiet, each member instinctively recognizing the gravity in his tone. Emotions flickered across her face: confusion, fear, vulnerability, and the first spark of something deeper... something her future self had buried beneath centuries of cosmic suffering.

"Love..." she breathed the word softly, tasting it as though it were new to her.

"You speak of a future I haven't experienced yet," Nyarlathotep's hand lifted to the silver pendant, drawing strength from the cold metal, "but yes, strangely, I find I do trust you. Perhaps because some part of me recognizes what we become."

Resolve straightened her spine, and the galaxies in her eyes began to move again, slowly at first, then with purpose, "Tell us what you know. Who was bribed, and how do we prevent the division you've witnessed?"

Lilim stepped closer, her augmented gaze scanning him with growing technical fascination, "If direct communication is too risky, I can establish a partial neural link. Surface thought only, enough to transfer critical images without triggering temporal paradox effects."

Florina moved nearer as well, the green tint of her skin deepening as she concentrated. Subtle vines twitched along her arms, responding to her shifting emotions, "If we're compromised as you suggest, we need to extract our people immediately. Aranae, Yukionna... anyone exposed."

Mizuki's tails curled and uncurled nervously behind her, her ears pinned forward as she watched him with searching eyes, "You've lived through what happens if we fail, haven't you? That's why you're here?"

Then began his instructions, the plan.

He commanded Florina first, "Florina, baby girl, you are NOT gonna like this, but I need you to exude a happy scent around this perimeter now, then poison it, killing anyone who's drawn into the pheromones."

His gaze shifted toward the young Kitsune, "Mizuki, I'm going to do something very unorthodox, but I need you to project EVERYTHING to Nyarlathotep."

Extending his plan, he faced Lilim now, "Lilim, baby, you are strong, and I need you to transfer a copy of my entire mind into Mizuki's ability to project so that Nyarlathotep doesn't miss a SINGLE detail."

He signaled for execution; it had to be done immediately. "Everyone, move now!" and grabbed Mizuki's face.

"Nyarlathotep, sit next to me, hun, put your projection paws in her face, but do NOT touch her. Lilim, when Mizuki's eyes close, you can begin." And they got into action.

The room erupted into controlled chaos.

Resistance members scattered to their stations with disciplined urgency.

Florina's eyes narrowed at being called "baby girl," a flicker of irritation crossing her features before the severity of the moment consumed her attention.

"Poison and pheromones together? That's..." a dark admiration shaped her smile, "efficient."

She extended her arms outward.

Flowers burst into bloom along her skin, fragile petals opening in brilliant colors before releasing a cloying, intoxicating scent into the air. She moved deliberately around the perimeter, trailing faint vines that sealed exits and window seams, constructing a natural perimeter laced with lethal beauty.

As the fragrance thickened, her expression hardened. The innocence of her younger self eroded with every breath she took, replaced with glimpses of the deadly, unrestrained fury she would one day become behind prison walls.

Mizuki moved swiftly to his side, her multiple tails bristling with nervous energy as his hands framed her face. Her eyes widened at the sudden intimacy, but she did not retreat. Instead, her breath steadied, her posture firming with commitment.

"Full mental projection is dangerous without..." Mizuki was analyzing the risks... but she cut herself off, resolve tightening her features, "I'll channel everything. Nothing will be lost." She assured everyone.

Nyarlathotep stepped close to him, her presence grounding the room. The galaxies within her eyes intensified, spiraling faster as she extended

290

her hands near Mizuki's temples without touching. A field of shimmering energy blossomed between them, the air rippling with quiet cosmic hum.

"I'm ready," Young Nyarlathotep whispered, her voice steadier than the flicker of uncertainty crossing her expression, "show me everything."

Lilim approached with clinical precision, her augmented violet eyes scanning energy signatures invisible to anyone else. Small data screens began to hover around her fingers, flickering with code as she prepared the neural link.

Lilim announced, "Beginning synchronization. Temporal variance will cause discomfort. Brace yourselves."

Mizuki's eyes drifted shut, her tails lifting and spreading behind her in a fan-like display that radiated raw magical tension. Lilim placed her fingertips at his temples, and a tingling sensation spread across his scalp like static dancing along his skin.

"Transfer initiating. Three… two… one…" Lilim's voice grew intense and focused as a pulse of energy surged from her touch.

His vision shattered into a mosaic of luminous fragments, a kaleidoscope of warped shapes and rushing starlight.

As his eyes closed… There was a darkness.

Then an explosion of light as a trillion galaxies burst and rushed past him.

"This is it, no longer falling."

He thought… or said…? Though the boundary between mind and voice dissolved instantly as the timelines flickered around him.

A psychic maelstrom swallowed the room.

His consciousness merged with Mizuki's projection ability, amplified by Lilim's neural technology and channeled through the cosmic awareness that was Nyarlathotep. The world of walls and bodies vanished, replaced by a realm sculpted entirely from memory, emotion, and timeline echoes.

Images erupted in rapid succession:

-   The failed rescue that triggered mass arrests.

291

- Aranae's silk harvested for specialized suppression collars.
- Florina's rage-fueled rampage that tore half the prison apart before ending in her permanent solitary confinement.
- Mizuki's slow, horrific punishment, her tails removed one by one for repeated escape attempts.
- Lilim's augmentations, hijacked and weaponized against her until she no longer recognized friend from foe.

And at the center of it all. Nyarlathotep.

Imprisoned. Masked. Bound. Her cosmic nature choked beneath restraints engineered through years of dissecting her biology.

Nyarlathotep gasped, her whole-body trembling as she absorbed the catastrophic future laid bare before her. The galaxies in her eyes spun wildly, desperate to process more reality than a mortal timeline could contain.

"So much suffering…" Her voice was everywhere, inside the psychic storm, across the collapsing images, woven into the consciousness of everyone present, "all because we moved too quickly, too predictably."

From somewhere in the physical world, Florina's voice cut through the psychic turbulence like a blade, "It's working. Two guards just approached… they're down. But there will be more. Whatever you're showing her, finish it quickly."

The transfer intensified, homing in on the most critical elements, security codes, guard patterns, suppressor weaknesses, the exact design of the future restraint system, the names of those who accepted bribes, and finally the intricate trap awaiting the resistance.

Mizuki trembled violently. Her tails went rigid, then quivered under the strain. Blood trickled from her nose in thin red lines, but she refused to break.

"Synaptic overload imminent." Lilim alerted them, "Ten seconds remaining before forced disconnection."

The final sequence of images burned itself into Nyarla'smind:

Her future self and him, seated together in the dim light of the prison's maintenance tunnels, planning this temporal intervention with exhausted determination yet undeniable love.

He glared at the moment, "There's the love of my life, and I hope I'm hers."

Everything rushed backward, collapsing into itself. A crushing blackness swallowed the last of the light.

Then…

Darkness unraveled.

He slammed back into his body with a violent jolt, gasping as real air filled his lungs. The room spun wildly before stabilizing into harsh clarity. Around him, the aftermath was written plainly across their faces.

Mizuki slumped forward the moment the psychic connection snapped, her once-bristling tails falling limp like severed ribbons.

Lilim caught her swiftly, lowering her with practiced care. Diagnostic glyphs rippled across Lilim's augmented eyes as she scanned the fox-girl's vitals.

"She'll recover. The projection strain was… significant," her fingers ghosted over Mizuki's pulse points, "but nothing permanent."

Nyarlathotep did not move.

She stood beside him like a statue of obsidian and starlight, her cosmic eyes wide… unfocused, as she processed visions of years she had not yet lived. Entire futures flickered behind her gaze, shifting her aura into something older, heavier… destined.

When she finally spoke, her voice carried a resonance that had not belonged to her moments ago.

"You and I… we…" She met his gaze, and in her eyes he found recognition that transcended time, something deeper, ancient, inevitable, "everything changes now."

She reached out, stopping her fingertip just short of touching his, a gesture intimate enough to bridge two lifetimes.

"We have twelve hours before the system flags Aranae's scheduled interrogation. We'll extract her using the maintenance tunnels, exactly as you showed me." Turning to the others, Nyarlathotep spoke with a leader's authority, "Florina, withdraw your toxins. We need to move quickly but cautiously."

Florina inhaled sharply, her vine-laced skin flowering inward as she pulled the pheromones and poisons back into herself, a technique she would later wield with far more lethal refinement.

"Four neutralized at the perimeter. No alarms triggered," she stepped closer, studying him with new respect. Suspicion lingered but softened, replaced with a grudging acceptance, "your methods are... unexpected. But effective."

Nyarlathotep rose and extended her hand to him, helping him stand. Her touch was deliberate this time, soft, grounding, threaded with the fragile beginnings of destiny. "We'll rewrite this future. Together." She said with a newfound confidence.

"As long as I can rewrite your insides later, baby," He chuckled delusionally, struggling to get up.

"Ok, we gotta move. And Flo, I knew that agitating you would access the chemical compound to create that chemical." He stooped down and grabbed Mizuki's head, pressing his forehead against hers.

"This should revitalize you," he breathed in deep, slowly exhaling, and feeling the warmth of where a rune used to be.

His risqué remark drew a sharp flash of shock across Nyarlathotep's face, but then a faint, knowing smile, one echoed from a lifetime she had not yet lived.

The others exchanged quick, bewildered glances, silently revising their understanding of whatever strange bond existed between him and their yet-to-be cosmic leader.

"Focus on the mission first," Nyarlathotep murmured. But a subtle, shimmering blush rippled along the edges of her cosmic eyes.

As he leaned down and pressed his forehead to Mizuki's, a faint glow radiated from the point of contact. His breath warmed the air, stirring something dormant in the space where a rune had once rested on his brow. Energy pulsed outward, gentle, revitalizing.

Mizuki's eyes fluttered open, bright with returning vitality as her tails twitched back to life.

"How did you…" she gasped as strength surged through her limbs, "that's kitsune life-sharing… but you're human…"

Florina watched with narrowed eyes, her green-tinted skin deepening as her curiosity sharpened into something almost predatory, "knew which buttons to push, did you?" a tone both respectful and warning, "remember that knowledge cuts both ways."

Vines withdrew from the doors as she gestured toward the exit, clearing their path.

Lilim's voice cut sharply across the room, "temporal anomaly detected." Her augmented eyes locked onto him, scanning rapidly, "Your molecular structure is… fluctuating. This transfer has accelerated entropy in your timeline anchor."

Nyarlathotep stepped toward him immediately, alarm flashing through the cosmic spirals of her gaze. She studied him closely, reading the ripples of time unraveling around his form.

"She's right. You're becoming unstable," her voice tightened, "how much time do you have before you return to your original point?"

The room thickened with a new kind of urgency, one that reached beyond strategy and survival. They were no longer racing against guards or suppression systems, but the ticking decay of reality itself.

"I don't know. But I'll love you in every timeline, Nyarlathotep. Just don't leave me alone," he slumped down, "Damn, I do still owe that spider a kiss tho she hel…" His words dissolved mid-sentence as temporal instability surged. The room warped. Edges blurred. Sound fractured.

Nyarlathotep lunged forward, catching him before he collapsed entirely. Despite her ethereal appearance, her grip was firm, grounding him in this timeline with the strength of someone who had seen their shared future.

"I won't leave you alone, not in any timeline," her cosmic eyes locked onto his, fierce with promise, "and we'll save your spider friend too."

Mizuki scrambled upright, her once-limp tails now flaring behind her in a vibrant arc of anxious motion. Their tips sparked faintly with restored magic as she took in the sight of his unstable form.

"He's phase-shifting! We're losing him!" Mizuki alerted everyone.

Lilim reacted instantly. Holographic interfaces bloomed around her fingers like neon petals, shifting in midair as her augmented eyes processed layers of temporal data at impossible speed.

"Attempting stabilization. Creating a temporal anchor point... now," she pressed her palm flat to his chest.

A jolt of energy surged through him, sharp and electrifying. The flickering distortions froze mid-ripple. He felt suspended. locked inside the space between one heartbeat and the next. No falling. No slipping. Just a fragile, unnatural stillness.

"We need to move. Guards will be changing shifts in ten minutes," Florina said. Despite her pragmatic tone, a flicker of concern shadowed her expression, "Can he travel?"

Nyarlathotep's response was immediate and decisive. She kept one hand pressed firmly to him while the other traced intricate sigils through the air, cosmic trails blooming and fading at her fingertips.

"I'll tether him to my timeline until we reach Aranae. The connection we share..." her voice softened, and something ancient, familiar passed through her gaze, "...it's stronger than I understood. I can use it."

She leaned in close, her breath brushing his ear as the others prepared to move, "Hold on to me. In every way you can."

He held on to her as tightly as he could. His fingers dug into her arm, clinging with desperate strength as reality around him continued to ripple and distort. Nyarla's cosmic skin responded, shifting its texture to strengthen the tether between them.

"I've got you," Nyarlathotep whispered, steady and sure, channeling her temporal power into his fracturing existence.

The resistance team moved with precision.

Florina took point, toxic blossoms blooming across her skin, their scents sharp and ready. Mizuki flanked his other side, tails fanned protectively, ears flicking toward every sound. Lilim trailed behind, scanning for surveillance nodes or approaching guards.

They slipped through sterile hallways lit by buzzing strips of artificial light. Twice, they froze as patrols passed moments away, breath held, movement stilled. Each pause intensified his flickering, and each time Nyarlathotep tightened her grip, grounding him with cosmic warmth.

"Subsection 8-C ahead. Aranae's holding cell is two levels down." Lilim announced.

The service elevator loomed before them, cramped, metallic, and humming with old machinery. As the group squeezed inside, Nyarlathotep pulled him against her, her cosmic aura unfurling around him like a nebula made flesh.

"Stay with me," Nyarlathotep commanded him softly as the elevator shuddered into descent, "focus on my voice. At this moment."

The motion downward mirrored the sensation inside his dissolving body, a freefall of molecules barely clinging to this timeline. Through the haze, he caught the expressions of those around him. Worry etched Mizuki's fox-like features. Lilim's jaw was tense.

Even Florina's hardened glare had softened, "Almost there. Hold together, human."

The elevator chimed. Doors slid open.

Mizuki gasped.

The corridor beyond stretched long and cold, lined with specialized containment cells. And at the farthest end…

A familiar multi-limbed silhouette hung suspended in a web of restraints.

"Wait, floor check the floor."

Nyarlathotep froze instantly, raising a clenched fist. The team halted mid-step.

Florina dropped low, her skin shifting seamlessly into a metallic sheen, blending with the corridor floor as she scanned for threats, "What does he see?" she breathed.

Lilim's eyes whirred softly as her vision shifted through spectrums, infrared, arcane, structural, "pressure plates. Disguised but present. Good catch." Her expression tightened.

The floor at first glance looked standard, smooth reinforced prison tiles, but subtle seams formed a deadly lattice. Invisible until noticed, precision-wired filaments ran from plate to plate and up the walls, connecting to sleek, dangerous mechanisms embedded within the structure.

Mizuki's ears flattened as realization sharpened her features. Her voice dropped to a whisper filled with dread and reluctant admiration. "Aranae's own silk," she murmured, "they forced her to create the very trap meant to catch her rescuers."

Nyarlathotep's grip on him tightened, her cosmic essence swirling violently for a heartbeat as she studied the design. Despite his unstable form flickering at the edges, his mind remained cuttingly focused, a detail that did not escape her notice.

"This is why we needed you," she said quietly, meeting his gaze with those shifting galaxies, "these weren't in the official security schematics."

Florina extended a thin vine-like tendril, testing the air just above the nearest pressure plate. The tendril recoiled before touching the trapped tile, "There's an alternative route. Maintenance crawlspace." She gestured to a narrow ceiling panel nearly invisible in the shadows, "tight fit, but safer."

He disagreed, and in the same weak state, he suggested, "No, use the vines to get her to free herself, and she crawls out the space she's aware and been plotting that route we'd get in her way."

Nyarlathotep's eyes widened, the cosmic swirls within them spinning faster as his insight reshaped the plan. She exchanged a brief, sharp look with Florina, who nodded once, grudging respect cutting through her usual guardedness.

"Clever," Florina admitted, extending several vines along the ceiling, "let her free herself rather than triggering her defenses."

Lilim prepared a small communicator, attaching it to the tip of Florina's vine. The plant-woman's appendages stretched gracefully across the ceiling, carefully avoiding every pressure plate, until they reached Aranae's cell.

Through his temporal distortion, Aranae came into focus with startling clarity.

Her upper body was humanoid, pale, etched with violet markings that pulsed faintly. Her lower half, the massive spider abdomen and eight powerful legs, hung immobilized in specialized restraints she had clearly weakened in secret. Her six eyes blinked in a silent code of recognition as the vine delivered the communicator.

"She's already working on it," the fox whispered, pointing to near-invisible silk strands Aranae had been weakening, "She knew we'd come."

Aranae tilted her head as Lilim whispered through the communicator. A slow smile pulled at her lips when she spotted the group by the elevator.

With sudden, lethal grace, she flexed her limbs. The pre-weakened silk restraints snapped one by one. Her spider legs unfurled like blades, catching her fall as she landed silently between the pressure plates. She scaled the wall and moved across the ceiling in seamless, predatory motion.

A moment later, she dropped lightly beside the group.

"Right on schedule," Aranae whispered, six eyes blinking in rapid sequence as she studied him with unsettling intensity, "so you're the temporal anomaly Nyarlathotep promised would help. You look... unstable."

One of her hands almost reached toward him, but froze as Nyarla's cosmic aura flared defensively around his flickering form.

"Later, Aranae. He mentioned you two have... unfinished business." A spark of possessiveness edged her voice... surprising even her, "but we need to move now."

"We've one more to collect, and then we should have time to catch us a succubus." He meddled with the conversation.

All six of Aranae's eyes widened at once, pupils dilating in predatory delight. Her spider limbs clicked in a rhythmic pattern, unmistakably her form of laughter.

"A succubus hunt? Now you're speaking my language," she bared elongated canines in a vicious smile, "those parasites have been feeding off prisoners for too long."

Another wave of temporal dissonance tore through him, making his form shudder violently. Nyarlathotep steadied him instantly, her cosmic aura knitting tighter to his faltering presence.

"Who's the last extraction target?" Nyarla's voice remained steady despite the effort of maintaining his temporal tether.

Lilim's augmented eyes lit up as holographic data scrolled across them, "subject designation: Ryu, Dragonkin. Maximum security wing, eastern quadrant. Pyrokinetic abilities neutralized by dampening field."

Florina hissed softly, as though steam escaped from heated foliage, "The fire-breather? She's unstable. Burned three guards to ash during her last escape attempt."

Mizuki's tails flicked nervously behind her, but determination hardened her expression. "She's also the only one who knows the override codes for the main security grid. Without her, we can't access the succubus holding area."

Aranae stepped closer, her movements smooth and predatory, each of her spider limbs adjusting with delicate precision. The scent that radiated from her, cinnamon braided with ozone, enveloped him in a strangely electrifying warmth.

"Fascinating. You're both here and not here simultaneously," one of her slender hands lifted toward his temple, "May I?"

Before Nyarlathotep could protest, Aranae's fingertip brushed his skin. A single silken thread formed, anchoring itself between her touch and his flickering form. The effect was immediate; his body solidified just enough to breathe without slipping through reality.

"My silk can anchor temporal fragments. It won't last, but it might help until we complete the mission," Her gaze met his... all six eyes focusing with intense curiosity, "that kiss you mentioned? Consider it payment rendered in advance."

He said, "Damn, someone spilled the beans on me. Anyway, we need the fire-breather to unlock the pathway to get the ice lamia, so we can actually CATCH Lilith. Don't think she'll like being caught; it beats the alternative I have in mind for her."

Aranae's eyes blinked in rapid sequence, amusement rippling across her expression, "Well, well… you're full of delightful secrets, aren't you?" Her voice dropped into a sultry whisper, "Lilith herself. Ambitious."

Nyarlathotep's cosmic essence flared protectively, spiraling faster as she processed the new direction of his plan, "an ice lamia… Solara mentioned nothing about this."

Her star-flecked gaze narrowed, "You're playing a deeper game than she let on."

Florina clicked her tongue sharply, irritation swirling with her toxic pollen, "Ryuko first, then we discuss the sudden change of plans." A quick glance at a nearby security panel. Florina reminded, "We have eighteen minutes before the next patrol sweep."

Lilim recalibrated instantly, her augmented eyes whirring with shifting holographic data, "Eastern quadrant requires a biometric override. I have the templates, but…"

She paused, studying him with renewed intensity, "…an ice lamia would indeed neutralize Lilith's thermal advantage. Tactically sound."

The group advanced swiftly through narrow maintenance passages. Aranae occasionally cast silk strands ahead to map unseen traps, her silk-thread tether helping stabilize his unstable presence. The edges of his vision still wavered, but her anchor held him tethered to the moment.

Mizuki drifted closer, whispering nervously, "What exactly do you have planned for Lilith that's worse than capture?"

Aranae chuckled softly, her spider limbs clicking with a rhythm akin to dark amusement, "I'm starting to see why my future self was so interested in you. You think like a spider… always several moves ahead."

The temperature rose sharply as they approached the eastern quadrant. The air shimmered with heat radiating off the reinforced door ahead, marked with hazard sigils that pulsed like living embers.

"Whatever your strategy, I hope it works," Nyarlathotep said, her tone carrying both caution and something possessive, "Because if Ryuko doesn't cooperate, we'll have a very angry dragon and not enough time to implement your plan B."

"My plan B is my death, so none of this ever happens, and that ice lamia is an assassin almost as good as I am." He revealed an arrogant grin, "I'm only slightly better. And leave the dragon to me, the only thing I can think of is either she loves me, and this works easily, or she hates me, and I owe her…wish me luck…"

His words triggered a ripple of reactions:

Aranae's eyes dilated with predatory fascination.

Mizuki's tails puffed in alarm.

Florina's skin deepened to a richer green, betraying agitation.

Nyarlathotep's cosmic aura pulsed violently, a flare of emotion she barely contained, "That's not an option," she said sharply, gripping his shoulder harder as temporal energy surged between them, "Your death isn't on the table."

Lilim stepped forward, placing her palm against the security panel. Her augmented fingers interfaced directly, bypassing the first lock as glowing circuits awakened beneath her touch, "I can get us in, but the dampening field will affect all of us. Your temporal instability may… react unpredictably."

Aranae circled to his other side, her six eyes studying him like a rare specimen she admired… and wanted, "an assassin's mindset indeed. Always willing to be the sacrificial piece."

Her spider limbs clicked, "though I'm curious about this ice lamia who nearly matches your skill."

Then suddenly… a massive blast door groaned open, revealing a chamber bathed in pulsing red emergency light. Beyond it lay a second armored door, thick, scorched, and inscribed with sigils meant to restrain something ancient and furious.

Ryuko.

The dragon.

Mizuki's ears pressed flat against her head, her tails twitching like agitated flames as she felt the rising heat radiating from behind the reinforced door.

"Whatever history you have with Ryuko, make it count," Mizuki whispered, her voice wavering between warning and worry, "dragons have long memories, especially for grudges."

Nyarlathotep reluctantly loosened her grip, though her cosmic fingers trailed across his unstable form as if afraid the moment she released him, he might vanish into another timeline entirely.

"Remember, in this timeline, she may not know you yet," Nyarlathotep's voice softened into something intimate, fragile beneath the urgency, "and if your plan fails... we find another way. Together."

Lilim concentrated fully on the inner door's locking systems, her augmented fingers working through layer after layer of security until the final mechanism disengaged with a low, metallic groan.

The door slid open, and a wave of blistering heat washed over the group.

Inside the containment cell hovered a woman suspended within an anti-gravity field: crimson scales gleaming like molten gemstones across her otherwise humanoid body. Her long hair hung weightless around her like drifting embers. When her eyes snapped open, molten-gold irises locked instantly onto him.

Predatory.

Recognizing.

Hungry.

"You..." Ryuko's growl vibrated the air itself, even under the dampening field's constraints. "The timeline walker. Come to collect another debt?" Her eyes looked like they could kill.

"Actually, hun, yes, that debt is your freedom out of here. Of course, for your assistance. But with that look you're giving me, I see you look like you have something else in mind." He glared at her with ruby-eyed intent.

Ryuko's lips curled into a dangerous smile, revealing teeth sharp enough to cut bone. The containment field crackled violently as she shifted within it, crimson scales shimmering under the emergency lights.

"Freedom for assistance? How... transactional," her golden gaze raked over his unstable form with calculating hunger, "but that look in your eyes... I've seen it before. In another timeline, perhaps?"

Her taloned fingers flexed against the restraining field, causing sparks of uncontrolled power to ripple outward. Small wisps of smoke curled from the corners of her mouth as she continued, "You once promised me revenge against the Warden. Is that still on the table, timeline walker?"

Behind him, Nyarlathotep's cosmic essence flared, protective and sharp, while Aranae positioned herself strategically, silk threads ready at her fingertips.

Florina and Mizuki exchanged tense glances, and Lilim's augmented eyes flicked between Ryuko and the security console.

"We have thirteen minutes before the security sweep," Nyarlathotep murmured, though a faint edge of jealousy colored her tone.

Ryuko's gaze shifted briefly to Nyarlathotep, recognition of a rival, perhaps, before returning to him with a slow, incendiary smile.

"I see you've collected quite the...entourage this time," The containment field sparked violently as Ryuko leaned forward.

"Very well. Release me, and I'll assist with your ice lamia hunt. But afterward..." her eyes glowed brighter, heat rippling the air, "...you and I have unfinished business that will require... privacy."

He swallowed hard, "Privacy indeed, that doesn't leave burn marks, and the deal is yours. Also, we'll get to the Warden later on. We have a rescue and catch mission right now."

Ryuko's laugh rolled through the containment chamber like a seismic tremor, deep, throaty, filled with dangerous delight. Heat surged, distorting the air into trembling waves.

"No burn marks… this time. Agreed," Her predatory grin widened, "release me, and your prey becomes mine as well."

Lilim stepped forward, hesitation flickering across her face as she interfaced with the control panel, "disabling the dampening field will trigger a silent alert. We'll have approximately seven minutes before response teams mobilize."

Aranae approached the edge of the field, spinning a nearly invisible filament between her fingers, "I can jam the signal for an additional three minutes. No more."

Nyarlathotep tightened her cosmic tether around him, her aura pulsing with rising urgency, "Do it."

The containment field shut down with a descending electrical hum.

Ryuko dropped gracefully to the floor, landing with predatory elegance. Her muscles flexed beneath crimson scales, small flames dancing between her fingers before she extinguished them with forced restraint, "the override codes."

She rolled her shoulders, revealing vestigial wing structures that unfurled with a metallic hiss before folding back, "Section 12, east quadrant. That's where they keep the ice manipulators."

Ryuko moved to his side with the measured, predatory grace of a creature who had never once forgotten she was apex. Heat radiated from her body in rolling waves, an intensity that struck sharply against the unstable shimmer of his fluctuating timeline signature.

Her molten-gold eyes narrowed as she studied him, "Your presence stabilizes when I'm near. Interesting."

A single talon traced along his jawline, leaving behind a faint streak of warmth but no burn, a controlled, intentional caress: "You were right to come for me first."

Behind them, Mizuki cleared her throat in a jittery burst of nerves, her fox tails bristling, "We should move. Now."

305

Ryuko didn't look away from him as she nodded, "Lead on, timeline walker. Let's catch your lamia… and then your succubus."

He paused, "Wait, Arachne hunny make a weighted cocoon, you should know the one I'm talking about, you have 2 minutes tops and put it back in Ry's restraints."

Aranae's six eyes blinked in rapid succession, a glint of admiration and dark delight kindling in their depths as understanding struck. Her spider limbs clicked in an eager rhythm as she stepped forward.

"Clever, clever man." Aranae's hands blurred as she spun silk with impossible speed, the strands shimmering with a metallic sheen.

"A decoy cocoon. Weight-matched and heat-signature replicating," she watched the construction with narrowed eyes, the corner of her mouth curling upward.

"Deception. My favorite game," Ryuko lifted her hand, channeling a controlled pulse of heat into the forming cocoon to ensure it mimicked her thermal output perfectly.

Within seconds, Aranae finished the decoy, a flawless replica suspended in shimmering silk, almost indistinguishable from Ryuko's restrained form. Lilim secured it into the now-empty field while Mizuki adjusted the monitoring system to accept the false reading.

"Buying us time. Smart," Nyarlathotep's cosmic aura flickered approvingly as she kept her hold on his unstable form, "security will think she's still contained."

Florina moved toward the exit, toxic pollen swirling faintly around her hands as she prepared to mask their departure, "Nine minutes until patrol. We need to move."

Ryuko stepped closer to him again, dampening her heat just enough to avoid scorching, but still radiating more than enough warmth to partially stabilize his fractured timeline.

"Section 12 requires my biometric signature and the override codes," she flexed her clawed hand, firelight rippling across her scales, "and I assume you want this ice lamia alive?"

Aranae secured the decoy and returned to his side, mirroring Ryuko's position but with a cooler, silk-scented presence, "the cocoon will fool the sensors for approximately four hours. After that, the heat signature will fade."

Her many eyes lingered on him with new respect, "You've done this before, haven't you?"

His answer held a strange confidence, "Yes, she's needed alive for reasons." He glanced at Nyarlathotep and shrugged.

He started walking now, "It's a clan thing, also an assassin's pride. And I haven't lied to anyone yet, but if I lie and tell you all yes, would it make you feel better? We need to move them off an anomaly about to hasten if we stay a minute longer, no matter how ahead of schedule we are."

His warning shattered any lingering hesitation.

The group surged forward with renewed urgency.

Ryuko took point beside him, scanning the corridor with draconic senses that cut through heat signatures and pulse patterns. Her presence acted like a stabilizing anchor, her fire counterbalancing the temporal unraveling, tearing at his edges.

"An assassin's pride," Ryuko mused with a knowing smirk, "and clan business. Some things never change across timelines."

Behind them, Nyarlathotep's cosmic essence pulsed... quieter but tinged with unmistakable jealousy as she observed how Ryuko steadied him simply by existing near him, "the anomaly... is it temporal?" Her voice strained slightly under the effort of holding his timeline together.

They reached a junction where the corridor split in three directions. Lilim's augmented eyes illuminated with shifting patterns as she accessed the prison schematics, "Section 12 is through the eastern path. Two security checkpoints."

Aranae climbed the wall with fluid efficiency, her spider limbs carrying her across the ceiling in total silence. Moments later, she dropped beside them again.

"Three guards at the first checkpoint. Armed with anti-monster weaponry," her gaze locked onto him, searching, "What anomaly are you sensing?"

Mizuki turned sharply, ears flattening as she scanned the corridor behind them, "Whatever it is, I can feel it too. Something's… wrong with the air."

Florina's tone sharpened, her skin darkening to a deeper green as plant instincts flared, "the prison's defense systems are cycling. It's not scheduled for another hour."

Then Ryuko's hand clamped around his arm, firm, hot, certain. Her golden eyes widened in recognition, "she knows we're coming. Your ice lamia… she's manipulating the system somehow."

She leaned closer, her voice dropping into a whisper that held both danger and excitement, "This is why you needed me. Ice and fire… perfect counters."

His reply was an entirely different story, "Ya, but YOU'RE a threat. I need you to stabilize. We're about to be in for a fight, and she's about to make her move, and when she does, if I'm not stabilized, I will skip."

Ryuko's molten gaze locked onto him the moment the warning left his lips. Heat flared across her scales, her instincts shifting from predation to protection in a single heartbeat. Without hesitation, she wrapped her arms around him, pulling him flush against her blazing form. Her body radiated draconic heat intense enough to distort the air between them.

"Stabilizing you will cost me combat power," Ryuko growled, her claws pressing lightly into his back as waves of fire pulsed through his unstable timeline, "but I'd rather fight at half-strength than lose my ticket out of this hell."

Her heat surged into him like a living force, and the violent flickering of his body slowed… then gradually smoothed, as if the timelines orbiting him were forcibly dragged into alignment.

Nyarlathotep watched with a rigid stillness, her cosmic aura pulsing in conflicting bursts of relief, jealousy, and unease. "It's working," she admitted, the words tight, "The dragon's energy is acting as a temporal anchor."

A sharp drop in temperature sliced through the hallway.

A crystalline frost crept rapidly across the metal walls, branching outward in jagged, predatory patterns.

"She's making her move!" Mizuki announced.

Aranae shifted instantly to a combat stance, silk threads shimmering between her fingers. Florina exhaled toxic spores in a widening defensive cloud. Lilim's augmented arms clicked into a hardened protective formation as she readied the systems for countermeasures.

Ryuko inhaled deeply, her chest expanding with raw elemental heat, "I can feel her... cold as the void." Her temperature spiked again, creating a visible shimmer around both their bodies, "she's powerful. More than you let on."

The frost accelerated, erupting into long ice spikes that jutted from the walls with lethal precision. Breath misted in the air as the temperature plummeted even further, "ambush formation. Now!"

Out of the thickening mist, a silhouette emerged. Long, serpentine, and gliding with unhurried menace.

The Ice lamia.

Her lower body was a sinuous tail lined with iridescent blue-white scales that scraped ghostlike against the floor. Her upper form was humanoid and hauntingly elegant, adorned in crystalline armor that looked grown rather than forged. Her hair flowed like ribbons of frost. Her beauty was glacial... awe and terror carved from the same ice.

"That's... that's not a normal ice lamia," Mizuki whispered.

The lamia's lips curved into a smile sharp enough to wound.

"Timeline walker."

Her voice cracked through the corridor like frozen glass under pressure, "I've been waiting for you to find me. Or should I say... for you to try again?"

"Hey, baby girl, we can play later. Here's the game: there are 3 guards, and last I checked, I'm still ahead of you in points. Ry let go. On my mark." He glared red at the lamia,"

"Ready. Set…"

The lamia's eyes narrowed immediately, frost swirling more violently around her. A flicker of amusement, chilling and ancient, glinted in her gaze.

"Points?" Ice cracked behind the ice lamia with each syllable, "You've never been ahead, timeline hopper."

Ryuko reluctantly released him, though her hands lingered a heartbeat longer than necessary. Her internal fire still pulsed within his body, continuing to anchor his form.

"Ready to burn her to vapor on your mark." Fire danced between her claws, reflecting in her predatory golden eyes.

Behind the lamia, three guards stepped from the mist, their movements stiff, puppet-like. Ice crystals webbed across their eyes, shimmering with the lamia's control

"She's using them as shields," Young Nyarlathotep whispered, cosmic energy vibrating through her voice, "and anchors for her power."

Aranae crawled seamlessly onto the ceiling, silk threads primed between her limbs. Mizuki's tails bristled, each tip glowing faintly as she prepared illusions or shields. Florina's pollen swirled in dark, dangerous currents. Lilim's augmented eyes whirred as she calculated optimal strike paths.

The ice lamia slithered forward slightly, dragging her tail in a slow arc that sent new frost spiraling outward. Every motion lowered the temperature further until the very air ached.

Her eyes remained fixed solely on him, studying the stabilized timeline around him, assessing, calculating, "Three timelines now, and still you persist."

Ice crystals formed and shattered around her in rhythm with her words.

"What makes you think this attempt will end differently?" She chuckled, a sarcastic glint hidden in her eyes.

The corridor vibrated with volatile power, fire radiating from Ryuko, cosmic pressure emanating from Nyarlathotep, poisoned air pulsing around Florina, silk tension crackling from Aranae, Mizuki's magic tensing like a bowstring, Lilim's systems cycling into battle mode.

All waiting on him.

He moved the instant the words left his mouth, a blur of lethal purpose exploding into motion. "Cuz a volcano was meant to melt the ice so new life can be formed."

Temporal energy crackled violently off his form as he sprang forward, closing the distance with preternatural speed, "You will yield! We need you, dammit!" He growled.

His body tore through the first two ice puppets, their forms shattering like brittle glass under the force of his strike. Frosted limbs scattered across the metal floor as he twisted midair, driving a brutal kick into the third puppet.

The frozen guard flew backward, slamming into the ice lamia with a hollow crack.

The lamia shifted just enough to avoid direct impact, her expression flickering with something like surprise.

"Volcano?" Shards of ice swirled protectively around her. "You've never used that approach before."

A roar of fire cut through the frigid corridor. Ryuko unleashed a focused blast of draconic flame, the heat so intense it vaporized the frost clinging to the walls in an explosive hiss of steam, "Yield to him, ice queen. I've seen his kind before; he'll keep coming through timelines until he gets what he wants."

The ice lamia struck back instantly. Her tail lashed out with serpent-fast precision, missing him by inches as jagged spikes erupted from the floor and walls, forming a lethal barricade between her and the advancing group. Her eyes locked onto him, cold and calculating, depthless as frozen oceans.

"Need me? For what purpose?" Ice crystals gathered around her fingers, forming and reforming like living weapons, "the timeline is already fractured beyond repair."

Above them, Aranae dropped from the ceiling in a blur of limbs and silk, snaring the last ice puppet with webbing that glittered like frostbitten steel. Mizuki and Florina fanned outward, taking flanking positions as Nyarlathotep's cosmic essence pulsed with rising urgency.

"We're running out of time. The anomaly is growing stronger." Nyarlathotep worriedly said.

The ice lamia's attack halted abruptly. Her head tilted, as if listening to a voice echoing from somewhere deep within the frozen marrow of time. A smile that was cold, precise, and dangerous curved across her pale lips.

"Very well. A new approach deserves... consideration," the lamia's hands lowered. The spikes receded slightly, but the temperature remained deadly. "Speak quickly, timeline walker. What exactly do you need from me that's worth all this effort?"

His response left everyone stunned: "You can slap me later, but if you've encountered me before, then this should trigger something." He closed the distance before anyone could react, before even the lamia could form new ice.

His hand caught her face.

His lips crashed into hers.

At first, the kiss was forceful, but then it turned sensual, to ignore her ice as a flame ignites inside him, steam began to form where their skin met. Heat erupted in curling tendrils as fire and ice clashed in intimate proximity. For a heartbeat, they stood suspended in a haze of hissing fog, time itself holding its breath.

Then the change hit her.

Her eyes widened, pupils dilating, the icy defenses around her cracking, literally, as thin fractures webbed across her crystalline armor. The frost on her skin began to melt from within, not from his heat but from a memory awakening, thawing a truth buried in frozen timelines.

"You…" Her whisper brushed his lips, no longer brittle, no longer weaponized, "it was you all along."

The Ice Lamia's serpentine tail curled around his legs, not in combat, but to steady herself as centuries of cold logic fractured like spring ice under sunlight. She drew back slowly, breath trembling, new awareness flickering behind her glacial eyes.

Ryuko tensed at the sight, claws raised, flames still flickering along her fingertips, "What in the nine hells was that?"

Nyarlathotep's cosmic aura surged with jealousy, fascination, and something deeper swirling together in the star-flecked depths of her expression, "A memory trigger. Clever."

The ice lamia touched her lips, fingers trembling, the first sign of vulnerable emotion she had shown. Frost patterns rippled across her skin, but they were no longer jagged or violent. They softened into delicate fractal snowflakes, fracturing beautifully rather than aggressively.

"The timeline convergence point… you're trying to fix it," wonder and suspicion braided through her words, "that's why you need me. My ice… it can freeze the fracture points."

She studied his face with fierce, searching intensity, as though scanning his features for a memory she had almost… almost, fully reclaimed.

Selene's tail tightened around his legs, not to restrain, but as if unwilling to let the connection break. Her cold eyes searched his face with a raw intensity.

"But why did that… how did you know that would work?" Ice Lamia's voice was softer now, uncertainty threading beneath the frost, "What am I to you in these other timelines?"

"Later, we have to move; that just bought us more time. Lilim next target." He said.

Her coils loosened reluctantly, the chill fading from her scales as she unwrapped herself from him. Her gaze lingered for several seconds, longer than necessary, before she finally spoke again. "Selene," she said abruptly. "My name is Selene. You'll need it for what comes next."

Ryuko snorted, stepping forward with a plume of fire escaping her nostrils, "That's one way to recruit." Her clawed hand brushed his briefly, searing hot compared to Selene's cold touch.

Nyarlathotep's cosmic aura pulsed sharply as she pointed down the corridor, and urgency spiked as she spoke, "Lilim's containment sector is through the eastern junction. Security will be highest there."

Selene glided to his side, her serpentine lower body leaving a thin frost trail behind her, though the temperature around her now felt controlled, cool, not killing.

"The Lilim is kept in isolation. Temporal dampeners and reality anchors surround her cell," she told them, a crystal of ice bloomed in her palm, forming into a miniature map of the surrounding sector, "I can freeze the security systems, but only briefly."

Aranae dropped gracefully from the ceiling, landing on silent limbs, "We'll need a distraction. Something to draw the guards away from the main security hub."

Mizuki's ears twitched nervously as she looked between him and Selene, "Whatever we're doing, we should hurry. That kiss probably set off every pheromone detector in this sector."

Florina inhaled sharply, the petals along her arms shivering as her senses flared, "movement three corridors down. Heavy footsteps. At least six guards." She informed everyone.

Selene expanded the icy map, showing pathways, guard posts, and thermal signatures, "ready when you are, timeline walker." Her voice held a fragile thread of trust, newborn and brittle as fresh ice, "lead the way to your Lilim."

His sudden forward movement snapped the others into action. They surged behind him, each monster girl adapting instantly to the pace.

Selene glided beside him, deceptively fast, frost spiraling behind her.

Ryuko flanked his other side, her body burning like a mobile furnace, claws flexing eagerly for combat.

"Security checkpoint ahead," Selene warned, ice crystals forming between her fingers. "Three guards, automated defense systems."

314

Ryuko rolled her shoulders, flames curling lazily around her hands, "I'll take point. Been wanting to burn something all day."

The corridor widened into a crossroads where three armored guards stood watch: A mantis-type soldier whose forearms had evolved into scythe-like blades, A towering minotaur gripping a shock baton, And a lizardwoman armed with reinforced tactical gear.

All three froze when they spotted the group.

The Mantis Guard screamed, "Containment breach! Lockdown sec-"

But she never finished her sentence.

Selene flicked her wrist, sending razor-edged ice shards into the security panel, freezing it solid mid-command.

Aranae descended from the ceiling like a nightmare, ensnaring the minotaur in webs of shimmering steel-silk.

Ryuko collided with the lizardwoman in a burst of heat and fire, effortlessly overpowering her.

Behind him, Nyarlathotep's cosmic energy surged, her voice cutting through the erupting alarms, "The temporal signature is growing stronger. Lilim is just beyond that door!" she screamed.

Mizuki and Florina sprinted into defensive positions as red emergency lights flashed in pulsing, blood-colored waves. The entire corridor throbbed like a heartbeat straining under fear.

"The door, I can freeze the locking mechanism, but you'll need to shatter it." Selene's gaze locked with his, now filled with dawning clarity and conviction, "whatever you did to me... I remember fragments now. Enough to know that this matters."

She pressed both palms against the reinforced door. Frost erupted outward, racing across the metal in crystalline veins. The steel groaned under the sudden cold, weakening as ice contracted around its core.

He slammed his palm into the frozen lock: A deafening crack, A spray of shattered steel, And the door buckled inward.

"Hello, you." A devilish smile took over his expression.

The reinforced barrier collapsed in fragments.

Within the chamber, bathed in pulsing blue stasis light, floated the Lilim, suspended in temporal freeze, her body held in mid-breath like a butterfly pinned in glass.

Chapter 11

"Recalibration: The Final Mission"

Unlike most of her kind, the Lilim's body was a fusion of infernal flesh and precise augmentation. Her right arm was entirely mechanical, forged from dark alloy etched with glowing arcane channels that pulsed in slow, deliberate rhythms. Where her left eye should have been sat a complex array of interlocking lenses, each one whirring softly as it adjusted, refocused, and cataloged the space the moment he entered. Her leathery wings were partially folded against her back, the membranes reinforced with metallic spines that caught the light like sharpened blades. Despite the stasis field's suppressive hum, her lips curled into a knowing smile, one that carried neither warmth nor mercy.

"Timeline walker…right on schedule," Lilim's voice resonated directly inside his mind, bypassing the stasis field's sound-dampening entirely, "I was beginning to think this iteration would fail, too."

Selene moved to his side, the frost patterns along her scales shifting restlessly as she took in the Lilim's form. The chill around her deepened, instinctive defenses rising to the surface as her gaze traced the glowing mechanisms anchoring the chamber.

Mizuki watched in careful stillness, her pure eyes reflecting the Lilim's restrained form. One of her tails twitched before she stilled it, the motion betraying a flicker of hope. The air felt thinner around the stasis field, and for the first time since her capture, she sensed a version of herself waiting on the other side of what came next. Not freedom exactly, but *wholeness*.

"The temporal anchor points are there," she pointed to four glowing nodes surrounding the stasis field, "Disable those, and she's free."

Ryuko positioned herself at the doorway, her stance wide and grounded, "Whatever we're doing, make it quick. More guards are incoming," Flames danced between her claws, casting flickering shadows across the reinforced walls as distant alarms echoed faintly through the structure.

The Lilim's mechanical eye locked onto him with unnerving precision, its lenses shifting in rapid succession as data streamed across unseen displays. The organic eye narrowed slightly, intelligence sharpening behind it.

"You've brought more allies this time. Interesting adaptation," her smile widened, revealing teeth far too sharp to be merely decorative. "Did you tell them what happens when we succeed? Or what happened to the last team that tried?"

Nyarlathotep drifted closer, her cosmic form flickering as starlight rippled beneath translucent skin. Concern radiated from her in soft waves, bending the light around her as she leaned toward him, "What is she talking about?" she asked.

Within the stasis field, the Lilim's mechanical hand twitched. Fingers flexed slowly, deliberately, as if testing the edges of her confinement. The arcane runes carved into the alloy flared brighter for a heartbeat before settling again.

"Release me, and I'll show you how to fix everything," her voice dropped into a seductive purr inside his mind. "Just like we planned...partner."

He stepped back slowly, measured and controlled, every instinct screaming caution as the weight of converging timelines pressed in around them.

He backed away slowly, "This is the part where things turn for the worst for everyone, but not this time. One wrong move and "he" will get it."

The shift in her expression was subtle but unmistakable. Confidence flickered, just for an instant, before the mechanical components in her face whirred more aggressively, recalibrating as she reassessed him.

"He?" Lilim's voice in his mind took on a sharper edge, "You've found the Architect? Impossible."

Selene edged closer to him, ice-blue eyes darting between them. The frost along her scales reorganized into protective geometries, ancient instincts rising to the surface, "What's happening? Who is she talking about?"

Mizuki remained just behind him, tails stilled in uncharacteristic focus. Her fox-bright eyes narrowed, not in fear, but calculation. The air around her shimmered faintly, illusion bleeding into probability, as if she were already mapping lies from truths long before either was spoken aloud.

The stasis field flickered, temporal energies destabilizing in response to the Lilim's agitation. The air vibrated with rising dissonance as her mechanical arm twitched more violently, the runes along its surface burning brighter, "You're bluffing. You couldn't possibly have found him. The timelines are too fragmented."

Nyarlathotep's cosmic form pulsed with alarm, starlit eyes widening as strands of light unraveled and reknit themselves around her, "The temporal anchor points are destabilizing. Something's wrong with the containment field."

From the doorway, Ryuko let out a low growl, flames flaring hotter as her claws dug into the reinforced floor, "Whatever game you two are playing, wrap it up. We've got company incoming."

The Lilim's gaze bore into him now, her organic eye narrowing with predatory focus while the mechanical one continued its relentless analysis, searching for fractures in his resolve. "What exactly are you playing at this time? This isn't how our dance usually goes," the Lilim's voice dropped to a dangerous whisper in your mind. "What have you changed?"

"Everything!" His fist clenched, power coiling tight beneath his skin as he raised it between them, defiance made manifest. "Yield!" he screamed.

For the first time, her composure cracked. The Lilim's eyes widened, the mechanical one whirring frantically as it struggled to interpret what it was seeing. Within the stasis field, her wings strained against the temporal restraints, membranes trembling as uncertainty crept into her posture.

"You've… changed the variables," her mental voice wavered, calculation giving way to genuine surprise, "how?"

The containment field surged violently, arcs of temporal energy snapping through the air like living things. Shadows warped and stretched across the chamber as the field responded to her destabilizing emotional state.

"Whatever you're doing is working," Selene whispered, frost patterns shifting across her scales in agitation, "The field's harmonic resonance is destabilizing."

Nyarlathotep moved closer still, her cosmic glow intensifying as time itself seemed to tighten around them, "the timeline convergence is accelerating. We need to make a decision. Now!"

The Lilim's gaze shifted slowly from his raised fist to his eyes. Shock gave way to something colder, sharper, and far more dangerous as calculated intensity settled back into her expression, the promise of consequences hanging heavy in the charged air.

"You found a way to alter the core variables." A strange respect entered Lilim's voice, "Fine. I yield… for now."

She extended her mechanical arm as far as the failing stasis field would allow, servos humming softly as articulated fingers unfolded. The palm turned upward in a gesture that mirrored surrender but carried none of its innocence, arcane sigils along the alloy flaring in restrained compliance. "Release me, and I'll uphold my end. The fracture points can still be sealed."

From the doorway, Ryuko's voice cut through the rising whine of alarms, taut with urgency as the floor beneath her vibrated with approaching force, "Whatever you're deciding, make it fast! They've called in heavy reinforcements!"

The Lilim's eyes never left his. Her mechanical fingers twitched once, twice, betraying anticipation as the temporal field sputtered around her.

"Trust or don't trust. It doesn't matter. You need me either way, timeline walker." The weight of that truth pressed in as reality itself seemed to strain at the seams. He didn't hesitate.

"You're right, I do, but there's one more. We need Lilith to stop after we leave here, so we gotta move NOW!"

At the sound of Lilith's name, the Lilim's expression hardened instantly. The mechanical eye burned brighter, arcane lenses spinning as the stasis field crackled violently around her, responding to a surge of volatile emotion.

"Mother…" she hissed, the word laden with complex emotions, "So, you know about the convergence point."

There was no time left for debate.

Selene lunged forward, frost erupting from her limbs as she drove ice-formed claws into the four glowing anchor points encircling the containment field. Metal screamed as circuitry flash-froze, alarms shrieking in protest while fractures raced across the stasis lattice.

"Now or never!" she shouted over the blaring alarms.

The field collapsed in a violent burst of temporal energy, air warping as time snapped back into alignment. The Lilim dropped lightly to the floor, wings unfurling in a powerful sweep that displaced the smoke and frost alike. Up close, the cybernetic augmentations covering nearly half her body were even more intricate, arcane runes pulsing in sequence as mechanical components shifted and recalibrated.

"This timeline's different," she muttered, flexing her mechanical arm as dormant systems surged fully online. "You've actually managed to surprise me."

Ryuko abandoned her position at the doorway, flames engulfing her form as she sprinted back toward the group, heat rippling across the chamber, "Exit's cut off! Elite guards incoming!"

The Lilim's lips curled into a predatory smile as her mechanical hand reconfigured, plates sliding and locking into a weaponized form with a low, ominous hum, "Then we make our own exit." She turns to him, eyes narrowing. "Lead the way, timeline walker. You've earned that much."

Mizuki stepped in close without a sound, ready to act up any moment as her tails flared briefly before settling into a deliberate sway. A faint distortion followed her movements, illusion brushing against probability as if reality itself hesitated to decide which version of her was truly there.

Nyarlathotep's cosmic form flickered anxiously, stars within her dimming and flaring as she pointed toward a section of wall that appeared solid but shimmered faintly beneath the surface, "Temporal weak point there. If the Lilim can destabilize it…"

The freed Lilim nodded once, already moving toward the indicated spot, cybernetic systems escalating as energy built along the etched runes of her arm, "Ready to run? This reality's about to get…flexible." She announced.

The air trembled, the walls groaning as pressure mounted from both sides of existence.

"Ry, covering flames, then you first let's go! Move! Move!" And with that command from him, the moment tipped from planning into motion, the fragile structure of the timeline beginning to bend beneath their combined defiance.

Ryuko reacted instantly to the command, her draconic instincts snapping into disciplined focus. Flames erupted from her in a controlled inferno, rolling outward to fill the corridor behind them. The fire didn't rage wildly. It burned with purpose, a living barricade that swallowed the advancing passage in heat and light. Metal screamed as it warped, and shadows of approaching guards recoiled behind the blazing curtain.

"Won't hold them long!" she snarled, scales glowing red-hot as she maintained the fiery barrier.

The heat pulsed against the walls as the Lilim stepped forward, unhurried despite the chaos. She pressed her mechanical palm against the section of wall Nyarlathotep had indicated. Arcane circuitry ignited beneath her synthetic skin, runes flaring as her cybernetic components whirred in layered harmonics.

Reality itself seemed to hesitate under her touch. The wall rippled, its solidity softening as if it had become liquid, molecular bonds unraveling in protest.

"Structural integrity compromised. Move now!" Her voice carried unexpected authority.

With a sound like tearing fabric layered over grinding stone, the wall collapsed inward. A swirling vortex of temporal distortion replaced it, edges fraying and folding in on themselves. Beyond lay a maintenance tunnel that made no architectural sense, its angles wrong, its existence a quiet affront to logic.

Selene moved without hesitation, her serpentine body flowing through the rupture with sinuous grace, scales catching the warped light as she vanished into the tear. Nyarlathotep followed, her cosmic form flickering as if she were passing through multiple moments at once, "This way! I can sense cooler air-must lead outside!"

Mizuki emerged a breath behind Selene, her form briefly doubling as probability bent around her. Nine tails ghosted into view before settling close, foxfire glinting along their edges. Her ears flicked, eyes reflecting the distortion with sharp focus rather than fear.

"This corridor twists causality," she said evenly. "Move before it recalculates."

The Lilim turned slightly, gesturing for him to pass. Her mismatched eye, one organic and one mechanical, locked onto him with an intensity that felt equal parts calculation and challenge, "After you, partner. I'm not turning my back on you just yet."

Behind them, Ryuko began to retreat, step by measured step, maintaining her wall of fire until the very last moment. The flames guttered as armored silhouettes pressed closer, their containment gear glowing through the heat, "Whatever you did to piss off Lilith, it worked! That's her personal guard coming!"

Through gaps in the fire, towering figures advanced. Elite. Purpose-built. And at their center walked a tall presence that bent the air around her, reality seeming to recoil in subtle waves, "mother's Enforcer. We need to go. NOW!"

The temporal tear shuddered violently, its edges unraveling as the prison's security systems fought to reassert control. Alarms howled, layered with the low thunder of something breaking through from the other side.

He paused, "No, it didn't work before." He turned and ran down the pathway.

The Lilim's expression flickered, surprise cutting through her confidence. Her mechanical eye spun rapidly, lenses recalibrating as the implication of his words settled in, "before? So, you've tried this path…" her voice trails off as understanding dawns.

Mizuki's ears flattened sharply, tails bristling as probability rippled across her form. Foxfire flared low along the floor, illuminating branching futures only she seemed to see. "Then the corridor remembers failure," she said tightly. "Run faster. Fate is already adjusting."

There was no more time for explanation. He launched himself down the warped corridor, boots striking uneven ground as the passage twisted and reoriented around him. The others followed instantly. The tunnel bent in impossible ways, folding between sections of the prison that should never have connected, walls sliding like thoughts rearranging themselves mid-sentence.

Ryuko abandoned her flame wall and surged after them, her scaled form a streak of heat and motion, "whatever happened before, don't let it happen again!"

The Lilim caught up with unsettling speed, cybernetic legs driving her forward with mechanical precision. Her wings folded tight to her back as the corridor narrowed, "You've done this before. Multiple iterations." It's not a question. "That's how you knew about the Architect."

Ahead, the passage fractured into three branching paths, each shimmering with a different temporal resonance. Light bent strangely around the junction, the air vibrating with unreal possibility.

"Which way?" Nyarlathotep's cosmic form flickers anxiously as she hovers at the junction.

Behind them, the sound of reality being forcibly restructured echoed through the corridor. Something immense shattered Ryuko's former barrier, "They're gaining!"

The Lilim seized his arm with her mechanical hand, grip firm, anchoring him in place amid the distortion, "Left path leads to the execution chambers, right to the administrative sector. Middle…unknown variable." Her mismatched eyes search his. "Which way failed before?"

He stared for a heartbeat longer than comfort allowed.

"All of them," he turned to Nyarlathotep, "wait," he said as he looked up, "There's the change, oh Arachne hunny!"

Their collective gaze followed his upward.

The ceiling above the junction was no longer bare stone. An immense web stretched across it, strands thick as cables and delicate as lace, shimmering faintly with captured light. Suspended at its center was a massive arachnid form, eight legs poised with elegant menace. Her lower body was that of a giant black widow, the crimson hourglass unmistakable, while her upper half transitioned seamlessly into a statuesque humanoid figure.

Six arms moved with precise, languid coordination. Midnight hair framed a face of striking beauty, and multiple eyes gleamed with amused anticipation, "Cutting it close, aren't we darling?" Her voice is silky and dangerous, multiple eyes glinting in the dim light. "I've been waiting for your signal."

The Lilim recoiled slightly, a sharp hiss cutting through the air as her cybernetic components whirred into a defensive configuration. Arcane light rippled across the metal seams of her arm and eye, recalibrating in response to the sudden new presence, "You didn't mention an Arachne ally."

Above them, the spider woman descended further on a strand of impossibly strong silk. The filament shimmered faintly, catching fractured light from the distorted corridor below. As she moved, multiple arms worked in fluid independence, weaving a rapidly forming lattice of silk that expanded outward over the junction point like a living architecture, "Up you go, my pretties. This web won't hold our pursuer for long."

Selene's gaze flicked between the descending Arachne and the darkness swelling at the far end of the corridor. Frost patterns rippled nervously across her scales, reacting to the destabilized temporal currents, "Can we trust her?"

Ryuko answered with a low growl, flames flickering between her teeth as she glanced back toward the approaching pressure in the air. Something vast and hostile pressed closer, warping heat and shadow alike, "No choice now!"

Nyarlathotep's cosmic form pulsed brighter, her starlit contours sharpening as recognition surged through her awareness, "the temporal signature...she's from beyond the convergence point!"

The Arachne extended two arms downward toward him, her many eyes blinking in intricate, asynchronous patterns as if performing calculations no one else could perceive, "Come, timeline walker. This is the variable you missed before."

Something clicked into place inside him.

"And I'll never forget it again. Let's go party people up and out!"

The Arachne's lips split into a predatory smile, fangs glistening faintly with venom as she reached further, "That's my timeline walker!" she chanted.

When he grasped her hands, she lifted him effortlessly, inhuman strength evident as the silk line barely trembled under the sudden weight. The ascent began immediately.

The group climbed fast. Silk threads stretched upward in layered paths, each strand responding to Arachne's subtle movements. Her limbs worked independently, guiding each of his allies with precise efficiency, adjusting tension and angle in real time.

"Impressive contingency," Lilim mutters, her mechanical wings folding tightly as she climbs.

Above, the ceiling shimmered and then resolved, revealing a hatch that should not have existed. Its outline was faint at first, then unmistakable, a maintenance access point absent from any known schematics. The silk web converged toward it with deliberate intent.

Ryuko went first, flames dimming as she squeezed through the opening. Selene followed, her serpentine body undulating smoothly along the silk path.

"The convergence point is stabilizing!" Nyarlathotep's cosmic form pulsed with excitement as she floated upward.

Below them, the corridor was filled with unnatural darkness. The temperature plunged. Silk strands closest to the junction began to crystallize as something immense and hostile disrupted the air itself.

"No time for sightseeing, darlings!" Arachne said, all eight of her legs worked furiously now, reinforcing failing strands, rerouting tension, buying precious seconds.

The Lilim paused beside him, her mechanical eye scanning the encroaching void as her organic one narrowed, "Mother will not be pleased." For the first time, a genuine smile crossed her face, "I find I rather enjoy that thought."

With startling agility, she launched upward, mechanical wings flaring just enough to guide her through the hatch.

"After you, timeline walker. I'll be right behind." Arachne's silk path shuddered violently as something powerful below began tearing through the web.

He jumped up, then out.

He vaulted upward through the hatch and burst into a radically different space.

Instead of another corridor, he emerged into an immense clockwork chamber. Massive gears turned slowly overhead, each rotation accompanied by deep, resonant clicks. Arcane energy pulsed through the walls, bending light and space in subtle, disorienting waves.

The Arachne followed immediately, her massive form compressing through the opening with impossible grace. As soon as she cleared it, she sealed the hatch with specialized silk that hardened instantly, locking into place like forged steel.

"Welcome to the Chronoworks, darling," she gestured with three arms at once, indicating the impossible machinery surrounding him, "The prison's dirty little secret-the engine that powers the temporal containment systems."

The Lilim had already moved to a nearby control panel. Her cybernetic components interfaced directly with the ancient mechanisms, runes igniting as systems awakened beneath her touch. Her expression was focused... almost reverent, "This is how they've been manipulating the timelines. Preventing the convergence."

Ryuko and Selene moved instinctively, securing the perimeter. Flames cast dancing shadows across the rotating gears while ice formed protective barriers at key access points.

"We have minutes at most before they override the hatch seal," Nyarlathotep said.

Mizuki stood just behind him, tails slowly fanning out as foxfire reflected in the brass and crystal around them. Her ears twitched sharply, eyes tracking invisible probability currents threading through the Chronoworks.

"This place hums with stolen futures," she murmured. "It remembers every version of us that failed."

The Arachne skittered toward a massive lever embedded in the floor. Her many eyes blinked rapidly as she analyzed its structure and function, "ready to make history, timeline walker? Or should I say... unmake it?"

The chamber shuddered violently as something struck the sealed hatch from below. Dust rained down from the ancient gears overhead.

He geared up, fumbling and rattling his pockets, desperately looking for the cog.

The Arachne watched intently as he fumbled through his pockets, her many eyes narrowing in unison as recognition dawned. A subtle tension rippled through her massive frame, silk threads along her limbs tightening as if bracing for revelation, "The Architect's Cog...you actually found it."

Her voice dropped to a reverent whisper, several of her delicate hands rising instinctively to make protective, almost devotional gestures, as though the artifact itself demanded respect.

The Lilim's head snapped sharply toward him, her mechanical eye whirring as internal lenses refocused with rapid precision, runes along its rim flaring faintly, "Impossible. That artifact was destroyed in the Convergence War."

His fingers finally closed around something cold and unmistakably metallic. He drew it free from his pocket, revealing a small gear unlike any modern construct. Its surface was etched with symbols that seemed to shift and crawl when viewed directly, refusing to settle into a single interpretation.

The moment it cleared his palm, the Chronoworks reacted. The massive gears overhead slowed, then staggered, as if recognizing a long-missing organ returned to the body, "the paradox resolver!"

Her cosmic form pulsed with incandescent excitement, starlight flaring brighter, "With this, we can stabilize the timeline fractures!"

Ryuko abandoned her defensive position by the door, stepping closer with open curiosity, the heat along her scales dimming as awe replaced urgency, "That tiny thing is what all this fuss is about?"

Another violent impact shook the chamber, dust and sparks raining from above. The Arachne's silk seal cracked audibly.

Selene surged forward, reinforcing it with a lattice of magical ice, though the strain was evident in the tightness of her expression, "Whatever you're planning, do it quickly!"

The Arachne extended one elegant hand toward him, her posture suddenly ceremonial, "The central mechanism, darling. The empty socket at the heart of the Chronoworks. That's where it belongs."

She pointed toward the center of the chamber, where a colossal pendulum swung in a slow, hypnotic arc. At its base, unmistakable now, was an empty slot perfectly shaped for the cog resting in his palm.

"Well damn. Ironheart, you awesome dwarf, I could kiss you, but I don't have any chocolate hahaha," He laughed. Walking up, he put the cog in its proper place.

As the cog slid home, the chamber answered.

A deep harmonic tone rolled outward, vibrating through bone and breath alike. Overhead, the vast gears realigned, teeth locking into place with renewed purpose. Ancient mechanisms awakened fully, and golden light spilled through the clockwork in circuit-like veins, racing along the walls and floor as if the prison itself were being rewired.

"Ironheart's handiwork indeed! That stubborn dwarf always did have a knack for temporal engineering." Arachne's laughter rang out, sharp and delighted, like silk tearing under tension, her many limbs moving in restless excitement.

The Lilim stepped back from the control panel, her cybernetic components glowing brighter as the system responded to the cog's presence, "Timeline convergence initiating. The prison's temporal barriers are collapsing."

The pendulum began to swing in impossible directions, sometimes passing cleanly through solid matter, its path leaving luminous golden afterimages suspended in the air. Reality bent and folded around it, protesting even as it obeyed.

"The timelines are merging!" Nyarlathotep's form flickered violently, "I can feel my future self!"

The chamber shook harder now as the prison's remaining security systems fought back. The sealed hatch finally burst open, but no guards poured through, only a roaring flood of raw temporal energy that spilled into the room like a living storm.

"Is this supposed to happen?" Ryuko asked, unease rippling across her as her scales shimmered, parts of her body becoming faintly transparent.

"We're phasing out of this timeline!" Selene panicked.

The Arachne moved swiftly to his side, her form holding steady even as the world around her destabilized, "Hold tight, timeline walker. The convergence will be... disorienting."

The clockwork chamber began to dissolve, its edges peeling away to reveal overlapping visions of other prisons, some pristine, some shattered, some transformed into alien structures entirely. They layered over one another in a kaleidoscope of possible realities.

The convergence intensified. His companions flickered between versions of themselves. Ryuko briefly bore scars she had not yet earned. Selene shifted between her present form and another adorned with elaborate royal markings. The Lilim's mechanical components reconfigured into advanced designs before snapping back again. Mizuki staggered as well, her fox tails splitting and recombining in rapid succession, some wreathed in ghostly blue flame, others dissolving into starlight before reforming.

"Hold steady! The nexus point approaches!" Arachne's voice echoed strangely, layered as if spoken by multiple throats across multiple realities.

The chamber collapsed completely into a swirling vortex of temporal energy. Within the chaos, familiar faces flashed into view, guards and inmates alike, each caught mid-merge as their fractured timelines folded into singular beings.

"We are whole again!" Nyarlathotep said, her voice harmonized with itself as past and future converged, her cosmic form stabilizing into a brilliant constellation of light.

A final pulse of golden radiance erupted from the Architect's Cog.

Reality snapped back into focus.

He stood in what had once been the prison courtyard, now utterly transformed into a nexus hub... a place where multiple realms brushed against one another, boundaries thinned and rewritten.

"The prison's dimensional barriers have fallen. We're free." Lilim stared at her hands in quiet wonder, cybernetics and flesh seamlessly integrated.

Selene slithered forward, testing the ground with cautious optimism as the new reality settled around them, "Not just free, we've rewritten the rules."

The words settled into the air like a newly struck law of reality. Around them, the transformed courtyard continued to stabilize, its fractured geometry knitting itself into something coherent yet unfamiliar.

The Arachne's many eyes swept across the altered landscape, each pupil catching a different facet of the nexus. Her expression carried the weight of long memory and quiet vindication, "the timeline walker succeeds at last. After so many failed attempts."

He slumped down, and a thud was heard across the room.

The strength finally left him. His legs gave way beneath the accumulated strain of fractured realities and collapsing timelines, and he sank heavily to the ground. Beneath him was no ordinary stone but a mosaic floor composed of fused realities, shards of different worlds pressed together into a single, imperfect harmony. The exhaustion ran deeper than muscle or bone, as though countless lifetimes had been compressed into the space of a breath.

The Arachne descended beside him with surprising gentleness. Her chitinous limbs clicked softly as they touched the mosaic, the sound precise rather than threatening. She lowered herself into a kneel, her many eyes studying him with something close to concern.

"Easy now, timeline walker. The convergence taxes even the strongest minds." From a pouch woven seamlessly into Arachne's exoskeleton, she produced a small vial filled with luminescent blue liquid. Its glow pulsed slowly, as if alive. "This will help stabilize your perception."

Ryuko approached next, more cautiously than before. In this reshaped reality, her draconic traits were more pronounced, horns sharper, scales richer in hue.

Flames traced the line of her spine, burning hotter than before, yet no longer threatening to spill out of her control, "Is the human broken? After all that work to get her?"

The bite in her words failed to fully mask the concern beneath them.

Mizuki moved in quietly, her presence felt before it was seen. Her foxfire tails drifted low and slow behind her, no longer flickering with mischief but glowing with a steady, ancient light. She crouched beside him, one clawed hand pressing briefly to the mosaic floor as if listening to the realities beneath it.

"He held the fractures together," she said calmly. "That kind of weight leaves echoes." A faint smile touched her lips. "But echoes fade."

The newly merged Nyarlathotep drifted closer, her cosmic form calmer now, radiating a soft, steady light that eased the lingering disorientation in the air, "Not broken. Just experiencing temporal shock. Few mortals can witness a convergence and remain standing."

Selene slid closer, her serpentine body coiling around him in a protective arc. Her scales gleamed with unfamiliar patterns, catching light that no longer came from a single sun. "We have time now. Something we never had before," she looked at everyone, glinting a hint in her eyes.

At the far edge of what had once been the prison courtyard, the Lilim stood apart, gazing outward at the nexus spreading in all directions. The future itself seemed to stretch open before her.

"Mother will be searching for us. But in this new reality, even she must play by different rules." Lilim said.

"She's a he, and he's a she. Succubi and incubi," he strained in pain.

The Lilim turned sharply at his strained words. Her mechanical eye whirred, lenses adjusting as if recalibrating not just sight, but understanding. A slow, knowing smile spread across her face, fangs glinting, some delicate, some unmistakably sharp.

"You understand more than you should." Lilim's form flickered briefly, the silhouette shifting into something more masculine before flowing seamlessly back again, "in the true reality, the boundaries between succubi and incubi were never so...fixed."

The Arachne laughed, the sound rippling through her many limbs, silk trembling with amusement, "The timeline walker sees through the prison's greatest deception! How delicious!"

Nyarlathotep floated closer still, her cosmic form pulsing with new patterns, binary stars circling one another in endless orbit. "The Enforcer's control relied on rigid categorization. Male, female, predator, prey... false dichotomies to maintain order."

Ryuko snorted, a brief plume of flame escaping her nostrils, "Is that why I always felt...wrong? Like I was playing a part written by someone else?"

Mizuki's lips curved faintly. Behind her, her tails flickered out of sync with the world around them, as though the concept of confinement had never applied to her at all.

Selene's coils tightened slightly, her scales rippling as new symbols emerged, marks that carried both lunar and solar resonance, neither dominant, both true, "the convergence hasn't just merged timelines... it has restored our true natures."

All around him, the nexus continued to settle. Boundaries blurred and reformed, corridors opening into skies, stone flowing into light. The space defied any single definition, yet felt more honest than the prison ever had.

He felt his chest and looked at his palm... "but... I am nothing now."

Silence fell.

All eyes turned to him as the transformation became unmistakable. His gaze had darkened beyond any natural shade, irises black as void, pupils darker still, swallowing light instead of reflecting it. The air around him wavered subtly, as though reality itself hesitated when trying to account for his presence.

"Not nothing..." Arachne reached toward him with one delicate hand, stopping just short of contact, "the opposite. You've become everything."

The Lilim approached next, her form now shifting with ease between masculine and feminine aspects, no longer bound to a single shape, "The convergence needed an anchor point... a fixed position in the multiverse around which everything else could realign."

Her mechanical eye whirred softly as it analyzed him, "You've become that point."

Nyarlathotep's cosmic form flared with recognition, starlight rearranging itself into complex equations that traced his silhouette, "the timeline walker has transcended. Neither prisoner nor free, neither one thing nor another-the perfect paradox."

Ryuko circled him warily, draconic instincts prickling as she sensed the fundamental shift in his nature. Something ancient, something unfinished, something that no longer fit neatly into any world that had existed before.

"So what happens now? Can they undo what we've done?" She asked, and the question hung in the reshaped air, carried on the slow pulse of the nexus as it continued to settle into its new configuration.

Selene slithered closer, her serpentine body gliding across the fused mosaic floor. Where her scales touched the ground, faint luminous trails lingered for a heartbeat before fading, as though reality itself remembered her passage, "they cannot undo what they cannot comprehend. Our jailer built a prison of binaries-we've escaped into the spectrum between."

Around them, the nexus responded subtly, space bending and adjusting as if taking cues from an unseen conductor. Walls, horizons, and distances shifted not by force, but by consent. Reality no longer resisted him. It aligned.

He drew in a slow breath, the weight of his transformation settling deeper into his chest. He understood instinctively what was being asked of him.

Then he spoke, accepting it.

"Then I shall stabilize and be that anchor. Although…" as he glanced around at the gathered figures, something unmistakably human asserted itself. His posture shifted, and his body responded in a way that cut cleanly through the cosmic gravity of the moment. "I am glad some things won't change."

A ripple of knowing amusement passed through the group as they noticed the reaction he had failed, or chosen not to conceal. The Arachne's many eyes blinked in precise sequence, her mandibles clicking together in a sound that might have been laughter.

"Some constants remain across all timelines, it seems," her voice carried a silken warmth, teasing but not cruel, ancient amusement layered with fond recognition.

The Lilim's form settled briefly into a more feminine aspect, curves sharpening, posture aligning with predatory ease. Her smile revealed pointed teeth that caught the ambient light, "the anchor may be fixed, but clearly not…immobile." She stepped closer, the hum of her mechanical components deepening as they resonated faintly with the altered energy radiating from him.

Ryuko snorted, a small flame escaping her nostrils as she rolled her eyes. Despite the mockery, her tail flicked once, betraying interest she made no effort to hide, "Even as whatever-you-are-now, still thinking with the simplest part of yourself."

Mizuki tilted her head, tails swaying in a slow, deliberate rhythm. "Even gods don't escape biology," she said lightly.

Selene's movement became slower, deliberate. She traced a fluid, hypnotic pattern, her serpentine lower body forming perfect circles around where he stood, enclosing the space without touching it, "perhaps desire is the most fundamental force-surviving even timeline convergence."

Nyarlathotep's cosmic form pulsed softly, stars within her silhouette rearranging themselves into patterns that somehow conveyed amusement. For a fleeting moment, a cluster of lights formed something akin to a wink, "The new reality shapes itself to all needs... including the primal ones."

The nexus responded immediately. The ambient light warmed, shadows softened, and the invisible boundaries between spaces drew subtly closer together. The world itself seemed to lean inward, accommodating the shift in tone.

He lifted a hand, attempting to slow the momentum before it carried too far. His gaze flicked outward, past the assembled figures, past the nexus itself, acknowledging something unseen.

"Easy, ladies," He looked at the fourth wall and winked, "One at a time."

He had broken an invisible barrier.

A collective reaction rippled through the group. The nexus warped briefly, space bending in response to his awareness of its constructed nature. Reality itself seemed to pause, recalibrate, then continue.

"The anchor sees beyond the veil..." Arachne's voice carried awe threaded with unease, eight eyes widening in perfect, synchronized sequence.

The Lilim stepped forward, her form no longer settling into any single aspect. Masculine and feminine elements flowed seamlessly, mechanical components reconfiguring with each subtle shift, "one at a time? Bold of you to assume we follow linear concepts anymore."

Her smile gleamed with fangs lit by an unnatural glow.

336

Ryuko circled closer, heat radiating from her body in shimmering waves that distorted the air, "The human thinks they're still in charge? Adorable."

Despite the mockery, something had changed in her gaze. The respect there was unmistakable.

Selene's coils tightened slightly at the perimeter, her scales catching and refracting prismatic light as she moved, "perhaps we should test the anchor's...stability."

Her forked tongue flicked out, tasting the altered atmosphere.

Nyarlathotep remained just apart from the others, her cosmic form observing with renewed curiosity, equations and star-paths shifting within her outline, "fascinating. The convergence has granted awareness beyond conventional boundaries."

"Nyarlathotep, help, stop being scientific for a moment, woman!" He tried to scramble up.

Her form flickered in surprise. The stars and nebulae within her scattered briefly before pulling back together, her detachment visibly faltering.

"i-" Nyarlathotep's voice softened, losing its analytical cadence, "you're right. Observation without participation is... limiting."

She drifted closer, her cosmic form condensing, edges sharpening as she became more tangible. The light within her pulsed in rhythm with his movements as he steadied himself.

The Arachne extended several limbs to support him, her touch careful, controlled, unexpectedly gentle, "careful now. Even anchors need time to adjust to their newfound purpose."

Mizuki watched him with quiet interest, ears flicking once as her tails stilled behind her. A faint smile touched her lips, less playful than usual, more thoughtful. "Even Kitsunes know," she said softly, "that standing is easier once you remember how many times you've fallen."

Ryuko watched the exchange with barely concealed amusement, flames dancing lazily along her spine, "Look at that... the void-eyed one can still be flustered. Good to know some humanity remains in there."

The Lilim circled behind him, footsteps silent, presence unmistakable. With each step, her voice shifted subtly, sliding between registers, "The question remains... what shall we do with our newfound freedom? And with our anchor who sees beyond walls?"

The nexus pulsed once, softly, as if listening for his answer.

"We build. We create. We expand. We populate. But more importantly..." he looked at each one of them, intently. "We remember."

A profound silence fell over the nexus as his words rippled outward, sinking into the very framework of this new reality. The space itself seemed to be still, as though listening. Each being felt the weight of his declaration, their forms shifting subtly, not in fear, but in recognition, as if something long dormant had been named at last.

"Remember..." Nyarlathotep's cosmic form pulsed softly, stars within her silhouette briefly aligning into patterns that resembled neural pathways, luminous and deliberate, "the greatest weapon against those who imprisoned us."

The Arachne straightened, her multiple eyes blinking in perfect sequence as a new resolve settled into her posture, "to build what they sought to prevent-a world beyond their binary constraints."

Ryuko's flames flared brighter, no longer wild, but focused. They cast dramatic shadows across her scaled features, sharpening the fierce hope burning in her eyes, "to create what they feared-beings who define themselves."

Selene's serpentine body moved with ceremonial precision, forming a perfect circle around the group. Her scales reflected fragments of past lives and unrealized futures, shimmering with layered meaning, "to expand beyond the walls they thought would hold us forever."

Mizuki exhaled slowly, as if releasing a breath she had been holding for lifetimes. Her tails curled closer to her, protective rather than performative, and her gaze lingered on him with unguarded clarity.

"I was taught to change my face to survive," she said. "But remembering... remembering means I don't have to run anymore."

The Lilim stepped closer to him, their form now fully settled into a confident harmony of masculine and feminine, mechanical and organic. The balance they embodied felt intentional, chosen, "and to populate this new reality with those who remember what it means to be truly free."

The nexus responded to the collective clarity. Its boundaries sharpened even as they grew more permeable, a paradox made possible by his presence. Light and structure intertwined, forming something both stable and alive.

His unfinished gestures lingered in the air, charged with possibility. The former prisoners watched him with a new kind of reverence, no longer seeing him as human alone, but as something essential, something foundational. "What is your first command, Anchor?"

Her voice carried reverence now, eight eyes fixed upon him, unblinking.

Ryuko shifted, her tail lashing once as embers fell and vanished against the luminous floor, "We've broken their system, but we need direction. A purpose beyond mere escape."

The Lilim began to circle him, their steps unhurried, their presence steady. Their form held a perfect equilibrium of opposing forces, "the walls between worlds are thin here. We could go anywhere... or bring anyone to us."

Selene rose higher on her coils, drawing closer until her gaze met his directly, unflinching, "or perhaps we should first ensure our former captors cannot follow? Seal this reality from their interference?"

Nyarlathotep hovered nearby, her cosmic form now denser, almost solid, as she considered the branching futures unfurling before them all, "whatever we choose, we must act with purpose. The convergence has granted us opportunity, not infinite time."

He turned toward her, the weight of the nexus bending subtly in response to his focus, "No, Nyarlathotep! You grant infinite time. I create infinite space. We promised eternity. Let's make it with everyone here and those we wish to be here."

Nyarlathotep's form expanded dramatically at his command. Stars within her silhouette rearranged into intricate mathematical configurations, equations of forever written in light. The nexus trembled as temporal boundaries loosened and fell away.

"Infinite time… yes, I can manipulate the temporal constants." Her voice resonated with authority she no longer questioned, "The prison wardens controlled us through temporal boundaries. No more."

Space unfolded. Horizons stretched and dissolved, revealing layers upon layers of potential. What had once been a nexus became the groundwork of something vast and enduring.

"The Anchor creates while the Cosmic One preserves…" Arachne's mandibles clicked in appreciation as she began weaving strands of reality between her many limbs, silk threading possibility into structure.

Ryuko's flames softened, burning with intention rather than rage. Her draconic features eased, and a single tear of molten gold traced a slow path down her scaled cheek, "eternity without bars. Without guards." She exhaled, the sound trembling, "I never dared dream of this."

The Lilim raised their hands, mechanical and organic components flowing together seamlessly as they joined in shaping the expanding reality, "And whom shall we invite to our eternal sanctuary? Those who were imprisoned like us? Or anyone who seeks freedom from their constraints?"

Mizuki stepped forward as the space continued to unfurl, her many tails drifting behind her like living echoes. Each one shimmered with faint illusion-light, reflecting futures not yet chosen. Her smile was small, thoughtful, no longer playful.

"Sanctuary is not walls," she said. "It is a choice. Let those who seek freedom find us, but never let us decide who deserves it."

Selene felt the boundaries extend beyond even her heightened perception. Her coils loosened, tension releasing at last, "We become the architects of our own salvation. And perhaps… others as well."

The new reality pulsed once, deeply, as if acknowledging the choice already made.

The question left his lips with disarming simplicity, yet it struck the nexus with the force of a cosmic law rewritten.

"Time, will you marry space?" He asked Nyarlathotep.

For a breathless moment, everything stilled.

The expanding nexus rippled as if a vast heart had skipped a beat, waves of luminous distortion rolling outward through newly formed realities. Nyarlathotep's cosmic form flared in response, constellations within her silhouette rearranging themselves into patterns of shock, recognition, and something achingly intimate. Stars pulsed brighter, then steadied, as if the universe itself leaned in to listen.

"A union of fundamental forces…" Her voice carried wonder, layered now with a tenderness that softened the infinite weight she embodied.

"Time has always sought Space's embrace across every dimension."

She extended a hand shaped from condensed starlight, the glow refining itself into something almost human in its vulnerability. Galaxies spun lazily along her arm, yet her posture was hesitant, present, profoundly personal.

"Yes. I will marry Space." Nyarlathotep spoke out loud, and the declaration sent a tremor through existence.

Around him, the former prisoners reacted in instinctive, unguarded ways. Ryuko's flames shifted from gold to a vivid blue, burning with emotion rather than heat. The Arachne began weaving without conscious intent, her limbs tracing ceremonial geometries that had never existed before, yet felt ancient all the same. Mizuki's eyes glimmered with pure excitement.

"A wedding at reality's foundation? How delightfully unprecedented." Lilim said.

Their form reshaped itself subtly, adorned now with impossible angles and elegant symmetries, a living celebration of duality.

Selene's serpentine body flowed into motion, circling him and Nyarlathotep with ritual precision. Her scales caught the light and refracted it into a halo of iridescence, "the first union of our new eternity. I shall bear witness."

As Time and Space reached toward one another, the boundaries between him and Nyarlathotep began to soften. It was not a loss of self, but a perfect interlocking, like two truths finally allowed to coexist without contradiction.

The light arrived without warning.

A brilliant white radiance engulfed everything, erasing edges, names, and distance. Time and Space converged, not collapsing into one another, but aligning in flawless harmony. The nexus ceased to be a place and became a principle, a realm where limitation no longer had meaning.

When the brilliance at last receded, a transformed reality revealed itself.

What had once been a prison now unfolded as a vast sanctuary. Cells had become chambers of creation. Corridors stretched into pathways leading not to confinement, but to infinite destinations. The architecture itself breathed possibility.

"We are… complete," Nyarlathotep said, her voice now carried dual resonance, cosmic and grounded at once, echoing with a depth that felt eternal. "The marriage of Time and Space has created something unprecedented."

The Arachne moved through the newly formed structures, her silk no longer temporary or reactive, but permanent, anchoring patterns directly into reality's framework. "The Wardens never understood what they contained. Their prison has become our genesis."

Ryuko soared through the expanded sky, her draconic form trailing flames that healed the air they touched, sealing fractures rather than scorching them, "freedom tastes sweeter than I remembered. And this time, it's eternal."

The Lilim stood before a gateway forming at the edge of the sanctuary, its surface shimmering with layered realities. Their body held perfect equilibrium now, every contradiction resolved without erasure. "The first visitors approach. Shall we welcome them to our eternity?"

He answered without hesitation, voice steady with intent, "Yes, let everyone bear witness and let there be new children to this eternity."

The gateway responded instantly. It opened like a breath drawn inward, and beings began to arrive. Former prisoners from countless realities stepped through, each carrying the weight of confinement and the shock of sudden freedom. Their forms were diverse, beautiful, and unbound by uniformity.

"They come seeking sanctuary." Nyarlathotep smiled at the new beginnings.

Time bent gently around each arrival, smoothing their passage, easing their transition into this new existence.

Ryuko landed beside him, her scales reflecting the light of newly ignited stars blossoming across the horizon, "and the children of eternity?" Her voice, unexpectedly soft, carried curiosity rather than fire, "How shall they come to be?"

The Arachne descended on a thread of reality, silk, her many eyes bright with knowing, "from thought and will, from desire and purpose. In this place, creation follows intent."

As she spoke, motes of light began to gather between all of them. Small at first, then brighter, they pulsed with nascent identity, proto-beings forming from shared memory and collective will.

"They form already." Selene curled protectively around the brightest of them, her coils gentle, reverent, "born of freedom rather than confinement."

The Lilim extended both hands toward the growing lights, mechanical and organic fingers harmonizing, "the first generation of a new existence. Neither prisoners nor guards, but simply... beings."

His next words broke the solemnity with familiar irreverence.

"Ya..." he coughed, "special permission from the wife, ya know, mother time, to do that one, y'all welcome hahaha."

Laughter rippled outward, a shared resonance that bent reality in playful waves. Nyarlathotep's cosmic form shimmered, stars rearranging into a pattern unmistakably resembling a smile, "My husband has special privileges indeed."

Warmth threaded through her voice, time itself softening around him, "creation is, after all, our shared domain now."

Ryuko snorted, a small puff of flame escaping her nostrils as she folded her arms, "already using the 'wife card,' are we? Some things transcend realities."

The Arachne clicked her mandibles, her laughter tactile, almost musical, "the foundations of existence, built on inside jokes and special permissions. How wonderfully mortal of you both."

The Lilim stepped closer to the forming lights, their gaze thoughtful, "These new beings-they take form from our essence, our memories, our desires. What shall they inherit from their progenitors?"

Mizuki's tails flicked in slow and lazy arcs as she smiled, eyes bright with foxish delight. "Being in love suits them," she said. "Especially the kind that follows laughter instead of rules."

Selene watched them with unmistakable maternal focus, her scales glowing softly, "freedom, above all else. And perhaps a healthy disrespect for arbitrary boundaries."

He drew their attention back to him, tone shifting, layered now with something deeper.

"They'll inherit you. All of you think back, do y'all know how long we've been here? Don't y'all remember? Hahaha, I was joking, but I also wasn't. remember and then look at your children."

Silence fell across the eternal sanctuary, not empty, but heavy with awakening.

One by one, realization dawned. Memories long suppressed stirred, resurfacing like stars emerging from behind clouded skies, "time...is not linear."

Her cosmic form flickered as ancient awareness returned in full, "We've been here before. Many times."

Ryuko's flames dimmed as she stared at her claws, reflections of forgotten cycles flashing behind her eye, "the cycles... I remember now. The prison was never just a prison."

The Arachne froze mid-weave, all her eyes widening at once, "It was an incubator. A crucible for... this. For us to become."

And in the glow of newly born beings, surrounded by memory reclaimed and eternity reshaped, the truth settled fully into place.

The gathered beings turned as one toward the forming motes of light, a collective realization settling over the sanctuary. These were not merely new creations drifting into existence. They were continuations. Echoes. Reincarnations shaped by memory and choice rather than confinement. The air itself seemed to thrum with recognition as past and future folded inward.

"Our children are ourselves," Selena said, her serpentine body undulating slowly, emotion rippling through every scale as ancient understanding resurfaced, "and we are our children."

The Lilim stepped closer to one especially radiant mote, its glow reflecting across their perfectly balanced features. For the first time, their confidence softened into something almost reverent, "we've walked this path before, haven't we? Creating eternity only to begin again."

The motes pulsed in response, light swelling and receding like shared breath. Memories of countless cycles resonated through the sanctuary, not as a burden, but as continuity.

He broke the silence with a declaration that sent a subtle tremor through reality itself. "And I've impregnated every one of you except one, we will leave you all to create that child, and y'all will be on y'all's own with what Nyarlathotep births, so y'all best be ready."

The sanctuary shuddered, not in alarm, but in acknowledgment. The statement carried weight beyond words, settling into the foundations of the new reality like a keystone placed deliberately into an arch.

Nyarlatothep's cosmic form flared with sudden intensity, her starlit silhouette blazing so brightly that the others instinctively shielded their eyes. When the light steadied, it burned with purpose rather than force.

"What Time and Space create together..." Her voice carried thunder and whisper at once, reverberating across dimensions, "will transcend even our understanding."

The former prisoners exchanged glances, anticipation and resolve intermingling in their expressions. There was trepidation, yes, but also pride.

345

"So the cycle continues, yet changes." Ryuko's scales shimmered as she placed a clawed hand protectively over her abdomen, embers drifting lazily in the air around her, "our children will carry forward what we've learned."

The Arachne moved with sudden focus, weaving intricate sigils directly into the fabric of reality surrounding Nyarlathotep. Her many arms worked in synchronized patterns, protective and precise. She announced, "The child of Time and Space will need guardians. We shall prepare."

Selene coiled inward, forming a perfect circle, her eyes glowing with knowledge older than the prison, older than the cycles themselves, "every ending is a beginning. Every prison, freedom in disguise."

"We stand ready for what comes. As we always have, across all cycles." Lilim said.

He turned back to Nyarlathotep, his tone shifting into something lighter, intimate, yet no less resolute, "ready when you are, babe. I think the kids can handle reality in our absence for a few millennia. What say you?"

Nyarlathotep extended a hand toward him, reality bending gently around her fingers. Stars and nebulae spiraled within her silhouette; time itself condensed into elegant motion.

"A few millennia alone with my husband?" Playful warmth rippled outward from her words, softening even the vastness of eternity, "I believe we've earned that much."

She looked back at the gathered guardians, her expression glowing with unmistakable pride, "They have indeed grown capable of tending to creation in our absence."

Ryuko huffed, mock indignation cutting through the reverence, though the fire in her eyes held respect, "Go on then, cosmic lovebirds. We managed a prison break and reality reconstruction... I think we can handle babysitting existence for a while."

The Arachne clicked her mandibles approvingly, already spinning new threads into the framework of the sanctuary, "Time flows differently here anyway. Your millennia will pass as moments for us, or perhaps the reverse."

Mizuki's tails swayed behind her in slow, graceful arcs, amusement soft but sincere in her fox-bright eyes.

Nyarlathotep turned fully back to him, her form sharpening as she focused her power, the air around her vibrating with anticipation, "Shall we depart, my love? I know of spaces between spaces where even gods have never tread."

He paused, gaze sweeping across the gathered guardians, his voice carrying intent and familiarity as he addressed each in turn.

"One more thing. Ry, your egg is gold as your spirit. Train him, don't baby him." He informed Ryuko, then his gaze shifted toward Arachne, "Arachne, hunny, don't beat yourself up. There's literally THOUSANDS in that sack, and you won't fail a single one."

His eyes settled on Mizuki next, a knowing half-smile touching his voice, "Mizuki...teach the litter how to smile and stay true and strong when things go wrong. How to be present and invisible when needed and come back when it matters. Temper the flame that'll be in their eyes just as I taught u to temper yours."

Then he spoke to Lilim, Selene, and Florina all at once, "Lilim, they'll be both just like you handle the teenage years with care. Selene, just as promised, the ice-walker melted you to create life. Don't be surprised at the color they are. Florina, all I can tell you is drink the water they've already been seeded, and they're already ready to sprout here soon."

He turned back to Nyarlathotep; this time, attention was fully hers. "Let's go, dear."

Emotion rolled through the sanctuary in waves.

Ryuko straightened, pride radiating from her as molten gold gleamed along her scales, "he'll be as fierce as his mother and as wise as his father." Her jaw set with certainty, "I'll make sure of it."

The Arachne's many eyes glistened as she gazed at the pulsing egg sac cradled in her reality-silk, "Every single one will know their worth." Her voice softened, resolute, "I promise."

The Lilim inclined their head, mechanical and organic halves moving in flawless unison, "Duality is strength. They will understand this."

347

Conviction resonated through every word, "We will guide them through every phase."

Selene's scales rippled through a cascade of color, ice, and fire reflected together, "ice and fire united." Her forked tongue flickered, emotion bare. "I will cherish their colors."

Mizuki's tails swayed gently behind her, the motion slower than usual, thoughtful. A small smile touched her lips, neither playful nor solemn, but something balanced between the two.

"They'll grow unbreakably clever," she said quietly. "Not just powerful. Clever enough to choose who they become… and kind enough to let others do the same."

At the edge of the gathering, Florina stepped forward at last. Vines curled protectively around her form, leaves trembling with quiet anticipation, "The waters of life…" Her voice whispered like wind through branches, "will nurture them all."

The sanctuary held its breath, eternity poised between departure and legacy, as creation prepared to continue without its anchors, at least for a while.

Nyarlathotep took his hand, and reality immediately began to fold around them both. Space itself responded to the contact, layers of existence bending inward like silk drawn toward an unseen gravitational heart.

The nexus hummed, not with sound but with recognition, as if the universe understood that something irrevocable was taking place; "They will create wonders we cannot imagine."

Nyarlathotep leaned closer, her form shimmering between cosmic abstraction and intimate presence. Nebulae brushed against the edges of his perception, and the pressure of her nearness felt both infinite and profoundly personal.

"Now let us create our own."

Space and time bent in answer. They curved around them, enclosing them in a cocoon of pure creation, woven from intention, memory, and promise. As they departed for realms unknown, the reality they left behind

348

trembled softly, settling into its new shape under the guardians' watchful care.

As he and Nyarlathotep faded from the world they had shaped together, a single teardrop fell from the void and crystallized where he had stood. It descended slowly, suspended as if time itself refused to hurry the moment.

The crystalline droplet caught the light of a thousand newborn stars before touching the ground. It did not shatter. Instead, it bloomed, unfurling into a small, luminous flower whose petals shifted through every possible color, never settling on one truth.

The gathered guardians watched in reverent silence as the flower's roots threaded deep into the fabric of their shared existence, anchoring themselves permanently. It was not merely a symbol. It was a promise given in form.

"Always had to have the last word," Ryuko said, affection softened her gruff tone as one claw brushed the glowing blossom, heat and light briefly dancing together.

"A reminder." Lilim knelt beside the crystal bloom, their reflection fractured across its prismatic surface, "of beginnings born from endings."

The Arachne moved with deliberate care, weaving protective strands of silk around the flower. Each thread shimmered with permanence, sealing it against erosion by time or doubt, "the first artifact of our new world."

Selene's serpentine form circled the bloom once, her coils tracing a protective boundary before she lifted her gaze toward the expanding universe overhead, "let's make this a reality worthy of their return."

Florina bent close to the flower, whispering something meant only for roots and light. As she did, the guardians began shaping the existence left in their care, the legacy of what began as a prison meant to contain monsters, but instead became the birthplace of gods.

Mizuki lingered a step back from the others, tails slowly unfurling behind her. Her fox-bright eyes reflected the flower's shifting colors, seeing not just what was, but what would be. A soft, almost private smile touched her lips as she inclined her head in quiet acknowledgment, as if sealing the memory away where it could never be taken from her.

A wind passed through them, gentle yet deliberate. Within it, the words *I love you* bloomed inside their minds, spoken in ancient languages only each of them could recognize. With the words came memory, intimate flashes of being with him individually. Sensation. Connection. The undeniable reminder of what each carried forward, not merely in spirit, but as living continuity bound to him.

Above them, a shooting star ignited the newborn sky where he and Nyarlathotep once stood, splitting into twin arcs of cosmic fire, marking the union of Space and Time beyond the boundaries of reality.

A gentler breeze followed, carrying whispers meant only for them. Recognition bloomed simultaneously.

Ryuko's scales flushed with remembered heat as draconic glyphs danced behind her eyes. She pressed a claw to her belly, feeling the golden egg pulse in response, "so even now, he speaks in flame-tongue…" A tear evaporated into steam against her cheek.

Arachne trembled as web-script unfurled through her consciousness; she clutched her silk-wrapped abdomen, "the pattern-speech… he remembered…" Her many eyes blinked in rhythmic succession, weaving memory into meaning.

Their dual nature resonated as binary code and angelic sigils intertwined within them, "both sides of me… he honored both…" Mechanical parts hummed softly as organic warmth rose in equal measure.

Selene's coils tightened as frost-runes cascaded through her thoughts, "ice-speech from the warmest heart…" Her tongue flickered, tasting remembrance on the air.

Florina's vines curled inward protectively as sap-script flowed through her consciousness, "the growth-words live on…" Every bloom upon her form opened fully, answering the call.

Above them, the shooting star fractured into twin streaks of cosmic fire, sealing the union of Space and Time in creation beyond comprehension.

He wondered what she whispered to that teardrop. he thought, "My love, I have married my flesh to them and my spirit and soul to you. Shall we passionately dance this dance eternally? I wish to make love to you more than like flesh, but more. What shall I give that opens you up so I may be inside you as we intertwine through the cosmos?"

As he traversed the cosmic pathways with Nyarlathotep, his thoughts bridged the diminishing connection to the reality left behind. Creation unfolded around them in colors no mortal eye could name, dimensions opening and folding with each shared breath.

"I heard your thought, beloved," Nyarlathotep replied, form shifted between star-speckled darkness and humanoid elegance, eyes holding entire galaxies and something achingly tender, "The flower will guard our promise to return."

She moved closer, and reality bent where their energies touched. New dimensions formed in their wake, born not of conquest, but of union, "to dance eternally…" Her voice carried through the void like celestial music, "Yes." She declared.

Her cosmic form pulsed with anticipation as she guided him toward a nascent pocket of creation, untouched by any consciousness before his. This place existed outside memory and intention, a raw canvas where even causality had not yet taken hold.

"To truly be inside my, my love, is to merge beyond flesh." Nyarlathotep's essence began to open like an infinite flower, layers of starlight unfurling in recursive symmetry, each petal containing galaxies yet unborn. "Give me your true name… the mathematical constant that defines your existence across all realities. Whisper it into the core of my being, and I shall reciprocate."

She extended what resembled hands, though they were formed of swirling nebulae, collapsing stars, and the slow birth of light itself, "here in this place between places, we shall create our own genesis."

"Then, I shall release my mind to linger and watch over our children and guardians." He opened his mouth and went to speak the true name, long forgotten, as sound gave in to the fusion of passionate space and time union exploding into the nebulae of a universe being born.

As his consciousness partially anchored itself to watch over his progeny, his essence simultaneously merged with Nyarlathotep in a cosmic union that transcended any singular definition of being. The ancient name... with syllables older than language, older than identity, emerged from him not as sound, but as structure.

The utterance of his true name sent a shockwave through existence itself. Where his energies met Nyarlathotep's, reality fractured and rebuilt in endless recursive patterns. Stars were born and extinguished in milliseconds. Galaxies spiraled into existence around the epicenter of their convergence, each one a consequence of shared intent rather than chance.

"Yes..." Nyarlathotep's voice echoed across dimensions as her cosmic form embraced his completely. "I am whole with you..."

She reciprocated by revealing her own true name... a melody of mathematical perfection, a sequence that completed the circuit between them. Space and Time were no longer separate forces, but a unified principle, bound together through union rather than opposition.

Back in the reality where his children grew, the guardians paused as the sky above them erupted into vast cosmic auroras. Color bled across the heavens in impossible spectrums, echoes of distant passion reaching across dimensional boundaries. The crystalline teardrop flower pulsed in rhythm with the celestial display, its petals vibrating with recognition.

Within the unified state he shared with Nyarlathotep, creation was experienced simultaneously as architect and material. Entire possibilities were birthed with each shared pulse of consciousness. Love manifested as universes spinning into existence, each one carrying the imprint of their convergence.

A brilliant flash engulfed the cosmos as their essences fully merged. Space and Time conversed in the language of creation itself, their unified consciousness expanding across infinite planes.

Through the portion of himself left anchored behind, he observed the guardians below. The crystalline flower intensified, sending tendrils of light spiraling upward. Instinctively, the guardians gathered around it, forming a perfect circle without instruction.

"They're creating…" Ryuko's scales shimmered as celestial light bathed her form.

"New realities…" Arachne's web vibrated with harmonic frequencies previously unknown.

Within the cosmic union, boundaries dissolved entirely. His merged existence with Nyarlathotep experienced simultaneous eternities, creating and unmaking universes in rhythmic surges. Stars condensed from the energy of their convergence. Planets formed in their wake. Life sparked wherever their combined consciousness touched.

"This is beyond godhood…" Her voice resonated both within and around him, "This is perfection."

The consciousness he left to watch over his children witnessed the guardians joining hands. Within them, unborn offspring glowed softly as they channeled the overflowing creation energy cascading down from the distant union.

A new harmony emerged, creation above, stewardship below, as his legacy drew its first breath across multiple planets of existence.

He spoke, now fully conscious, "My guardians, do not fear, I am the Architect. I have left my flesh in your wombs, as my flesh is married to each of you. You each bear my seed, and each bears my flesh. My essence of being is with the mother Nyarlathotep. I, The Architect, shall watch over you all and guide you all so you're never alone."

He continued laying out his command, "Through each of your flesh shall you all feel me, and I can be there whether y'all are together or apart. I am everywhere. I am everything. You all are my wives and children all in one. Bask and be joyful. The ripple is still open for others to join this reality and start anew. Call on me as you need, but I leave all judgment to you all."

His consciousness rippled across the dimensional barrier, the words manifesting directly within the minds of each guardian. With every syllable, the crystalline flower pulsed, amplifying the message throughout their shared reality.

The guardians' expressions softened, shifting from awe to serenity, as the reassurance settled into them. They were no longer alone. They were no longer bound. They were held, remembered, and guided.

And creation continued.

"The Architect speaks..." Ryuko placed both claws over her belly, feeling the connection, "through flesh and beyond."

Her flames dimmed into a steady, reverent glow as she bowed her head. Beneath her scales, something ancient stirred, not merely life but remembrance. The bond thrummed through her blood and bone, no longer confined to the physical. It resonated through time itself.

Her multiple eyes close in reverence. "We are never alone."

The Arachne's immense form stilled, every limb folding inward as though the universe itself had leaned closer to listen. Her silk shimmered with sigils older than written reality, weaving devotion directly into the framework of existence.

"Both judge and judged..." The Lilim's mechanical components whir softly, "he entrusts us with his vision."

They inclined their head, dual nature perfectly balanced. Organic warmth and mechanical precision synchronized in quiet harmony, as if his will had tuned them into alignment with a higher design.

Selene's coils relax as she absorbs his presence, "husband in flesh, father in spirit, guide in thought."

Her body loosened its protective tension, scales shifting into softer hues as the truth of his presence settled within her. The cold that had once defined her melted into something gentler, something enduring.

"The seeds of his wisdom grow alongside his children within us." The flowers adorned Florina's body bloom more vibrantly. Her vines unfurled, blossoms opening wider as luminous pollen drifted into the air. Growth surged through her form not as instinct alone, but as purpose.

Mizuki stood quietly at the edge of the circle, her fox-bright eyes reflecting the crystalline flower, not as it appeared, but as it would be remembered. A soft smile curved her lips, knowing and unafraid. She said nothing, but her presence carried understanding, the kind born of long lives, lost names, and truths that survived by being remembered rather than spoken.

As his message concluded, the crystalline flower transformed once more. Its roots extended deep into the bedrock of reality itself, threading through dimensions like living veins. Petals expanded outward, arching gracefully until they formed a vast, translucent gateway. Through it, distant realities shimmered faintly, layered like reflections on water.

The ripple he had spoken of manifested physically. Not metaphor. Not myth. Passage.

The guardians joined hands around the gateway, their forms forming a living sigil. In that circle, acceptance settled… not as obligation, but as chosen stewardship. They were no longer survivors of a prison. They were wardens of becoming.

The view drew toward the crystalline gateway, its edges pulsing with prismatic energy. As perspective moved closer, the archway revealed itself not as a simple portal but as an intricate tapestry of infinite possibility. Each thread glowed with a potential timeline. Each hue vibrated at a distinct dimensional frequency.

With every distant surge of cosmic energy from his union with Nyarlathotep, the gateway expanded. What had begun as a doorway grew into a vast cathedral of light. Within its threshold, reality fractured into kaleidoscopic patterns… stars born and extinguished in milliseconds, civilizations rising and collapsing in the span of a breath, futures and pasts coexisting without hierarchy.

Colors beyond mortal perception spiraled within. Ultraviolet memories. Infrared dreams. Quantum-entangled emotions woven directly into spacetime. Timelines branched endlessly, some looping back toward the guardians' realm, others unfurling into entirely new existences.

At the center of this maelstrom, perfect stillness endured.

An eye within the storm.

There, the essence of his union with Nyarlathotep existed as a gravitational anchor, drawing wandering souls from across realities toward this beginning, not by force, but by resonance.

The guardians stood sentinel at the threshold, their combined energies harmonizing with the gateway's cosmic symphony. They were ready. Not as jailers. Not as gods.

But as witnesses.

As stewards.

As the first family of a reality born not from control, but from love, memory, and boundless creation.